MISS McKIRDY'S DAUGHTERS
WILL NOW DANCE THE
HIGHLAND FLING

MISS McKIRDY'S DAUGHTERS WILL NOW DANCE THE HIGHLAND FLING

Barbara Kinghorn

St. Martin's Press ☙ New York

'I BELIEVE'
Words and Music by Ervin Drake, Irvin Graham, Jimmy Shirl, and
Al Stillman. Copyright © 1952 (renewed), © 1953 (renewed)
Hampshire House Publishing Corp., New York, N.Y.
Used by Permission.

Library of Congress Cataloging-in-Publication Data

Kinghorn, Barbara.
Miss McKirdy's daughters will now dance the Highland fling / by
Barbara Kinghorn.
p.   cm.
ISBN 0-312-14016-9
1. Kinghorn, Barbara.   2. Dancers—Biography.   3. Highland
fling (Dance)   I. Title.
GV1785.K486A3   1996
792.8'028'092—dc20   [B]   95-47523   CIP

First published in Great Britain by Black Swan Books

First U.S. Edition: April 1996

10 9 8 7 6 5 4 3 2 1

THIS BOOK IS DEDICATED TO MY DAUGHTER AND
MISS McKIRDY'S GRANDDAUGHTER, ALEXANDRA
LOUISE, WITHOUT WHOSE UNCONDITIONAL LOVE,
OLD SOUL WISDOM AND DEDICATED PARENTING I
DON'T THINK I'D HAVE MADE IT.

Acknowledgements

This book was seven years in the writing. Throughout that time my friend, Jack Klaff, has been a source of encouragement and support. During the first year we worked on it together and Jack not only gave unstintingly of his time and labour but actually made me believe that it was a story worth telling. I have him to thank for its very existence. For getting the manuscript onto a word processor and assisting with the endless re-writes I have my friends, Dalmae Adkins and Carol Rickard to thank – I could not have done it without them.

I would also like to acknowledge my niece, Sheena, who has so generously allowed me to print her letters and who has given me such love and support over the years as have my many dear friends who also read the book and gave their honest and caring appraisals, especially Michael Fitzgerald and Dillie Keane.

Finally, I have Life itself to thank because without its experiences there wouldn't be a story to tell.

Barbara Kinghorn 1994

Part One

Miss McKirdy lives with her three daughters, Jilly, Annie and me, in a dutch-gabled house on the outskirts of Johannesburg. The corrugated iron roof is painted red and the bricks are the colour of dried blood. The house is guarded by four strong palm trees and surrounded by a perimeter fence of stone and spiky steel. Our father lives with us, sort of.

The most important thing in our house is Highland dancing. My mother and Auntie Edie teach it and we three girls are champions at it. (I won my first medal when I was three years and four months old.) We practise every day and go to classes three times a week. My mother has founded the Highland Dancing Association of the Transvaal and is on the South African Official Board of Highland Dancing (which is affiliated to the Scottish Board of Control). She also teaches elocution. My father is bored to death by it all.

Jilly's dancing reminds me of the way Daddy eats his porridge. Neat, measured mouthfuls – but instead of sprinkling sugar on top he insists on salt. Jilly is what Mummy calls a 'technician'. She likes to get her foot in exactly the right position on her leg and her precision placing in the Sword Dance is famous. She says the Sword Dance is her favourite because it's logical like maths, which is her best school subject. One thing she absolutely refuses to do is smile. The Highland Fling is about joy, so when you dance it you should show people just how happy and victorious you are. Showing facial expression is something new they started doing in the colonies; the purists in Scotland don't believe in it.

9

Jilly and Annie and I must have won over a thousand medals and trophies between us. When Mummy used to dance she won hundreds too. In those days, in Johannesburg, the medals she won were made of 18-carat gold, and she also won tea-sets, books, tortoiseshell hairbrushes, leather suitcases, clocks, and all sorts of things that go in display cabinets.

I love the way Annie dances, everyone does. Mummy and Auntie Edie shout, 'Be more accurate with your positions!' But when Annie gets going she couldn't care less about technique, all she thinks of is having a wonderful time. She smiles and flings her legs and leaps. She's like a young buck running free. Maybe that's how they danced the first Highland Fling. I don't know how I dance. Mummy says I'm a jelly, which makes me cry, and then she says, 'What do you expect – bouquets?'

We have to go to Highland dancing on Wednesdays and Fridays after school from two until six, and Saturday mornings from eight till twelve. There are other dancing studios in Arts House but ours is the only one teaching Highland and Irish dancing. The others teach exciting things like ballet, tap and Spanish. They have pretty costumes and learn lots of different dances. We just practise the same ones over and over again. I get so sick of it all.

I'm also so sick of the lectures about 'sacrifice', 'the family name' and 'duty'. Mummy is always telling us how 'dancing sprang from man's natural emotions'. It doesn't feel like that when you're doing the toe and heel step for the twentieth time. She says the conquering Highlanders crossed their swords in triumph and danced over them. I'm sure it wouldn't have mattered to them if they'd kicked their swords. But if we so much as even touch ours we're disqualified from the competition.

In the afternoons and at night we have private lessons at home. Mummy teaches us in the front room or the kitchen. When we're learning to smile Mummy always says, 'Copy Annie. People love that smile.'

Jilly can't and won't do it. Jilly's a great giggler but only when it comes naturally and not to order. I can do it but it makes my lips tremble.

In our house there isn't always a fight at suppertime, but there's nearly always an argument. Mummy says Daddy's liverish and has black moods. Also Daddy can't stand Auntie Edie and she stays with us nearly every night. We all hate it when Auntie Edie says, 'I just want a wee bit,' because she eats more than anybody. She even steals some when she's helping to clear away the dishes.

Daddy's never hungry so he takes a long time cutting everything up small but even then he doesn't eat it.

And Mummy says, 'Duncan, is there something the matter with your food?'

'What did you say?'

'I said, is there something the matter with your food? Why are you pushing it around your plate?'

'Is that what I'm doing?'

'You know that's what you're doing. You're certainly not eating it. You are pushing it.'

'I'm chewing it. We don't all gobble our food in this house.'

'And what is that supposed to mean?' she says, putting her head on one side.

Daddy hums quietly.

'I suppose that nasty little remark is referring to my sister?'

'What nasty little remark?'

'We ALL know what you're getting at.'

'Oh, you know what's going on in my mind, do you?'

'I know your lemonish little remarks.'

'Oh, of course, you know everything about every-thing. There's nothing you don't know about.'

This calls for a slight change of tactics from my mother. 'You can be very nasty, Duncan.'

11

'Well, of course, as per usual, I'm the big bad wolf around here.'

'You're your own worst enemy.'

'OK, OK. Get up on your soap-box. Let's have a lecture. No meal could possibly be complete without a lecture.'

'I am not LECTURING, Duncan. I am simply speaking the truth which, of course, you do not wish to hear.'

'Oh? So you're an expert on the truth now, are you?'

Mummy gets her teacher's voice and she closes her eyes as she speaks.

'You've been drinking, Duncan. You've been drinking and you're liverish. And I am fed up to the teeth with it. Do you hear me? I AM FED UP AND I DON'T THINK I CAN TAKE MUCH MORE OF IT.'

Daddy whistles to himself and stares at her. He doesn't blink.

'DO YOU HEAR ME?' Mummy's eyes are open now. She beats the table with her finger. 'Either you cut out that poison or I am walking out through that door and I won't come back.' You can hear there are tears in her voice.

'That's right, go on, turn on the waterworks. That's what you women do every time. Petticoat government. I don't know. What's the point?'

And he puts his plate down on the floor for the cat.

Granny Mac is my mother's mother. She lives in a mine house on the Robinson Deep gold-mine with her daughter, Auntie Edie, and her son, Uncle Rob, and his wife, Betty. They have a son who's already grown up and gone away.

Granny hates Betty and Betty hates her. They've stayed together in the same house for over twenty years without ever talking to each other.

They live separate lives in their bedrooms. Nobody ever goes into the sitting-room. The bathroom isn't used very often either. Granny thinks cleanliness is next

12

to godliness but too much washing destroys the natural oils in your skin. Betty never washes because she hates to waste money on soap. Granny thinks she's disgusting. Uncle Rob washes at the gold-mine after work.

They have to share the kitchen but as they eat mainly soups and stews they can prepare their meals at different times. Auntie Betty and Granny Mac like poking in their cooking pots a lot of the time but they listen out for each other, so they don't do it at the same time. Granny clumps and Auntie Betty shuffles.

When it comes to the table, they each have their own side. They enter in silence. Betty goes to her sideboard and Granny Mac goes to hers. Betty opens the centre drawer of her sideboard and takes out a blue and white checked tablecloth and knives and forks. From her sideboard, Granny Mac takes out a white cloth with mauve thistles around the border and her knives and forks. Granny keeps Epsom salts, bicarbonate of soda, prayer books and a Bible in the bottom drawer. The tablecloths are folded and put across each half of the table. 'No woman's land' is a strip of teak, an inch wide, in the middle.

When Uncle Rob comes home, Betty dishes up his meal, and he sits down at the head of his half of the table. Auntie Betty stands behind him. Granny Mac sits at the head of her half, with Auntie Edie beside her, and dishes up for them.

After dinner, Uncle Rob goes to his masonic lodge and Betty has her food, eating straight from the pot. Granny Mac usually goes straight to bed while Auntie Edie does their washing up. If Granny Mac isn't around, Auntie Edie sometimes talks to Betty.

We are Scots. Mummy and Daddy were born in Scotland. We are Presbyterians, Calvinists, living in a calvinist land. But Mummy earns her daily bread working for Catholic nuns. And Daddy earns his working for Jews. We three protestant girls are educated at

13

the convent where Miss McKirdy started teaching when she was just eighteen years old. We have to be grateful that Mummy teaches there because the nuns give her a special rate – three for the price of one.

Mummy is very good at lying to the nuns. 'Remember you are Protestants,' she always says to us. 'You're not to believe all that Catholic nonsense. Just do as the nuns tell you, because you're well brought-up girls.'

In my photograph album I have a Kodak snapshot of Jilly, Annio and me – Daddy's three smart girls. We are standing in the miniature Japanese gardens in Durban dressed in our McGregor tartan kilts, white hand-crocheted socks, cream satin blouses and black patent-leather shoes. Our hair is clean and shining and cut in the page-boy style. We are smiling.

At the outbreak of the First World War Miss McKirdy was nine years old. She stood on the steps of the Johannesburg city hall, dressed in a red velvet coat trimmed with swansdown and recited, 'You're a better man than I am, Gunga Din' so movingly that scores of young men dashed off to the recruiting office to join the army. Years later she would say to us, 'In my whole life that is the one thing I wish I'd never done.'

Miss McKirdy and my father were introduced to each other at the Johannesburg Caledonian society. Right from the start, Granny Mac disliked him. She thought him too old, too much of a drinker and from the wrong part of Glasgow. She tried her best to stop my mother seeing him but Miss McKirdy, like her sister Mary, had a mind of her own. Mary had defied Granny and run away with a Cockney bus conductor called Alf and Granny never saw them again. She didn't push too hard because Mummy was her favourite daughter and anyway Daddy was, at least, a Scot.

Mummy believed it was her duty to stay with her parents for as long as she could and insisted on a five-year engagement while she saved up enough money to pay for her own wedding. Years later she would say to us, 'Every woman should have a nest-egg that her husband doesn't know about.'

However, her nest-egg was only half laid when a nasty rumour spread through the Scottish fraternity. It was whispered that her fiancé already had a wife and children in Scotland.

When the gossip reached Granny Mac, she packed a bag, took a train to Cape Town and set sail for Scotland on a Union Castle mail ship. She also had a nest-egg her husband didn't know about.

Granny Mac's seven-week fact-finding mission was twofold. If the rumour proved true she would be able to put a stop to the wedding. If not, she would at least have cleared her daughter's name.

On arrival in Glasgow she took a taxi to the address she'd been given and demanded to be told the truth. It turned out that it was my father's brother, Ian, who was married with three children. Satisfied, Granny Mac sailed on the next ship back to Cape Town and took the train to Johannesburg. She threatened to knock the teeth down the throat of any person who ever mentioned it again.

Right from the very beginning, Daddy loathed Granny Mac. 'A bloody old battle-axe,' is what he called her. In fact, the only member of my mother's family that Daddy liked was Grandpa Mac. He was a gentle man who dealt with Granny Mac by following a policy of passive resistance. She punished his placidity by refusing to talk to him, sometimes keeping up the silence for as long as two years, communicating only through their children.

However badly he was treated at home, Grandpa Mac was respected at work. Whenever there was a seemingly insoluble problem, the bosses would send someone to the workshops to 'fetch Mac'.

He had started work in Scotland at the age of eleven and was what was known as a 'half-timer'; half day at school, half day down the coal mines. By the age of twenty, he was working in John Brown's shipyard on the Clyde, where they were building the *Queen Mary* and many other great liners. The propellers on the *Lusitania* were made by a team led by my Grandpa Mac. He had no degrees after his name but, in our family, he was always referred to as 'your grandfather – who built the propellers on the *Lusitania*'.

By the time Grandpa Mac was thirty his lungs were so damaged that he was told to emigrate to a warm, dry climate. He left Granny Mac and their five children in Glasgow and set sail for sunny South Africa where the Witwatersrand gold-mines were snapping up Scots. They needed men with the courage to go down in cages, six thousand feet below the ground, to crawl through tunnels no more than two feet wide, to drill the rockface and bring up the gold which was then melted, moulded and locked up again, in vaults underground.

Grandpa lived in single quarters and sent money home for twenty-two months. In October 1913, he could afford to buy a house and bring his family out to the Transvaal where Granny Mac discovered the joy of riding to market in a rickshaw and drying her washing in the sun.

But the very next year her two sons, Rob and Billy, were sent up north to Abyssinia to fight in the First World War. Most of their acquaintances had at least one son up north.

Every evening at sundown, people came out of their houses and stood talking quietly at their garden gates, waiting for the sound of a motorcycle. They fell silent as the dispatch-rider, in a cloud of dust, appeared at the top of the street. He had come to deliver telegrams from the army headquarters. If the messenger stopped at your garden gate, there was still the tiniest of hopes; you prayed for the word 'wounded'. One friend of Granny's lost five sons before they sent her sixth son home. There was an army rule which limited the number of fatalities in any one family to five.

The first time Granny Mac didn't get a telegram. The boy himself was sent home to die. Billy wasn't wounded, he was suffering from blackwater fever which had already killed thousands. But Granny Mac, medicine woman of the clan, didn't believe in doctors and declared, 'No fever is going to get the better of me!'

She prepared strained barley broth, boiled up bones for beef tea and beat countless eggs into delicate custards. Gradually, the emaciated boy, who needed at first to be lifted up and cradled whilst being fed, began to recover. Eventually, after months, Billy was restored to perfect health and was ordered back to Abyssinia. The day after he stepped off the train he was shot dead.

When the Presbyterian minister came to offer comfort to Granny in her grief, he tried to console her by saying, 'You must remember, Mrs McKirdy, you're not alone in your suffering. Millions of mothers have lost their sons.'

'Reverend,' she replied, 'millions of mothers might have lost their sons, but only I know what it feels like to lose mine.' And she started looking for another church.

Granny Mac's first born, Rob, who was four years older than Billy, came through the Great War without a scratch.

Uncle Rob is the member of my mother's family Daddy hates the most. He calls him 'Bandy Big Conk' because Uncle Rob is bow-legged and has a huge nose. In fact, the whole McKirdy family is bandy-legged and big-nosed, except for Mummy who has an elegant nose and gorgeous legs.

When Daddy is being particularly lemonish to her, he says, 'Your mother claims to have lost your birth certificate – but I wonder sometimes if you ever had one.'

Daddy has a birth certificate but he doesn't have a mother. He has a stepmother who is also his aunt. His mother died when he was two and his older brother was three. Almost immediately his father, Grandpa James, married his mother's sister.

Daddy is very fond of saying that he was treated like a bloody servant by his stepmother. He always calls her 'she'. While 'she' had babies and their father worked, the two wee boys did all the fetching and carrying.

He does have some happy memories though of those early days in Glasgow, most of them to do with funerals. He enjoyed riding up front with the driver on the horse-drawn hearse each time 'she' lost another child (six in all).

After his demob from the Royal Navy in 1919, my father couldn't find work in Glasgow and took the boat to South Africa where he got a job electrifying a town called Vereeniging, which means 'union'.

His letters home to Scotland were full of enthusiasm for life in what he called 'the land of milk and honey'. So much so that his father and stepmother packed up their few possessions and set sail, too, taking with them their surviving younger children.

Five hundred guests had RSVP'd the invitation. The matron of honour and the eight bridesmaids had had their final dress fittings.

Miss McKirdy and her fiancé were supposed to be having a wedding rehearsal. They waited and waited but he didn't turn up. Eventually she decided to go to his lodging house in Braamfontein. She had never been there before and was shaken by its shabbiness. She asked to be taken to his room and when the 'boy' opened the door she saw him, lying across the bed, dead drunk.

She didn't mention this incident to anyone but remembered her mother's words, 'I'd rather sleep with a pig than a drunk man.'

One week later, on a freezing cold day in June, they were married in the St George's Presbyterian church, Noord Street, Johannesburg. On the marriage certificate she signed McKirdy, and that's what she remained, declining to take my father's name. The pipes and

18

drums of the Caledonian society played 'Scotland the Brave' as they cut the cake and everyone congratulated Granny and Grandpa Mac on the fine send-off they had given their youngest daughter.

I'm pretty sure it was Daddy who started the feud between him and Uncle Rob. They both do the rounds of the British clubs in Johannesburg: the Sons of England, the Cambrians, the Orangemen, and of course, the Caledonians. Both men are also staunch masons.

Uncle Rob sings and plays the violin, off-key, according to Daddy, and Daddy sings and tells jokes (one Scottish for every two Irish and three Jewish). Among the many things the two enemies have in common is that each sings as his finale, Robert Burns's song, 'A Man's a Man's for a' That' which ends with the words ' 'tis coming yet for all that, that man to man the world o'er shall brothers be for a-that'.

When it comes to hating, Granny Mac and Uncle Rob are only silver medallists. Daddy takes the gold hands down.

Granny Mac hates Afrikaners. She connects them with the Germans who killed Billy and sank the *Lusitania*. By supporting Hitler in the Second World War, the Afrikaners have shown their true colours.

Granny Mac is a Geordie. She was born in Newcastle-upon-Tyne but went to live in Scotland when she was little so she considers herself Scottish; she thinks the English are stuck-up, the Welsh treacherous and the Irish mad.

My father hates the Germans too. During the First World War they torpedoed him twice and each time he ended up in the North Sea.

After the Germans, Daddy hates German Jews and after them, all other Jews. Next come the Afrikaners followed by nearly everyone else.

He also has specific hatreds: petrol-pump attendants and dustbin 'boys'; newsreaders; sports commentators; members of the Oxo Brain's Trust; women who don't

19

put their arms in their sleeves, who drive cars and who smoke; customers who are always coming in and wanting things; crooners, especially Frank Sinatra – who'd be nothing without his mike; Indian waiters; Lawrence Harvey – a Jewish show-off from Orange Grove whose real name was Larusschka Skikne; anyone who eats onions and garlic; men who put their hands in their pockets; women who wear sunglasses; all his daughters' boyfriends; boys who ride motor bikes; politicians – especially prime ministers; referees; people with bad table manners; motor mechanics and all violinists. But most of all Daddy hates Granny Mac, because, he says, all men hate their mothers-in-law.

Mummy had to be the breadwinner when Daddy's partner in their vacuum cleaner business disappeared with all the machines and Daddy's money. They had been married for five years and were staying in the back bedroom of Granny Mac's mine house.

One night Daddy was out at a masonic do when Mummy miscarried. The midwife was called and cleaned out her insides with hot irons. When she left, Mummy sobbed quietly into the pillow. It was well after three in the morning when Daddy finally staggered in and was told what had happened.

'Well that's that then,' he said. 'You'll never have children now.' That remark hurt her much more than the hot irons and she was determined to prove him wrong.

And two years later she does. At six o'clock in the morning, on the eighteenth day of October in the year 1937, she produces a big-boned baby girl. Miss McKirdy's first born, my sister Jilly, has arrived in the front bedroom of their newly built dutch-gabled house, bought with the entire proceeds of Mummy's second nest-egg and a little help from Granny Mac.

Another three years pass and it is the eighteenth of February in 1940, a Sunday night, and the configuration of the stars in the heavens are not good. The world is at war and the humidity is high. It is close, very close. February is the suicide month in South Africa. Around five in the evening the heavy black storm clouds gather. The thunder rolls across the heavens and the sky cracks open. First single, isolated drops fall, big and heavy. Then they join together and suddenly the hail is pounding, hammering, battering against the thin corrugated iron roof. As fast as it begins, it ends. A few final plops and it's all over. The hot air melts the icy hailstones within minutes, and apart from the smashed fruit and the broken roses, you wouldn't know there'd been a storm at all. The smell remains for a while; wet earth mixed with the perfume of flowering shrubs.

In the dutch-gabled house the atmosphere is tense as Mummy's baby is due any minute and she is cleaning out cupboards like a cat preparing for kittens. Granny Mac and Auntie Edie are staying to help her look after Jilly.

Around six Daddy comes into the kitchen. He has been sleeping all afternoon and now he is hungry. Mummy is standing on a chair putting freshly-washed cake tins back up on a shelf in the pantry. Granny Mac and Auntie Edie are in their room listening to the Oxo Brains Trust on the wireless. Daddy roars, 'Where the hell is everyone in this damn house?' Mummy freezes in mid-stretch, seething but remaining silent. 'What I want to know,' foolishly continues my father, 'is when I can expect to get something to eat around here tonight.'

Mummy takes aim with a cake tin. The weight of her heavy belly tilts her forward and nearly brings her down off the chair.

'What was all that about?' asks Daddy staring at the missile as it hits the floor. He has always been mystified by the eccentricity of womankind. 'All I said was, when can a man expect to get something to eat. Is there something wrong with that?'

But Mummy isn't listening. She is concentrating on the warm trickle running down her legs. Her silence shuts Daddy up.

Granny Mac waddles into the kitchen carrying a cold cup of tea and a plate with crumbs on it. She has eaten her scone at the start of the programme but when the questions become too exciting she lets her tea go cold. Auntie Edie is having a widdle in the bathroom.

When Granny Mac sees Mummy's face she stops in her tracks. It doesn't take great psychic powers to realize something is up. She flings down the crockery and rushes to the phone.

The midwife arrives in her neat grey Austin. They get Mummy onto the bed in the front room and see the baby's head poking out like a tortoise peeping out of its shell. Suddenly Mummy lets out a scream and the baby catapults into the world. The midwife can't believe it. She has brought hundreds of babies into the world but has never seen one arrive like this. 'Like a pea shot from a pea-shooter,' she says. And then they see the blood, gushing out, changing the colour of the sheets from white to red in seconds. 'Bricks and stones! Fetch bricks and stones, or she'll die,' screams the midwife.

Daddy has been hovering outside the door. He dashes out into the back garden and shouts at the garden boy to fetch whatever he can find. Inside, the newborn baby, still covered in blood and mucous, is bundled up in a towel and thrown down onto a chair. Being a Protestant household, the concern is all for the mother; the child's survival is of secondary importance. Lifting the bottom of the bed reverses the flow of blood and an hour later they are able to turn their attention to the wee one on the chair.

Miss McKirdy's second born, the child born on the Sabbath day, is 'bonny and bright and good and gay'. They name her Annie.

*   *   *

My mother is forty when she finds herself pregnant with me. Just when she thought all 'that' was over. At first she mistakes me for the change of life. But she is experienced enough to recognize a foetal kick when she gets one. With a sinking heart she remembers a particular night the previous March when it had turned unexpectedly chilly and she and Daddy had cuddled up.

On 21 November 1944, as the Allies advance across Europe, Miss McKirdy gives birth to a third daughter in the front bedroom of the dutch-gabled house. I am no beauty. Years later, Mummy will say, 'I really can't remember when you were born, dear. It may have been the morning. But I do remember your Granny Mac looking at you and saying, "This one's been here before." '

My teacher, Sister Angelica, is the only grown-up who is prettier than my mother but that is only because she's younger. She is also closer to God than Mummy because she is more holy. She is married to Jesus. Mummy is married to Daddy. Daddy is a drunkard – I can see it when he comes home. Sister Angelica tells us about drunkards and sinners. She says, 'God loves them too and forgives them.' I think Sister Angelica is kinder than Mummy about drunkards.

But then Mummy says, 'That's because Sister Angelica hasn't ever lived with one, so she doesn't know what she's talking about.'

You can see why Jesus wanted to marry Sister Angelica. She's so young, and her voice is high and sweet and she's got the kind of face you want to stare at all the time. How does she get her skin to shine like that? We don't know if she has any hair. Marie Speck says her head's shaved but if her hair grew long you could be sure she'd look like a fairy princess. Her eyes are the same blue as the dress the Virgin Mary wears all the time.

You want to do everything the way Sister Angelica does, the way she walks, the way she writes on the blackboard, the way she holds things, the way she unlocks cupboards. You want to copy the way she stands so very still and you want to wear small shoes like that when you're big. When we pray, I keep my eyes open so I can watch her. Sister Angelica's got long, curly eyelashes, and soft, pink hands. All I ever want is to have hands like that; and to be so clean.

Wherever Sister Angelica goes, there are groups of children around her. 'Please, Sis-ta, can I carry your keys, your pencils, your jotters?'

Sister Angelica gives out stars. When you get a gold star, Sister writes VG. I don't get many gold stars. I don't think I'm very good. I try very hard but I get mostly silver. Even if I got a million gold stars I'd never be in charge of the Holy Water. You only get put in charge of that if you're a Catholic. Sister doesn't say, 'Only if you're a Catholic,' you just know it. The girl with the most gold stars pours the Holy Water. The girl with the most gold stars is always a Catholic. That's how the convent is. Catholic girls get gold stars.

If I tell Mummy she only says, 'They're like that, the Catholics. I know it's not fair but that's the way they do things.'

I don't know if I love Sister Angelica, and I don't know if the other children love her, but we are all pretending we do and I've got to be like the others. When she's happy, we're happy. And when she's cross, we're scared.

I tell Sister Angelica that the Catholic way is best. When I say that she smiles at me and says, 'Yes, but don't let your mother hear you say that.' The other children laugh, give me some of their sweets and ask me to play with them. Sister even lets me carry her books.

I hate catholicism. But I want a first Holy Communion dress. I'll never get one, of course.

The Catholic children tell the non-Catholics that they

24

know secrets that they can't tell us. They also have rosaries and religious pictures and their first Holy Communion dresses have lots of frills and matching veils.

Sister Angelica taps at her catechism chart with her wooden cane. 'This little soul has not been baptized. It is still covered with original sin and CANNOT go to heaven. God has prepared a place for souls like this. Do you know where they go to?'

'Yeees Sis-ta!'

There are twenty-two children in my class. Five of us sit at the back. We're the non-Catholics. So we don't have to say everything out loud all together like the Catholics do and we haven't got little catechism books like they have, but we learn the answers when they sing them. I say it in my head and nod to the tune, and sometimes I join in. I don't think Sister minds.

'Venial sin' sounds as though it tastes like Marmite, and isn't too bad. Venial is not as bad as murder. That's mortal. Sister Angelica doesn't show us in pictures but I think venial is black spots on white and mortal is black all over.

'This soul will never go to Heaven.' Sister Angelica looks up at the sky, and closes her eyes, 'It will go to Hell.' And she slowly bows her head like Mummy does when she says, 'The subject is closed.'

The soul is on the head, sort of on top there. Not above it. On it. The Catholic soul and the Protestant soul are both on the head. Because of halos and things; and the head's the closest thing to heaven. But in our classroom at the convent there's a picture of Catholic Jesus with his front cut open and showing his sacred heart. So there must be a bit of soul on the chest, too . . . but only if you're a Catholic. When I'm unhappy, like when Ginger, my cat, got run over, or when my mother smacks me and locks me in my room, I get a pain in my heart and my throat hurts, so the Protestant chest also has a bit of soul in it. But not bleeding like the sacred heart. And it's white, not red, so it's better. On the head the Protestant soul is white. The Catholic soul on the head is also white but a more colourful white, and it glows. No. No. No. No. When a Catholic soul is clean, it's red. It has to be because the sacred heart is red. And the Protestant soul is a nice, simple white. And I'm not sure about the head any more.

'Souls which are still covered in Original Sin and have not received the Sacrament of Baptism go to Limbo. That's right, children. Limbo.'

When Sister Angelica talks about limbo she doesn't look up or down. So where is it? I ask my mother if I might have to go there because I haven't received the sacrament of baptism but Mummy always says, 'Don't pay any attention to that kind of stuff. It's all a load of rubbish.'

Mummy says, 'We don't believe like the Catholics. They dwell on the crucifixion which is so negative.' But she also says, 'Oh, the crosses I have to bear!'

And she sometimes refers to the nuns as Uriah Heeps. But when she talks to them she says, 'You're absolutely right, Sister,' and 'Oh yes, of course, Sister,' and 'Precisely, Sister!'

Whenever my mother tells the nuns that Daddy puts the bottle before his family the nuns say, 'Well now, Miss McKirdy. It's because God loves you so much that He tests you so.'

And Mummy says, 'Yes, Sister, that's true you know, that's very true, Sister.'

I think she likes it when the nuns say she's a saint.

Granny Mac went looking for a new church. After sampling the Spiritualist church which she found 'too hot', she tried the Christian Science church which was 'too cold', and finally settled on School of Truth which she said is 'just right'.

We all like going to the School of Truth because it's in a bioscope. We're not allowed to have films on Sundays in South Africa. That's why they have it there. The seats

26

are comfy and we don't have to sing hymns.

Daddy doesn't come with us. He prefers to listen to his wireless in the bedroom. He lies on the bed and shouts at the Jewish panellist on the Oxo Brains Trust. Daddy always argues with the wireless.

At the School of Truth they tell you that you are responsible for your own life and that you mustn't blame God or anybody else for your troubles. But the Catholics say He sends pain to test you because He loves you. They say suffering is a sign of His love.

And at the School of Truth they tell us that God is love and health and happiness, and it is man who creates his own pain and suffering by thinking negative thoughts.

Sometimes, if it's Caledonian or family business, we have to go to the Presbyterian church, where it feels like a Transvaal winter, cold and dry. There's no colour except for the blue hats in the front row. They look like budgies on a branch and smell of lavender.

The minister is Dr Waddell. When he talks about God, he is angry. Is God angry? To be hugged by Dr Waddell would be torture because all his bones would stick into you. I think he's sick with something. He looks like my mother when she says, 'I'm at the end of my tether.' He's got a face like a vulture and he thumps the pulpit. The noise wakes up Granny Mac and her chins wobble.

'And now . . . for the benefit of the devoted few who have, this Sabbath, managed to pass up earthly pursuits such as tennis, or golf, or bowls, or the Grand Prix, or swimming, or picnicking (or drinking, in Daddy's case, although he never comes with us) in the hope of saving their souls, I shall deal with the question of love.'

Dr Waddell goes on, and on, and on, and on. All the words sound the same. He makes me want to scream back at him. I would if I were bigger. When he talks about blood, and sacrificial lambs and smiting, his eyes and mouth go thin in a sort of smile. Now Dr Waddell is coming down the stairs of the pulpit so he's not

27

very far away from us. Maybe we're close to the end. I blink hard to wake my eyes up.

Auntie Joan and Uncle Ian rush forward with a bundle. A christening! Oh yes . . . that's what we're here for! The baby is dozing in its hand-crocheted shawl. Its soul must be stained with a lot of original sin to make Dr Waddell twitch like that. I hope we'll see the dirt. Maybe the water will be like it is in the tanks at Granny's place after a storm.

I wonder if Dr Waddell will have to rub hard to get the soul clean? I hate that, when my mom rubs my face with a hanky that she spat on, to wipe off the jam and the chocolate and ink and everything. When she doesn't use a lot of spit, it's worse, because she has to rub much harder and it takes longer. So please God, thank you, if Dr Waddell uses a lot of water and a facecloth.

Oh! Dr Waddell doesn't even wash the baby at all. He just sprinkles some water on its head. (That won't do any good.) The baby screams. Granny Mac shakes her head. 'Poor devil!' she says. Granny loves babies. Dr Waddell gives the bundle back, takes out a hanky and wipes his hands.

When I've done something Mummy thinks is naughty she whacks me, stinging slaps on my bottom and legs. And then she puts me into my bedroom. And just before she locks the door she says, 'When you've stopped crying and pulled yourself together, I'll come and open this door.' The whacks aren't very sore. But she talks to me from far away and she is very cold. She doesn't say, 'Knock on the door three times when you've stopped crying and then you'll be let out.'

She goes away. Then you have to wait until she comes back. You can hear your friends having fun in the garden next door but you have to stay inside the bedroom. And she closes the curtains so it's dark.

Even when you've stopped crying, you may still have

to wait for another half an hour before you are let out, because Mummy is giving an elocution or a dancing lesson. It's up to her when you'll be let out. She says, 'I'm the parent, I'll decide.'

My mother loves telling this story. It happened to my sister Jilly before Annie was born. 'Jilly couldn't have been more than two years old when one Saturday afternoon we came back from a wedding, and that little lady took off her brand-new shoes and threw them at me – she was a very strong-willed child. I said, "You come here and pick up these shoes." The little devil just looked at me and said, "No." Can you believe that? "NO"!

'Well, I battled with that child for four hours. I whacked her bottom. I boxed her ears. I put her head under the cold tap. I was determined she would pick them up. In the end I won. Oh, she was a sobbing wreck all right, but she finally bent down and picked up those little white shoes and handed them to me. You've got to, with children. It's for their own good. If they get the better of you, you've had it. You've got to keep the upper hand. And, I'm happy to say, we never had a performance like that again.'

Only once does Jilly steal the show. She is playing Grumpy in Miss McKirdy's production of *Snow White and the Seven Dwarfs*. At rehearsals the dwarfs just mimed eating their dinner. But on the opening night they suddenly discover real food on the table. Once Grumpy starts eating she just won't stop. She scoffs down her plateful in no time at all and then sets about mopping up all the other dwarfs' supper. Undeterred by the threats from the wings or the cheers from the audience, she eats on, determined to see it through to the bitter end.

After that one performance as Grumpy, Jilly is left at home with Daddy and me. Eating the props showed she was no real pro.

But Annie is. She makes the perfect Snow White. Apple cheeks and curls the colour of dark milk chocolate. She is the star of Mummy's production even though she is the younger of the two. Mummy says, 'You just can't keep that child off the stage.'

Auntie Edie says, 'And people just can't keep their hands off her either.'

Annie says she hates having to rest in the afternoons to be fresh for a show at night.

Auntie Edie rolls Annie's hair in rags and then makes her lie down in the back bedroom every afternoon from two till four. Annie says she can't sleep because it gets too hot with the curtains drawn. She just lies there and tells herself stories about princesses who don't have to practise their songs and dances a thousand times. Her princesses get everything perfect straightaway and their hair is always naturally curly. They are waited on by pretty fairies and not ugly aunties with hairs on their chins.

Auntie Edie looks like an aardvark. There is a picture of one in my nature study book. It has very small eyes and a big snout, like a pig, which goes flat at the bottom. The aardvark has tusks on either side of its face rather like the prickly hairs that grow out of Auntie Edie's cheeks.

We three girls hate Auntie Edie. We wish she didn't have to look after us when Mummy has too much on her plate, which is most of the time. She is always saying, 'Get a move on' and 'Hurry up' and shoving us around. Everything she does from scoffing her food to thumping the hell out of the piano is ugly.

She can't even dance properly. When she teaches us the Highland Fling, she has to hang onto the piano to balance on one bandy leg. Her feet are covered in bunions and corns and she can't point her toes.

Once Jilly dropped her school milk bottle on Auntie Edie's corns and Auntie Edie chased her around the house with the broom. Jilly managed to climb into the dirty clothes cupboard and hid there until it was dark and Mummy came home. Auntie Edie can't hit us when Mummy's here because Mummy always does the hitting.

Auntie Edie never takes a bath. When she goes to the bathroom, she says, 'I think I'll just have a wee wash.' She has to be careful not to wet her black petticoat because she sleeps in it. She stands at the basin and rubs Lifebuoy soap under her arms, then she makes the towel into a kind of knob and uses it to wipe away the soap with water. Even though she's got quite a few dresses, she puts on the same one day after day and never puts it out for Jane to wash.

Her hair is thick with grease and when she asks us to plait it, we want to vomit.

This is the way she eats her food: she pushes her chair back and bends her body forward to rest her mouth on the plate. Then she uses her spoon or her knife or her fork to shovel it in. Sometimes her food drops from her mouth and she catches the bits with her hand and stuffs them in with the rest. At the same time as she's eating she's drinking tea. She pours the tea from her cup into her saucer and then she lifts it up with both hands and slurps it up like a dog.

At breakfast she drops gingernuts or toast into her tea before she pours it into the saucer.

Daddy says things like, 'We have very musical soup, tonight.'

And once I said, 'Do you know, Auntie, my Daddy says you eat like a pig.' Mummy pretended that I was choking. She pushed a serviette over my mouth and thumped me on the back.

We get so sick of the way Auntie only ever puts fishpaste and Marmite on our sandwiches and she always cooks mince and barley. Just that, no carrot, nothing. Just mince and barley. If Mummy ever makes a sandwich she always trims the plate with lettuce and puts a cube of tomato on top.

Mummy is light and Auntie is dark. Mummy's shoes and handbags are new and white and Auntie's are old and black. Mummy's dresses are pink and blue and Auntie's are brown and grey. Auntie smells of dirty stockings and stale sweat and Mummy smells of April Violets.

I want to love Mummy so much but she won't let me. She's never there. She's always out at work. So now I've got a nanny called Lena because Daddy doesn't want Auntie Edie staying here all the time. Lena's a servant and black and I'm not allowed to kiss and hug her. So what good is she to me?

Sometimes I come home from school and I lie on my bed and cry and cry. When Lena tells me not to dirty the candlewick bedspread I get really angry and start to scream and kick.

'I want my mummy, I want my mummy! I don't want you, I want my mummy.'

'You can't have her,' says Lena. 'She doesn't want a naughty child like you. If you don't stop being naughty she'll never come home.' And she gives me a smack on my bottom even though she's not supposed to. I don't care that she hits me because I don't care about anything but wanting my mother. I cry and cry until I fall asleep.

Today Mummy comes into my room with Lena and says, 'What is all this nonsense Lena has been telling me about?' I get up from the bed and run to my mummy. I am happy now she is home. But my mummy is cross with me. She smacks my bottom as hard as she can and says, 'You are a naughty little girl giving Lena so much trouble. Don't ever, ever, ever do that again.' And she smacks me each time she says a word.

My heart is sore and I'll never forgive my mummy for that. Never, never, never.

Lena Mashlanghu's husband is called Axel. My mummy and daddy say he's a good boy so they let him sleep in the *kaya* with Lena even though it's not allowed and if the police raid they'll arrest him.

Mummy says, 'It's the law and they're only doing their job.'

Lena and Axel are Zulus. She wears a white cloth wrapped around her head, her *doek*, she calls it. Her uniforms are pink or green check and she wears a big white apron.

I spend a lot of time with Lena. She allows me to play in the house while she cleans, but when she polishes the wooden floors and washes the linoleum in the kitchen then I must get outside into the back garden.

'Heh, Terri-bull, don't you mess my floors,' she shouts. 'No child makes marks on my floors. Terri-bull, you stay in the garden.'

She and Jane, the wash-girl, and Joseph Kabendo, the garden boy, eat their lunch in the afternoon under the palm tree in the back garden. I am allowed to sit with them. There is a great big cooking pot of mealie meal which is white and stiff enough to take in your fingers and roll into little balls, stewing steak, onions and tomatoes in a thick sauce. I never ask for any because I don't think I am allowed to but it looks nicer than our mince and mash.

They talk and laugh together, speaking in Zulu, which I don't understand. But when I hear them say 'Master' and 'Madam', I know they're talking about my family.

After lunch I go with Lena and sit in her *kaya*. Sometimes other nannies visit her. We all sit on the floor and Lena sits on a little stool because she says sitting on the floor gives her a sore wee-wee. Lena's bed stands on bricks to keep her safe from the bogey-man who comes to get you in the night. Lena's bogey-man is black like her and looks like a monkey. She calls him the *Tokoloshe*. Her bed is covered with a big embroidered cloth. All the nannies have cloths on their beds which they sew themselves. They buy them from a man who

33

comes round on a bicycle. He wears a hat and has an old suitcase strapped to the back of his bike. We all gather in the street and I try to see into his suitcase when he is showing the nannies the cloths. After they have decided which ones they want, the man writes in his 'money' book. The nannies don't have very much cash and so they always owe him from last time. And everybody laughs and shouts all the time.

Lena's cloth has flowers and butterflies and 'Home Sweet Home' and 'Jesus Loves Us' and some bees, all in bright colours.

Lena decorates the wooden shelves on the walls in her *kaya* with newspaper cut into patterns. Everything that gets thrown out from our house she puts on her shelves. My favourite is a little china house that got chipped in the spring-cleaning. Mummy says Lena chips things on purpose so that she can have them, but I love it when she gets our ornaments because then I can touch them. In our house they are either up on the ornament rail or locked up in the glass display cabinet.

Mrs Brink, my music teacher, locks everything away so her children have to say, 'Ag, Mammie, please can I have an apple?'

Then she takes a huge bunch of keys off the belt around her waist and says, 'OK, but just one, hey! And then lock it up again and bring the keys straight back to me.'

All the nannies visiting Lena in her *kaya* have children of their own but they don't look after them, just like my mummy doesn't look after me. They also have to work to pay for things for their children like my mummy does. My mummy pays Lena to look after me while she is out earning money because private school education and extras like dancing and music don't grow on trees. She says, 'It is my duty to give you the best, whatever the sacrifice.'

*   *   *

It's Sunday night and I've been staying at Granny Mac's house for the weekend. Auntie Edie, Granny Mac and I are on our way to Mr Ferreira's fish and chip shop, the Seabreeze, even though the sea is hundreds of miles away. I am pushing my blue doll's pram. I'm glad we're going out to buy our supper. By the time we get back, Auntie Betty will be in her room, Uncle Bob will be out, and the kitchen's all right then. I also like to smell Granny's hotpot and her baking. Granny has a big mine house with a veranda. In the garden there are lots of nooks and crannies where you can play housey-housey, very tall mealie plants that you hide amongst and a little bird-bath with stone birds that even the real birds think are real birds.

Inside the house are hundreds of cupboards that people don't use and you can climb into. Once in a while, if I'm very good, Granny lets me go into the front room where there are locked display cabinets with miniature furniture, real Scottish heather and a little black doll in Zulu skirt and beads.

When I'm in bed, I hear the trains trundling in the mines and the hooters blasting. And now, as I walk along between Granny Mac and Auntie Edie, the men are switching on the golden lights which make a fairy queen's crown all around the mines. It is so pretty.

As we pass Booysen's Police Station someone is making a terrible noise inside. It sounds as if a dog has been run over and it is howling. I stop pushing my pram. 'Get a move on,' says Auntie Edie.

'What's happening?' I ask.

Auntie whispers crossly, she's scared too, 'It's only the natives getting a hiding.'

Mummy says, 'Right is something inside you. It may not be the popular choice, it will never be the easy choice, but it will reap rewards in the end. Right will need the hardest work and the greatest effort. The easy thing to do is always the wrong thing.'

35

I understand this because fools always do the wrong thing. The fools that don't listen to Mummy. Sister Angelica and Mummy say the same. They agree about right and wrong when they're together. 'That is correct, Sister, I completely agree. She deserves to be punished.'

Sister Angelica says she always expects Mummy to agree because both of them want to do right and it's only by showing the child the wrong that she will come to love the right. Mummy says she is so right. They never show you that they aren't together.

Mummy says some of the things that the nuns think are really wrong but we mustn't tell them. I think it's because they've got to find out for themselves. She says they will. Besides, we go to the convent nearly for free so we should show appreciation and gratitude, and anyway, it would be cheeky to tell them they're wrong. Mummy says it's not that she has anything against the Virgin Mary, but it is wrong to pray to her because it's breaking God's commandment about having images. But it's the Catholic teaching. It's not Sister Angelica's fault. Mummy would rather not go into all that. Sister Angelica says it's right to pray to the Virgin Mary because a son is closest to his mother so he's bound to pay more attention to her intercessions.

I think that's bunkum. I like to talk to God straight. I like to have God as a friend and companion and I don't like all that incense, all that ringing of bells and tinkling and swinging. I think it's a load of old rubbish. And Mummy says that the way the Virgin Mary's eyes are so downcast as she sits on the donkey shows that she hasn't got an awful lot of gumption. Granny Mac and Auntie Edie agree.

Sister Angelica can make her whole arm disappear underneath her clothes; you can see lots of movement under the white starched cardboard and the black cloth, and somewhere there she finds her big bunch of keys. Bringing them out takes another little while.

Every morning the Catholic girl with the most gold

stars goes to the front of the class and takes the bunch of keys from Sister Angelica and opens the cupboard where all the boxes of white and coloured chalk are kept, and the elastic bands and the yellow HB pencils. That's my favourite cupboard because all the new things are in it and there are interesting boxes packed on every shelf. I'd like to steal them and put them in my cupboard at home. On the second shelf, in a corner, is a bottle with a holy picture pasted on it, and a label that says, 'Holy Water'. Sister Angelica's handwriting is just perfect with all curls like on a peacock – you can't believe it's been done by a person.

The girl takes the bottle and unscrews the top and goes to a place near the door where there's a bowl hanging on the wall. It's like a budgie's bowl and it's nailed there, and it's got a sponge in it. If you're a Catholic, every time you come in or go out, you dip your finger into the bowl and cross yourself, even if you're just going to the toilet. The Catholic girl pours the water very slowly into the budgie bowl. She has to be careful not to spill any, then she puts the top back on and puts the bottle into the cupboard and locks it. And when Sister Angelica gets the keys again she takes them back to that safe place inside her clothes.

At home I've got my own secret bottle of holy water and I practise with it. It's from one of the cupboards in Granny Mac's house. On it there's my own holy picture and my own holy water label. The water's from the cold tap in the bathroom so I don't really think it works.

I wear a curtain ring on my finger and I put a towel on my head and I collect all the hair ribbons like Sister does when we go swimming. I use my six hair ribbons and go round collecting them again and again. I mark the work in all my story books; I use my red pen, and all the time I keep my curtain hook finger curved out. I take all the keys out of all the cupboards in our house and I tie them together with string so that they make a big bunch and they jangle. (My mother and father get cross because I don't always put them back.) I take all my dolls and line them up and I use a bamboo stick from Daddy's toolshed and I smack their hands. The dolls don't hold out their hands when I tell them so I have to pull them out for them. It's three good whacks on each doll's hand because they are such naughty children! I make their hands red. They deserve it! Some are fat and lazy! And there are bold and ugly ones too. Especially the teddy bear who never cries, no matter how hard I hit. They never answer me back and if any of the dolls whine after I've smacked them, I hit them again and after that I whisper, 'There you are. Just so you'll know.'

Dolls can't puff out their cheeks or look upset so I have to do that for them too. I make all the noises. If I tease a doll I have to do the teasing sounds that all the other dolls make and I do the sobbing too. And then I pray.

Sacred Heart of Jesus, I place my trust in thee
Sacred Heart of Jesus, I place my trust in thee
Sacred Heart of Jesus, I place my trust in thee

I worry a lot because I have to get things right for Sister Angelica. She sometimes hits me and I don't know why. Sister Angelica whacks me from behind, on the back of my head. We have to look at the blackboard all the time. She never shouts, she just comes behind you and you don't know if you're going to get hit.

Mummy hits you from the front so you can see her coming. Mummy hits you with her hand, Sister hits you with the ruler.

She may ask a question from the back of the classroom and you can't see the answer on the blackboard. And you're scared when she calls your name. But you don't answer because you don't know what the answer is and that's when you get a whack. 'Wake up!' she says.

She's different when she's doing things with the Virgin Mary at the altar. She's kinder then. When she's teaching us, she's cross.

But she can be funny, especially when she says things like, 'Did you ever see such a sluggard?' Or, 'At last, Miss Snail.' And we children laugh when she calls Pamela Hogg fat and ugly. We laugh because we're on her side.

Sister Angelica's cross with me. I don't know why. She doesn't frown. She doesn't shout. She just looks at me. For about half an hour. I don't know how she does it without blinking. What am I doing wrong? I feel sick. She keeps on looking. The scared lump is starting to come up inside me. All the other children stop breathing. They're glad it's not them. What am I doing? Why does Sister hate me so much. All I can think is, 'Please Sister, take your eyes away.' I can feel the other children smiling now. They must know what I'm doing wrong. I must be doing something so ugly she doesn't want to say what it is.

Have I got something hanging out of my nose? Aren't I put together right? Sister Angelica is put together so right! Everything about her fits. Is there something missing in me? Maybe it's the same thing that makes Mummy not want to hug me. I know I'm not pretty. Jilly and Annie call me the pink rat. Daddy says, 'Stop calling her that!'

And my mother says, 'There's nothing the matter with her.' But she doesn't sound too sure.

I want to wee. But then Sister would be disgusted and she hates me so much already. I want to run up to her and say, 'Sis-ta! It's me! I carried your books for you yesterday!' I'm still not breathing. I think I'm going to faint. Suddenly I have to let the air in so fast that my voice goes into me backwards. Then I'm crying. Every time I turn my head back to Sister her eyes are still very wide, still looking at me. Doesn't she know who I am? What I'm doing must be something from a long time ago. When? From when I first came here? From the very beginning?

ORIGINAL SIN is big, dark, brown smudges. Sister Angelica has made a painting of Africa for the wall chart that shows how much money we have given to feed the black babies. And that's what it is. Original sin is smudgy shapes like Africa on a white soul.

I don't have any smudgy shapes on my soul. Mine is just simple white. The Protestant soul is just much nicer. Granny and Mummy and Auntie Edie say there's nothing wrong with Catholics, but God loves simplicity best. He's not interested in rosaries and holy pictures and that. And that's why it's best to be a Protestant, I think. After they've been christened and they're clean, Protestants don't have to worry about those other sins.

'Come here.' Mummy is looking very cross. 'Lena tells me you've been a very naughty girl! The ground's covered with apricots. They'll all go to waste.'

'I didn't do anything . . .'

'Don't you pretend you don't know what I'm talking about. You know you've been a very, very naughty girl. Lena says you were swinging on the branches of the apricot tree.'

'I wasn't Mummy . . .'

But she's already started hitting. I am covering my bottom with my hands and trying to get out of her way. But she's stronger than me. She can hold both my hands in one of hers and then my bottom's free for a really good hiding.

'It's not fair! I didn't do it! It's not fair!'

'Don't lie to me, my girl. I . . . WILL . . . NOT . . . TOLERATE . . . LIES.'

I've got a friend called Carbolic. Nobody knows about her. She sleeps in the passage cupboard. I tell her, 'And this is your room, Carbolic.' She's a good friend, you know. We talk a lot while we're playing. 'Carbolic,' I say, 'be a dear and fetch that stick for me.' I teach Carbolic Scottish dancing. I lose my patience with her.

40

'I've told you time and time again to turn your knees out and watch your supporting foot. Your arms are all wrong, they look like a scarecrow stuck up in the air like that. And can't you get some control into your body? It's like a jelly, wobbling all over the place. You'll never win any medals at this rate. Unless you're prepared to concentrate and listen to constructive criticism, you'll never get anywhere in this life. Oh, we're crying now, are we? What do you expect me to do? Hand out bouquets? Well I can tell you, life is no bed of roses and tears won't get you anywhere, either. Hard work and getting the job done – that's the answer. So stop that snivelling now and let's get stuck in and try and make something out of you. Mark my words, one day you'll thank me.'

Whatever I say to Carbolic she loves me and always lets me be in charge.

A girl with frizzy hair has come to our school. It's very curly and smudgy brown like her skin. We all say 'Poo' at her and we laugh and hide her sandwiches. One day, to make them all laugh more, I throw them into a muddy puddle. I don't want a friend with frizzy hair and dirty skin.

We've just sprinkled birdseed on the dead nun and I don't know why. Sister Joseph says, 'Well, children, you are blessed. Reverend Mother is allowing you, all, without exception, to pay your respects to our dearly departed Sister Mary Theresa, and say a prayer for her. So line up. Come on. In line. Make a line. Come on.'
I don't want to. But if I don't I'll be an ungrateful, wicked, callous, unnatural girl.

'Do you know,' Sister Joseph goes on, 'Sister Mary Theresa lived to the grand old age of ninety-three. And now look at her there, she's so peaceful and serene. Oh! She's just beautiful! Like a bride!'

I look in the coffin. Sister Mary Theresa's skin is blackish-blue with purple spots and yellow blotches. She looks like the chicken Lena left in the sun too long. Mummy smelt it and said, 'No. Oh no, no, no.'

When I come home from school, Lena isn't waiting for me at the bus stop like she usually does, with my cat, Ginger, in the shopping basket. The bus must be early so I walk down the road alone. I go round the house to the back door. The front door's always locked, because of burglars, and only Mummy's pupils come to it anyway. Nobody ever comes to visit. I go past Daddy's roses and the apricot tree and the birdbath to the back door.

But it's locked! The back door's locked! I bang on the kitchen window but the venetian blinds are down and closed. Then I run to Lena's *kaya* and the padlock's on the door. And I run to the back lane and call, 'Lena! Lena!' but there's no-one there.

They've left me! Mummy and Daddy and Jilly and Annie and Auntie Edie. They've all gone. And now Lena's gone too. They've gone to live somewhere else. And left me here.

I'll have to stay sitting on the kitchen steps till it's dark and then I'll go into the toolshed with no lights. But the toolshed's locked. I try the garage but it's empty. Mummy always takes the car anyway, but this time they must've all gone away in it. My doll's house in the garden is locked too, and the key's in the kitchen.

I can't do my homework. I can't play. Maybe if darkness comes I'll have to tell Mrs Weizman across the road. I don't want to, I don't want anybody to know they've left me. I'll stay here till I die.

Is that her laugh? I run. I see Lena! She's coming in the back gates. On her head she's balancing the basket with bread in it and some soup greens. She says, 'Why didn't you wait? I was frightened for you!'

And I say, 'The bus came early. I thought you'd be home.'

Lena says, 'I was running, running from the shops to catch you.'

Yes, she's always there. Lena's always there. She always waits for me, except for today. I think people

42

who wait are not very important. I think you can be cheeky to them and rude. I think you can. Other girls are cheeky to their mothers. Sharon Weinstein shouts at hers which is a disgrace. My mother wouldn't stand for it.

But sometimes you feel like shouting at someone and so I shout at Lena. And then she chases me and when she catches me she laughs and puts her hand inside my pants and squeezes hard. She says she's holding my cake.

My mother isn't just my mother. She's Miss McKirdy, the elocution teacher. She doesn't go to the classroom to teach like other teachers; the nuns take the children up to the big hall for her. They're always saying, 'Get a move on! Get a move on, girls! Don't keep Miss McKirdy waiting.'

My mother doesn't have time to wait, she teaches so many children. It's not just a question of me and my convent, she's got five convents. She's GOT to get on. She can't wait.

My mother can't knit, or sew or cook, but I wish just once I could take sandwiches that she had made. Even fishpaste sandwiches would taste nice if they had been made by her, but she's got too much on her plate, so it's always Auntie Edie who makes them or Lena. I hate fishpaste sandwiches.

I love flowers and gardens that don't have walls around them with sharp metal spikes to keep burglars out. The lady down the road doesn't even have a fence. There are roses climbing everywhere up hedges and round the trees. It's like a jungle with lots of secret paths.

I'm so hot. I wish I could be a leaf and play in the water from the sprinklers. In my storybooks England looks like her garden, wet and green.

I like our garden because it's our garden. But it's not fun to play in because Daddy never lets things grow big. He cuts them back. And he uses a ruler to measure where to plant the flowers. First he kneels on an old green velvet cushion and pours a packet of seeds into a tea strainer. Then he makes a hole exactly an inch deep in the soil with a pencil and drops a seed into each hole using a pair of tweezers.

My mother goes mad. She opens the fly screen door and shouts, 'For God's sake, Duncan, throw the whole packet in and let's get some abundance.'

There's crazy paving and cement up the driveway and down the pathway and there are concrete rings around Daddy's rose bushes. I keep grazing my knees and elbows, or getting scratched or tearing something.

Sometimes I raid Daddy's flower beds and steal nasturtiums and dahlias. I stick them in old ink bottles and fishpaste jars and arrange them on the furniture all over my room. I tie the curtains with bows and arrange my dolls on the bed. When all is ready I go outside and climb up onto the back wall so that I can look into the room and I sit there, gazing at my work and pretending that I am a poor, homeless child looking into a cosy cottage on a cold winter's night.

One day, on my way home from school I spy a beautiful pink flower in the lady's garden. It looks like a ballet dress. When I dance at the eisteddfod I see children whose mothers carry their ballet dresses in zipped-up plastic bags. They powder their daughters' feet and dress them in pink socks and pink satin shoes. But my mother doesn't come with me. I have to change my shoes alone.

There's no-one in the street. Can the lady see me? I must have that flower. I can just reach. Pull. Tug. Snap! I've got it. Run! Run!

Mummy drives like a maniac when she takes us to school in the morning. Very often she gets a speeding ticket and she always says to the traffic cop, 'But officer, how can I get up that hill if I don't accelerate down this one?'

44

On Monday and Tuesday afternoons Mummy teaches in the big lounge at home. On Wednesday, Thursday and Friday Mummy has private pupils at school so she doesn't get home till late. Jilly and Annie mostly come home with Mummy on those days because they've got things to do like hockey and singing lessons.

When I play at home, I make my friends sing 'God save the King' because if you go to see a film that's what you do at the end. Mummy always sings out loud. In the bioscope people laugh at her but she stands like a soldier and sings.

My best friends are Maureen and Peter and when we've finished singing 'God save the King' their mother calls, 'OK kids, that's it. Into the bath now.' And Maureen and Peter climb over the back wall.

I pick up my toys and put them in the doll's house and then I go into the house and into the bathroom and I call myself inside, shouting out of the window, 'OK, that's it now. Come inside and have your bath.'

And then I bath myself. I don't like Lena bathing me because she always wants to touch my cake. She says nannies are allowed to do that to children they look after.

Lena has her bath before me. Every day at five o'clock she boils a bucket of water on the stove and I go with her to her toilet in the back lane where she keeps her tin bath. She fills the bath with water from the outside tap and then puts the hot water into it. She says that makes it not so cold. After she's dried herself and dressed, she rubs some Vaseline into her hands and puts it on her face. Then it shines like Sister Angelica's, only Sister's doesn't need Vaseline.

We have Palmolive soap but I would rather have Lifebuoy. Sister Angelica smells of Lifebuoy. When I've finished, Lena cleans out the bath and picks up the towels. I put on my jammies and my red slippers with the blue cats' faces on them and the red dressing gown which used to be Jilly's and Annie's and then I sit with Lena at the kitchen table waiting for Mummy to come home.

I help her shell the peas. When she's not looking I pinch some and Lena says, 'Heh! Suga, wena!' and pretends to be cross. She never says, 'Heh!' to Mummy and Daddy but they never talk to her like they talk to me either. They say, 'Please, Lena do this.' When they talk to me they say, 'Do it.'

When it's already dark and you think Mummy will never come home you hear her car's hooter and then Lena has to run out and tip up the garage door and run up the drive and open the gates. Mummy drives straight in and up the drive and into the garage. When Mummy comes in the lights go on in the house.

I wake up. People are moving on the ceiling. They are dancing with the burglar bars and laughing and talking in native. They are Zulu impis, hordes of them. They fill the ceiling. I'm surrounded. They're going to murder me! They come closer and closer. They're a township of natives with spears and hats and sticks and stones.

'Please Lena. You are my nanny. Help me! Don't let them kill me. Mummy pays you, it's your job! Stop laughing.'

I have this dream a lot. But my parents will be cross if I wake them. It's not important enough.

I like Jesus when I look at his picture in my *Bible Story Book*. I like how He sits on the hillside in the sun. I like how He is surrounded by people, in the open air, talking to them. He's such a soft, kind man. I'd like to be there to listen to him. It looks like everyone wants to be there. I'm sure He never shouts or is too busy. In the picture in my book, a young child is asking Jesus a question. And Jesus is sitting on the ground. He doesn't have a throne or stand up high. Some of the people in the crowd are looking at the child who is asking the question and some are looking at Jesus. No-one is looking at the end of their tether. Jesus is in a loose white robe. His hair is being blown about by the breeze; He is leaning forward. Listening.

Jesus is listening carefully; He doesn't want to miss a single word of what the child is saying; what the child is saying must be very important for a grown-up to look so interested. His right hand is slightly raised as if to ask the crowd to let the child speak. You want to tell him everything. And you feel safe. I know this sounds silly, and I wouldn't tell anyone, but I want to swim in the tears of his eyes. You just know those tears would be warm.

The children at the convent tease us because our mother is the elocution teacher. They mimic her and say, 'How Now Brown Cow,' and 'Sister Susan's Sewing Shirts for Sailors'.

What makes it worse is that Mummy makes Annie and me do monologues and recitations. We have to copy her way of speaking and pronounce the words after her and copy her gestures and stress the word she says to stress. She goes over it, and over it, and over it with us. She's always saying, 'Practice makes perfect. The great Harry Lauder would practise a number a thousand times before performing it in public. If you're not prepared to put the work in don't expect bouquets.'

Miss McKirdy says that in all the world there are only two kinds of people – those who love being on a stage and those who don't.

Annie is a born showman. She was known as 'South Africa's Shirley Temple' because she was singing and dancing by the time she was three. She wore a pink ballet frock and pink bows clipped to her sausage curls and she twirled a pink parasol. She sang on the steps of the Johannesburg city hall and at the Johannesburg railway station as the troop trains arrived and left. Mummy and Auntie taught her to sing all the old war songs like 'It's a Long Way to Tipperary' and 'Pack Up Your Troubles in Your Old Kit Bag'.

The men would all go mad. It reminded them of their own little girls back home in Britain and they would

47

all shout and cheer and throw their caps in the air.

I never saw any of this because I hadn't been born yet, but the pictures are hanging on the walls in the passage.

I take her costume out of the costume cupboard and dress up in it but I can't sing so I don't get to do any numbers. Daddy says, 'That child's tone deaf. I don't know why. It's a complete mystery to me.'

Jilly refuses to put a number over or under or any-whoro at all. Mummy says if something is white, Jilly will insist it is black. They are always fighting, those two. 'You'd be better off trying to get a mule to sing and dance,' says Mummy to Auntie Edie.

'Best thing,' says Auntie Edie, 'is to completely ignore her. Just let her get on with it. She'll soon notice who's getting all the attention.'

Jilly and I have to take the bus. There isn't enough room in the old Dodge for Mummy, Auntie, Annie, the costumes and us. Annie has reached the final of the Grand Curzon Bioscope Talent Contest and everyone is hoping she'll win the big prize. The Curzon is very popular because it runs these contests before the feature film. The manager is a Scot from Glasgow. He adores Annie and has given her the best spot in the final. Everyone loves Annie. You just can't help it.

Each contestant has a chance to appear twice and Annie's first number is her hillbilly. The outfit consists of a pair of hide pants, leather boots, old leather holster with two guns in the pockets, a checked shirt, sheepskin bolero, kerchief tied at the neck and a ten gallon hat. She wears a comedy moustache which wiggles and jiggles. She sings 'She'll Be Coming Round The Mountain' and the audience joins in the chorus singing, 'Ai yai, yippee yippee yai'. Then she pulls out her guns and 'sticks 'em up'.

Her second number is her Harry Lauder. For this she wears a kilt, tartan socks, brogues, a tartan tie, white shirt, tweed jacket. Her hat comes down over one eye and she carries a crooked stick. She wears false, bushy eyebrows to make her look like an old man and she walks like Daddy when Mummy says he's had too much to drink. She sings a medley of 'I belong to Glasgow', 'Stop Yer Ticklin' Jock' and 'Keep Right on to the End of the Road'.

Mummy always stands in the wings when Annie performs. She winks and nods and laughs and claps and afterwards gives lots of constructive criticism in the dressing room. Sometimes Annie cries and says, 'What more do you want?'

And Mummy answers in one word, 'Perfection.'

Daddy doesn't come to the final. He says he wants to forget the whole entertainment business. Years ago my dad was very famous in Johannesburg. He played all the leading roles in the Operatic and Dramatic society. When he played Benny in 'The Desert Song' he came onto the stage riding backwards on a donkey. He likes telling us how one night a woman in the audience laughed so much at his antics that she had to be carried out of the theatre and given oxygen by the St John's ambulance man. I have never seen my dad on a big stage with other people. But I have seen the photographs of him in funny costumes and he doesn't look like my dad at all. He looks so young and happy and full of fun!

Tonight the Curzon is jam-packed and everyone is very excited and buying popcorn and Eskimo pies. Outside on the pavement there are crowds of nannies and Zulu flat cleaners who wear thick rubber sandals made from old tyres and have leather discs in their ear lobes. Of course they won't be allowed into the bioscope because that's for whites only.

Annie is running neck and neck with a Jewish boy who tells jokes and does magic. Mummy says he is precocious and has a very pushy mother who is only out for number one. Apart from Annie and the Jewish joke teller, there is a boy who can whistle like a bird and one who can yodel. The audience doesn't like them very much but they do like the girl in the snakeskin bathing costume who does acrobatics. She can rest her head on the floor of the stage and let her body run around it in circles which Mummy says is 'cheap and nasty and just the sort of thing you'd expect an Afrikaner to do'.

The Jewish boy has added a little surprise to his first turn. As well as magic and jokes, he is going to play a miniature mouth organ. Mummy thinks this is against tho rulos and she complains to her friend, the manager, who is also from Scotland, but he says there's nothing he can do about it. When the boy's mother finds out about Mummy's complaint she brushes past Auntie Edie so hard that she knocks a tin of hairpins to the ground.

'Petty,' says Mummy as she escorts Annie to the stage for her hillbilly.

Mummy is good at measuring audience applause and she can tell that the first round went to the Jewish boy. Maybe Annie didn't get a good night's sleep, or maybe she's showing that 'old unreliability'. Mummy isn't sure but her performance lacks 'it'. She takes Annie into the lavatory for a pep talk. 'Do you realize you've let your whole family down? You are a bloody disgrace, that's what you are. Well, I can tell you, tonight's the finish of it. There'll be no more performing after this. I'll sell your costumes and pay for an orphan to have music lessons instead.'

Annie always ends up crying, but Mummy says it's a tactic that works and that in no time at all Annie's a different child.

In the second half the Jewish boy has gone a step further and added a trumpet solo to the end of his jokes. Luckily he goes really wrong on the last note and the noise is so horrible that the audience has to cover their ears with their hands.

'You should have seen his mother's face,' says Mummy, laughing afterwards. 'Like a thundercloud, poor kid. He must have got hell when he got home.'

After the interval Annie comes on and is really good. She is a star shining in the heavens.

The audience stands and cheers and there is no doubt who will be the Curzon Star of 1951. Jilly and I clap until our hands are red as we watch our sister climbing to the top of the gold-painted dais to receive first prize, a silver trophy and a Raleigh sports bike.

Jilly is wild. She smokes and drinks and kisses boys in the orchard. She has lots and lots of boyfriends even though boyfriends are forbidden in our house. One day when she is suntanning in the garden a boy walks past and whistles at her. At first she doesn't realize he is the postman on his rounds because he doesn't carry a bag. That's carried for him by a piccanin who walks behind. The postman takes the letters from the little black boy and pops them in the boxes. He walks along the pavement with his hands in his pockets and Jilly thinks he is just a nice guy who lives down the road. They don't talk a lot to each other because he is Afrikaans and Jilly can't speak Afrikaans even though she learns it at school.

'Who could be bothered to learn such a stupid language?' she always says. So she and the boy just do a bit of smooching in the orchard.

When Annie's conscience gets the better of her she tells Mummy about Jilly's affair with the postman. Mummy is disgusted. 'Why are you always attracted to the underdog?' she asks.

Jilly is forbidden to ride on motorbikes so she does. She also gets a lift home in a car with a boy from Maritz Brothers College. Annie knows about it so it won't be a secret much longer. Annie is hopeless at keeping her mouth shut. She is so scared of Mummy she tells her everything even before she's been asked. Mummy is waiting for Jilly as she steps out of the car around the corner. Jilly doesn't seem to be scared of Mummy or the nuns. She'll never cry in front of them. In fact, Jilly never cries at all. I don't think she knows how to, not since she was a little girl, anyway. She just gives them a look which Mummy and the nuns call 'dumb insolence'. Jilly is a born leader. The girls at school adore her. They voted her head girl but the nuns wouldn't have her.

She is captain of the first hockey team and very naughty. Miss Schultz teaches Afrikaans and in the middle of her lessons Jilly jumps up and shouts, 'Walls!' Then all the girls run down into the senior cloakroom to hold them up.

She sits upstairs in the back seat of the bus and smokes. She puts peroxide in her hair and wears her schoolgym four inches above her knees. The nuns call her bold and ugly, which is rubbish. She is the prettiest girl in her class and has lots of boyfriends. One of them is called Billy.

One night Mummy and Daddy are out and Auntie Edie is in charge. When we hear the 'broomph' of Billy's motorbike through the sound of 'Highland Laddie' Auntie Edie stops playing the piano and gathers us three girls together in the small lounge. 'I'm going to put out all the lights in the house, so he'll think there's no-one at home.' And she goes from room to room clicking off all the switches.

'She's bloody barmy,' says Jilly. 'He already knows we're all at home.'

When we are in the dark Auntie Edie peeps through the venetians. 'Oh my God,' she mutters, 'he's still there. I can see him sitting under the lamppost. Let's get under the beds!' With that she shoves us all into the front bedroom and makes us crawl amongst the dust and fluff. We have to lie in the pitch dark while Billy rides his motorbike slowly up and down in front of our house. It is so frightening but I don't know what I'm scared of – I don't think any of us do. Then Jilly starts giggling and she can't stop even when Auntie Edie threatens to slap her. I start giggling too.

*   *   *

Daddy is getting thinner and thinner and he's started vomiting. Daddy drinks on the hour, every hour. Right through the night you can hear his footsteps going down the passage, making the floorboards squeak. He goes into the bathroom and you hear the tap turn and then silence and then the tap turns again as he washes the glass out. You can smell it on his breath at breakfast and as he walks up the path to go to work he leans over to one side and nearly falls into the flower beds.

'Born on the side of a mountain,' says Jilly.

He lets the garden go to pot. Joseph cuts the lawn when he's not in jail for pass offences, but it's up to Daddy to buy the plants and shrubs. When he's drinking he forgets to do that. He is always so fussy about his clothes but now he drops mince and marmalade on his Royal Navy tie. He doesn't care about anything. Mummy doesn't care about him, that's for sure. She says the only women who get things out of men are the ones who simper. Strong women are losers every time. Auntie Edie agrees, although I don't know what she knows about it all.

Mummy prays that Daddy will one day find the truth that will set him free and that she, thank God, has found. She says that Daddy is not essentially bad. Just weak.

Peter Peter pumpkin eater
Had a wife and couldn't keep her.

Mummy is going away. She's taking Annie and they're going to spend the summer in Scotland. Annie is going to compete at the Highland Games and the Edinburgh Festival and Mummy is going to take her fellowship which will make her the most highly qualified person in Highland dancing in South Africa. As well as answering a lot of questions, Mummy has to dance the Highland Fling, the Sword Dance, the Seann Triubhas

53

and the Strathspey and Reel of Tulloch. She says it's not surprising that a woman in her late forties is a bit out of puff. But the official board say she must 'execute six steps in each dance from start to finish in one continuous movement'. It is very funny seeing Mummy dance. She's a bit like a jelly.

Granny Mac and Auntie Edie took Jilly overseas when she was twelve. She did very well at the Highland Games and came back with quite a few medals. On the whole, they said, she behaved quite well, except for the young stewards onboard ship. They told us how poor the people in Britain were after the war and how lucky we were to live in the land of milk and honey. They were very embarrassed when an old white woman in Ireland cleaned their shoes just like Lena cleans ours.

Mummy and Annie are going in June, and they will be gone till early September when they'll return to the African spring. This makes me feel very, very sad. A whole three months without my mother and sister.

Lena is going to look after my Dad and Jilly and me. Mummy wanted Auntie Edie to move in lock, stock and barrel and take over the running of our house. But Daddy said, 'If she comes, I go.' And Mummy knew he meant it.

The cabin trunks have been taken down from the cupboard in the roof. The old labels have been washed off and clean brown paper has been spread inside. One of the trunks is for costumes and one is for summer clothes.

I love going to Park station because there is a goldfish pond and fountains. I like to kneel down and draw my finger through the water. This brings the big fish to the top and they nibble my nails.

Because my mother is president of the Caledonian Society and the Dancing Association, the Johannesburg pipe band is playing and dancers, holding broadswords, are forming an oranges and lemons tunnel for her and Annie to march through. Daddy is walking squiffy because he's just popped into the United Party Club across the road in de Villiers Street. Mummy doesn't stop talking to her committee members as he weaves down the platform towards us. She just gives him one of her looks.

Black people are not allowed into the white part of the station so the porters are old Afrikaans men with no teeth. Ours can hardly manage to get the heavy trunks into the compartment. Mummy and Annie have one to themselves because Mummy has bribed the head steward. Annie is so excited. She is running around kissing everyone and telling them that she will bring them white heather for luck from Scotland. She keeps thinking the train will leave without them.

Mummy says, 'Calm down, will you, the station master has to blow the whistle three times and he's only blown it twice so far.' The band has started playing 'Will ye no come back again' and Mummy bends down to kiss me and tell me to be a good girl and to look after my dad. She smells of April Violets and the fur collar of her coat is soft and warm. Everyone is singing 'Auld Lang Syne' and my father is trying to wrap his arms around her but she is waving and shaking people's hands and she doesn't see him.

The boat train is pulling out now and we are all crying as we watch it getting smaller and smaller until it disappears behind the grey, concrete pillars.

I sleep in Mummy's bed which Daddy pulls alongside his. If I'm feeling very sad Daddy says, 'Come and snuggle up,' and I get into his bed with him. I love being warm with Daddy. The only thing I don't like is most of the time he smells of drink. He licks his lips, and after he's kissed me I want to wipe my mouth. And sometimes he's crying and that's even wetter.

Orange Grove Junior School looks like a fairground. There are streamers and flags flying and striped tents. There isn't a ticket collector at the gate but policemen in khaki uniforms with guns. It's the day white people are choosing the new South African government and Daddy has taken me along when he goes to vote. 'Of course it will be the same old crowd getting in as usual. That's a foregone conclusion,' he says.

We live in an English-speaking suburb of Johannesburg so our member of parliament is United Party which is the official opposition party to the Nationalists. The Nats have won the last two elections and they'll win this one, hands down. But Orange Grove will be won by 'us'. Daddy knows the UP candidate because they drink together at the United Party Club.

The ones Daddy really can't stand are the Liberals. 'Troublemaking buggers,' he calls them, 'sucking up to the blacks, pretending to be do-gooders but in the meantime feathering their own nests. They want to keep in with the natives so that when trouble comes they'll be in the pound seats.'

There is only one man standing alone in front of the Liberal tent. A woman is shouting at him. 'It's people like you who will cause a blood-bath in this country.' He smiles and shakes his head, but she carries on: 'If we don't have pass laws we'll be overrun by them. Give them an inch and they'll take a mile.'

Other people have gathered now and they are joining in. 'Why don't you go and live in Russia, you bloody Communist. We don't want you here,' shouts a man smoking a cigar.

'You tell me why we should hand our country over to a bunch of savages who can't even read or write?' asks a fat man with a moustache.

'Because,' replies the man in front of the Liberal tent, 'it's their country.'

'Jesus,' shouts the man with the moustache, 'let me at that bastard. I'll kill him.'

Someone else holds him back. 'Don't waste your punches. He's just a kaffir-boetie. A real man wouldn't talk such junk.'

People have started pulling down the Liberal posters and tearing them up. The policemen standing around are killing themselves laughing. I'm scared but I want to stay and see what happens. Daddy takes my hand and pulls me away. 'Things could turn nasty. Let's get back to the car.'

As I go through the gates of the school I turn around and stick my tongue out at the Liberal.

Peter Peter pumpkin eater
Had a wife and couldn't keep her
He put her in a pumpkin shell
And there forever she did dwell.
AMEN

I cover my mouth as soon as I say it. I am laughing and I think all the other girls will laugh too. But they don't. We are sitting on the long seat at the front of the bus, the one where you have your back to the driver. Grown-ups want to face the way the bus is going, so that seat's always free and we can all squash up together on it. I know most of the people on the bus because they're on it every day and I give them all names.

Mrs Tapioca is my favourite. I want to eat her face because the powder and the freckles look delicious, like a pudding. She always sits in the same seat and she always smiles at me; I know she likes me. Mrs Tapioca knits very fast.

Pamela Hogg says, 'You swore. That's swearing. You said "amen".'

'It's not.'

'It is!' they all shout. And they click their fingers and chant, 'We're going to tell Sis-ta!'

'No, don't, please.'

Pamela Hogg says, 'Amen is swearing. We're going to tell Sister Angelica on Monday morning.'

I beg them not to tell, but they say it is their duty.

I can't sleep. If Pamela Hogg or someone else tells

Sister Angelica, I don't know what will happen to me. I might be taken up onto the balcony at assembly. That's worse than being hit because everyone laughs and it goes on for much longer. When I had ink stains in my arithmetic book and rubbed them out till I made a hole in the paper, Sister Angelica pinned the pages up on the noticeboard. But for saying that rhyme and then amen, she might nail me up instead.

'Self-willed, pig-headed and mulish,' writes Mummy. Annie is proving extremely difficult to handle on the trip. 'Trying to get her to practise is a constant nightmare. Not to mention getting her to dance in the rain.' In Scotland they don't cancel the Highland Games if the weather is bad like they do in South Africa. And the Scottish judges are marking her down on technique. Apparently Annie is smiling till her face nearly cracks but they seem to be made of stone.

Eating fish and chips and scones and jam and fruitcake is about the one thing Annie likes in Scotland. And she's put on so much weight she can hardly lift herself off the ground. They are both pretty down in the mouth when they go to stay with Dad's brother, Uncle Ian, and Auntie Maisie who now have five children.

Annie becomes very friendly with our cousin, Ailsa, who is also twelve. One drizzly Saturday afternoon the two girls are playing on the golf course nearby when an elderly gentleman comes up and says, 'Wee lassies, come here a moment. I was playing golf this morning and I've gone and lost two of my balls somewhere over there. Which of you two young ladies will help me find them. There's a shilling for the one that does.'

He leads them to a bunker behind some heather and the girls start looking for the ball. Suddenly the man grabs Annie and pulls her down into the sand. For a moment she thinks they must have tripped and fallen. But when Ailsa sees that the man is holding Annie down and trying to do something naughty, she takes fright and runs. Annie is struggling to hold on to her clothes and can't think of anything to say except, 'Please, dear man, don't hurt me.'

Suddenly the man makes a funny noise and pushes Annie away. He says crossly, 'What a fuss about nothing,' and marches off, putting his cloth cap back on his head.

Annie tries to stand up but her legs keep giving way beneath her like a newborn pony. Eventually she crawls out of the bunker on all fours and starts stumbling towards the house when she sees Ailsa and all the adults running towards her. Annie starts screaming and hitting and kicking my uncle because he's holding her just the same way the man did. Mummy is embarrassed at Annie's wild behaviour and gives her a crack across the face to stop her becoming hysterical. 'For God's sake child, pull yourself together.' She shakes Annie over and over. 'Stop all this nonsense and tell us what happened.' But Annie is sobbing so loudly she can't hear anything at all.

'I think we'd better get the police,' says my uncle.

'Is that really necessary?' says Mummy. 'She does have such a vivid imagination and we don't want any fuss.'

'And it would be most terribly embarrassing if it was one of the members of the golf club,' says my aunt.

However, Uncle Ian has made up his mind and the police are called. The two girls are put into separate bedrooms upstairs and are then questioned by the police. Afterwards the inspector tells the adults that their descriptions of the man and what he did are identical so he's sure the attack took place.

But there's a problem. Because Annie is only visiting Scotland, there would be no point in hunting down the man, arresting him and putting him on trial without the star witness. Anyway, Annie has still got to dance at the Edinburgh Festival so Mummy thinks it's best if the subject is closed.

'Just when you think she's down, she'll come up,' says my mother. Annie is suddenly winning again even though the competition is stiff. There are dancers from Australia, Canada, New Zealand. But Annie sails through and wins the Colonial Champion of Champions Cup. Her picture is in every newspaper and she is the toast of the town.

Then it is time for them to come home. 'And not before time,' says my mother, 'I'd had it up to here. This girl is up and down like a Jack-in-the-box. One minute she's on top of the world and the next she's in the doldrums. There have been times when I've just wanted to walk away and leave her, she's been so difficult.'

However, as Mummy climbs the gangway of the Union Castle liner berthed at Southampton, her heart is heavy. Despite the drizzling summer weather and Annie's moods, she has enjoyed being away from Daddy. She is so sick and tired of him and his drinking. She pays the school fees and buys the groceries and our clothes. He has no-one to look after but himself and he can't even do that. She knows he goes to work under the weather and comes home under the weather and she worries about his job and how much longer the Lipman brothers will put up with it all. Daddy has worked for them in their gramophone saloon for twenty years. There are three Lipman brothers, Harry, Max and Sam. Daddy ran the store for their father when he was alive. He is the only one to know the combination of the safe. Harry, Max and Sam trust him more than they trust each other. 'Their patience and understanding is amazing,' says Mummy, 'but it can't go on forever.'

Mummy and Annie are not even talking to each other when they get on the ship at Southampton. Annie stays up on the deck while Mummy unpacks in their cabin. It's not as exciting as the sailing from Cape Town but the band is playing and people are throwing streamers and singing 'Auld Lang Syne'. Mummy and Annie are good sailors and they are both dressed and ready for dinner when the first sitting gong goes. Mummy is very impressed with the food. 'Lovely, lush English vegetables. So much tastier than those you get in South Africa and served by young men who really know how to treat a woman like a queen.'

Mummy is invited to sit at the captain's table. 'Such a fine looking man. So fresh! And what a charming manner. He puts everyone he meets at their ease. The sort of man of whom Kipling said, "Here is a man who can walk with kings, but never loses the common touch. A man amongst men and a dedicated sailor."' He invites Mummy to judge the fancy dress competition with him and she suggests that Annie perform the Sailor's Hornpipe. But Annie refuses to practise and Mummy decides to ignore her. The night of the fancy dress ball Mummy and Annie have a terrible fight. Annie really cops it from Mummy and that seems to do the trick.

By the time the Union Castle liner has docked in Cape Town, Annie has quietened down. In fact, she seems to be quite a different person.

Part Two

It is the day before my tenth birthday. Ephraim, the painter, has come back again. He's been away a very long time and Daddy says it's his own fault. 'I've told that boy time and time again not to go in the street. He doesn't listen. So he ends up getting picked up by the police.' And Daddy sighs. 'You can't help these people. They want to do things their way but if we let them, we might as well just pack and leave this country. There'd be nothing but bloody chaos.'

'Don't swear, Duncan,' says Mummy.

Daddy gets Ephraim painting jobs. The people pay Daddy and he takes some of that money for letting Ephraim sleep in the toolshed. He says it's an agent's fee.

'Whatever you like to say about these people,' he goes on, 'Ephraim's a damned fine painter. Fast and clean. But unfortunately very unreliable, like the rest of them. Unreliable and irresponsible, no matter how old they are. He knows that the government will never give him a pass. They want him to go back to Swaziland where he belongs. I've told him time and time again not to go out into the street, because the police will just arrest him. He must stay in the toolshed when he's not working. But he wants to do things his way so there's no point in trying to talk sense to him.'

Ephraim knows he'll get into trouble if he goes into the street or anywhere away from the toolshed but he still does. Then he disappears for a long time. When you see Ephraim again he's looking very thin and there's no hair on his head because it's been shaved. When Daddy looks at him through the fly-screen door Ephraim puts his hands over his head. 'So you're back are you? Which prison did you get sent to this time? Didn't get much to eat, I see.'

Ephraim shakes his head and giggles.

'Have you learned your lesson? Are you going to do as I tell you now?'

Ephraim nods. He's still smiling behind his hands.

'OK,' says Daddy, 'I'm going to have my dinner. So I'll see you tomorrow morning. I've got a job for you, Ephraim. All right? A lady wants her house painted – quickly, quickly. So tonight you stay in the toolshed! You hear?'

Now Ephraim is using just one hand to cover his face. He mumbles something through his fingers and he giggles.

'Money?' says Daddy. 'You do the job first and then we'll talk about money.' And Daddy steps inside and puts the catch on the fly-screen door. 'It's hopeless trying to help these people,' he says. 'Why bloody bother? You're beaten before you've begun.'

'My family and I have been victimized and ostracized. And it's nothing but pure jealousy on the part of Elsie McKintosh and her satellites.' Mummy says we girls suffer because there is a deep and tragic division in the Highland dancing world brought about entirely by Elsie McKintosh. She was once Miss McKirdy's star pupil.

South African by birth, she came from a broken home and was more or less taken in by Granny Mac. Not only did they teach her free of charge but Granny Mac gave her a family kilt with matching tartan stockings. Shortly after Elsie won her first big championship, she married a young piper and then she fell into the most common of human traps. She got too big for her boots.

'Pure ingratitude,' says Mummy. The next thing they knew was that Elsie had set up in opposition. Not only had she started her own dancing studio, but she had lured away several of Mummy's best pupils. From then on it was war.

When he was still very young, Elsie's husband committed suicide which Mummy said was a great shame since he was such a nice chap. Elsie's daughter is Jilly's strongest opponent, even though she's quite a bit younger.

The rift in the dancing world means that there are McKirdy judges and McKintosh judges. According to Mummy and Auntie Edie, 'our' judges are loyal, efficient and fair whilst 'their' judges are biased, incompetent and blind. If Betty Brown, who was one of Mummy's bridesmaids, is on the judging panel then justice will prevail and either Jilly or Annie will get the gold. But if that snake-in-the-grass, Reggie Strydom, is in the judging seat then corruption is the order of the day and we girls can come home empty-handed.

Mummy doesn't let us off the hook just because the judges are crooked. If we don't win she gives us a lecture and her cold treatment. Shrugging her shoulders and sighing to God, she says in a voice that is very soft and sad, 'It's no good crying over spilt milk. You've missed the boat. In life, you only get out of it what you put into it.' She takes off her spectacles, flesh-coloured, because she's not too keen on people knowing she's wearing them. She rubs her eyes and puts the cashbook down on the invoices and receipts to stop them blowing about. Then she goes into her room and locks the door.

We girls start talking in whispers. We don't know what to do, like at a funeral. You wish she'd come back but she can stay there all that night and the whole of Sunday. And when she does come out, she doesn't talk.

If you say, 'Mummy, would you like— ' she says, 'No thank you.'

Sometimes we can make up to her by setting her hair and painting her nails but mostly there's nothing you can give her, nothing you can do. You just have to make sure that next time you win.

65

Winning is the way to Mummy's heart.

By five o'clock on Sunday evening she might phone one of her allies on the South African Board of Control for a post-mortem of Saturday's Highland gathering. She likes to get to the bottom of things.

'Aha!' she says, 'I knew it. I just knew it! It's as plain as the nose on my face. I recognize the forces that are at work here. It's the same old story, my family and I have been victimized and ostracized!'

On most Friday and Saturday nights our family entertains at old-age homes, Caledonian societies, masonic lodges and mental hospitals.

My mother plays the piano and sings duets with Daddy. She gets all the chords wrong but to make up for her bad piano playing she puts in all sorts of flourishes and twiddly bits. Jilly and I perform Highland and Irish dances. Annie does her 'turns' and Daddy sings humorous songs and compères the show. We three girls are packed around the costumes in the back seat of the old Dodge.

Mummy and Daddy sit in the front and fight all the way to the venue. On stage we smile and laugh at all the old jokes until we are facing upstage and then Jilly and I pull such terrible faces that Annie nearly falls off her chair laughing. Sometimes you can hear the giggle in her voice as she sings.

There are always envious remarks from the audience. How lucky we are to be such a lovely, talented family.

Mummy and Daddy fight all the way home. Sometimes Daddy stops the car and gets out, and then Mummy climbs over into the driver's seat and grates the gears all the way back to the dutch-gabled house. Daddy stays away for several hours. He walks the streets all night or sits at a bus-stop. I can never go to sleep until I hear him come in in the early hours of the morning.

I love to stand at the gate of Granny Mac's weekend cottage at Henley and gaze across the veld at the native *kayas*. The people who live in them work in the Portuguese market garden as vegetable pickers. Life in those huts just seems so different to ours. From the gate you can see their fires and their candles burning. You can smell the wood smoke and hear their chatter and their calls. It is that time of evening. You know that they are standing around the fire that is cooking their meat and mealie meal and they are laughing and singing and drinking kaffir beer.

Sometimes our Afrikaans neighbours, the Murrays, have a *braaivleis* and they also stand around drinking beer and cooking their meat on an open fire. All the adults in my family have false teeth so they don't like barbecues.

When the stars of the Southern Cross come out I go inside to have my supper, mince and mash.

We spend nearly every weekend and most of our school holidays at Henley. Grandpa Mac built the house himself in 1925. He used thick stone which was carried by ox-wagon from a quarry fifteen miles away. Even on the hottest Transvaal day the rooms are cool inside. Ice-cold water is brought up in a bucket from the well in the back yard and Granny Mac has planted mint outside the kitchen door. Henley-on-Klip is a tiny settlement about thirty miles outside of Johannesburg, on the banks of the Klip river, a tributary of the mighty Vaal. It was given its name after Henley-on-Thames in England because there are so many willow trees. Granny Mac has called their acre of land 'Aberfoyle' to remind her of Scotland and it runs from the dirt road at the top of the property to the bank of the river where thousands of brightly coloured birds live in the reeds. The soil is dark red and is covered with thick kikuyu grass. The driveway starts at the iron gate and runs around both sides of the house and down to the river. Pine trees are planted on either side of it and there are flowerbeds filled with orange nasturtiums and purple portulaca. The verandah is covered in the palest mauve wisteria and there are two Pride of India trees, one purple and one red, in front of the house. On either side of it there are lots of fruit trees laden with apricots, peaches and plums.

Sometimes bats get in through the wire mesh verandah door and fly into the stone walls. If that doesn't kill them, we thwack them with tennis rackets because Granny Mac says if they get into your hair you'll have to have it all shaved off.

At night you can hear bull-frogs and see something moving on the river. That's Mr Murray fishing by torchlight. Mr Murray looks like a film-star. He has four little sons and a wife who drinks. Mummy says it's an absolute tragedy because she is such a lovely young woman. When Mr Murray's pet bulldog, Lady, was bitten by a snake and died, he drove off in a cloud of dust and didn't come back until the next day. Mr Murray and Daddy talk over the barbed-wire fence that divides the two properties. Mr Murray told Daddy that if we were English he and his family would have nothing to do with us. But as his great-grandparents came from Scotland and he is also a mason, he is prepared to 'extend the hand of friendship and speak in English'.

On Saturday nights Mr Murray takes us girls to the bioscope which he runs in the Meyerton town-hall. The seats are so hard they make our bottoms numb and we have to take cushions to sit on. Afterwards Mr Murray buys us milkshakes at the Pickin a Chickin roadhouse. I have strawberry, Jilly has lime and Annie has a brown-cow – Pepsi-cola and a blob of ice cream.

Mummy hates Christmas. There is so much for her to do what with shopping for presents and wrapping them up and ordering food. She has to do it by herself because Daddy is always drunk.

Daddy's drinking has got very bad and on Boxing Night we think he is going to die. Granny Mac, Auntie

Edie, Jilly, Annie and I are all sitting around the paraffin lamp on the verandah at Henley. There is a breeze blowing through the Pride of India trees cooling the hot night air, but our hearts are heavy as we listen to the conversation between Mummy and Daddy in the front bedroom. The window opens out onto the verandah so we can hear them clearly.

Daddy is trying to be sick into a basin. But there isn't anything in his stomach except whisky. And there's not too much of that because he's too weak to get up and go to the bathroom where he hides his secret supply. Mummy certainly won't get that for him. She has already poured one bottle over the mint patch outside the kitchen door. Daddy knows when he's beaten. His body can take no more and he has run out of hiding places. Mummy knows them all. She puts the tin basin down on the dusty floor.

'Well Duncan, what's it to be?'

Daddy lies back on his greyish pillow. The bed linen doesn't get washed all that often and it always looks grubby. In the candlelight Daddy looks as grey as his pillow. His voice is tiny like a mouse's. 'It's the end of me, I'm finished.'

When I hear this I want to be sick. I don't want my dad to die. I love him. I want him to live. I can hear Mummy standing up now and I know exactly how she is wagging her finger when she speaks. 'Duncan, if I have to drag you through this by the scruff of the neck, you're going to live.'

Daddy doesn't answer, or at least we can't hear him. We lean forward to hear what is said next. We needn't bother because Mummy's voice is strong and clear. 'Did you hear what I said?'

The mouse-voice says, 'It's too late.'

'For God's sake man, where's your gumption. You've got years of life in you yet, if you will only turn on this demon and confront it. Turn on it and tell it to get out of your life.'

'Get thee behind me, Satan,' says Daddy in his small voice. But I can hear a little laugh running through the words.

When we children hear that little laugh we get up and go into the bedroom. Mummy is sitting on the bed and holding Daddy's thin hand in hers. Annie puts her arm around Mummy. I climb onto the bed to be near my dad. Jilly stands over by the window. Daddy's cheeks are all caved in and he hasn't shaved for days. He smiles a little smile and says, 'My three smart girls.'

'Please don't die, Daddy,' I say, cuddling into his arms.

'He's not going to die,' says Mummy, 'not if I've got anything to do with it.' And she heaves him up into a sitting position.

'Your mother wins every argument and no doubt she will win this one too,' says Daddy, already starting to look better.

My heart is flying now because I know it's going to be all right. Mummy's in charge and Daddy will do as he's told. We all start laughing and hugging and someone goes to make tea and someone else to get some warm water to sponge Daddy's face. Mummy rubs cologne into his forehead and straightens the sheets.

'Mrs Holmes at the convent has told me of a wonderful man near Hartebeestpoort Dam who does faith healing. When we get back on Monday I'm going to give him a ring and we're going to see him and we're going to get you cured once and for all.' Daddy nods.

Oh, it's wonderful when your parents agree. It makes me so happy to see them being kind to each other. Daddy is enjoying being fussed over by Mummy, being the centre of her attention. She's even kissed him on the forehead and he's agreed to try to eat some toast and Marmite.

Jilly suggests that we girls have a game of monopoly and I help her get out the board and sort the money.

We play by the light of the paraffin lamp until it's late. We can hear the bullfrogs down in the reeds. We can also hear Mummy and Daddy whispering in the front bedroom. They are making plans for the future. Granny and Aunt Edie are getting ready for bed in the back room, glasses of water for their teeth, bicarbonate of soda for their indigestion and prayer books on their bedside tables. Finally we put away our game, clean our teeth in the tin basin in the bathroom and climb into our iron beds with their old horse-hair mattresses.

Jane, our washgirl, loathes me, my family and the entire white race. Jilly says she looks like Madame Defarge in *A Tale of Two Cities*. She has piercing black eyes and cheekbones jutting out like cliffs that you could fall hundreds of feet off.

In order to iron our shirts, trousers, shorts, dresses, skirts, blouses, vests, panties, sheets, pillowcases, tablecloths, doilies, bras and handkerchiefs, Jane has to get up at about four-thirty in the morning in her shack in Alexandra township. She has a cold wash in her tin basin and then lights a paraffin stove to boil water for tea. Then she walks nearly a mile to the bus stop and queues for about an hour for the bus. She says that there are so many people travelling on the buses that you don't even have to hold on and often there are *tsotsies* who steal your money when they're squashed up against you. When Mummy shouts at her for arriving late, Jane clicks her tongue and says under her breath, 'Suga!'

She leaves at six o'clock in the evening and gets home between eight and nine. Then she cooks mealie meal for herself and her children and does her own washing and cleaning before going to bed.

We spend a lot of time trying to get Jane to smile. Once Annie went dancing past her in the kitchen where she was ironing and sang, '*Pack up all your cares and woes, here I go singing low, bye-bye blackbird.*' Then

71

she put her hand over her mouth and said, 'Hell, I'm sorry!'

Jane just went on with her ironing.

Thursday is when most white women go out because it is their nanny's day off. Mummy always takes us to John Orr's for afternoon tea on the last Thursday of the school holidays. The tea lounge is on the fourth floor and the manageress, who Mummy says looks as if she's just stepped out of a band-box, escorts you to your table. Tea at John Orr's is more expensive than anywhere else in Johannesburg because they have white waitresses. They are old women who need the money because their husbands are dead, or they are divorced or haven't had a proper education.

We are served by the same woman every time because she recognizes Mummy who always says to her, 'Aren't your feet killing you, dear?' When she goes to fetch our order Mummy says, 'Imagine having to earn your bread and butter doing this.'

I think it must be quite nice because you can eat lots of chocolate cake in the kitchen. We order our favourite food: toasted chicken sandwiches with mayonnaise, lettuce and tomato, and slices of gherkin. The bread is cut into quarters and we have four small sandwiches each. While we are eating, mannequins twirl around the tables showing the customers the latest fashions. They never smile because smiling isn't chic but they pause at the tables to let the women customers feel the material. A man in a silvery suit plays music from the shows at the grand piano. Mummy is a great favourite of his because she sings along, waving her hand in the air to the music which embarrasses us terribly. People at the other tables smile and encourage her which is even worse. We are thankful when the cake trolley comes along because if Mummy's mouth is full of black forest gateau she won't be able to sing.

After she has eaten her cake, she smokes two

Rothman's Kingsize Filter cigarettes and stubs them out in her saucer. Mummy has a very funny way of smoking. She doesn't inhale, she puffs on her cigarette like a goldfish in a bowl until the ash gets so long that it falls off into her tea or onto her clothes. We have to say, 'Ash, your ash,' all the time.

She also has a very faraway look in her eyes when she smokes, as though she is remembering things long ago and miles away.

Daddy gets very irritated by her smoking even though he used to be a chain smoker himself. 'Sixty a day at one time,' he says. 'How can anyone smoke all those cigarettes and not inhale?'

I agree with him. I've smoked every day since I was seven years old, either in the back lane or up on the toolshed roof. One day I inhaled so deeply that I got sick and dizzy and fell off the roof. Luckily I just made it to the mint patch in the back garden before I passed out. Mummy was sitting on the lavatory looking out of the bathroom window. She saw me collapse and yelled for Lena to come and help her pick me up.

I came around just in time to stuff a few mint leaves into my mouth so she wouldn't be able to smell cigarettes on my breath. I don't think it even entered her head to think I'd been smoking. Lena and Mummy carried me into the bedroom and Mummy fetched a face-cloth rinsed in cold water from the bathroom and patted my face with it. Then she got her bottle of Eau de Cologne and rubbed a few drops on my forehead. I groaned and squirmed on the bed.

'Poor little devil,' said Mummy. 'It's the heat. Too much for her. She never was any good at being in it.'

Being sick is a good way to get Mummy's attention.

I am playing Voortrekkers and Zulus with Maureen and Peter, the children who live next door. It has been raining and we have been slipping and sliding in the mud. We finish off our game and I go inside to have my bath. My white socks are all covered in mud and my knickers are muddy too. The next morning the brown colour has turned to red and it is there again on my pyjamas. Mummy comes into the bathroom and when she sees it she goes and fetches me what looks like a little tissue case. She says even though it's perfectly normal to bleed, I can stay away from school just this once.

Annie bleeds like meat on the butcher's block. Once I have to hold the ladder whilst she climbs onto the roof to clear the hailstones out of the gutters and I see the blood, bright red, like stewing steak, running down her legs. I want to be sick but she doesn't seem to notice. I wonder if you can bleed to death and not notice.

> *My little dolly is sick, sick, sick,*
> *Run for the doctor quick, quick, quick,*
> *The doctor came with a tat-a-tat-tat,*
> *He came with his stick and he came with his hat.*
> *He looked at dolly and shook his head:*
> *Now little girl, you must put her to bed;*
> *Keep her very, very warm and very, very still*
> *And when I come tomorrow you must pay my bill.*

Jilly no longer cares how much trouble she gets into. She says she dares the nuns to expel her. Jilly has met the boy she will marry. Terry is at trade school learning to be a motor mechanic. He is tall and blond and meets her in the orchard under the plum tree. If he sits on the high saddle of his sport's bike he can kiss her over the spikes on the fence. He is very good at sport, just like Jilly. He plays cricket and soccer but not rugby. Jilly plays hockey and tennis and she swims. I like the way Jilly's muscles move. You can't take your eyes off her legs when she runs. You can't take your eyes off her anyway, she's so beautiful. She has lots of golden hair that I want to touch and her eyes are green with brown speckles sprinkled in them. She always smells lovely, like clean sheets and baby powder and the roses in

Daddy's garden after it's rained and the grass has just been cut.

Annie and I call her China because she is so perfect. She looks just like a china doll even though she is so sporty and strong.

I am sitting at my Dolly Varden dressing table, cutting a picture out of the *Rand Daily Mail* newspaper to paste into my scrapbook. In the photograph a black woman is holding a baby on her lap and looking at the camera. Around her neck, on a piece of string, she is wearing a cardboard number plate. Above the picture is written PASSBOOKS FOR AFRICAN WOMEN BECOMES LAW.

Nearly every night now the police are raiding the servants' *kayas* in our suburb. When you're fast asleep the noise of the big trucks wakes you up and you can hear dogs barking, women screaming and sometimes a baby crying.

'They know the law,' says Daddy. 'It's up to them to abide by it.'

'For God's sake, Duncan,' says Mummy, 'they're only human.'

Auntie Edie is so frightened of men she either says 'Yes, yes, yes, yes' to everything they say or she scuttles out of the room when one of them comes in. She hates boys and parties and having fun. She peeps through the bottom of the Venetian blinds and listens outside windows. She's a *schloop*. She sucks up to Granny Mac and Mummy and would to Daddy, if he'd let her. He calls her 'the yes woman' and says if she opened her purse the moths would fly out. But Auntie Edie says she doesn't have any money except the handouts she gets from Granny Mac and a little bit from teaching Highland dancing.

Auntie Edie's studio smells of sweat and fish and chips and it's where I meet my dancing friends. My best friends are Elizabeth and the Harding twins. Even though they are twins they don't look like each other.

75

She has blond ringlets and his hair is carrot-red. Their mother never wanted a boy so she pretends he isn't one. She curls his hair and puts lipstick and powder on him. Auntie Edie plays the piano and teaches her pupils at the same time. She bangs the tunes out very loudly because she says it helps the dancers to jump higher.

The Harding twins have to sit next to their mother with their hands folded and their feet crossed. Elizabeth and I don't have mothers who watch, so we can do really naughty things. Our favourite thing is riding up and down in the lift, pushing all the buttons to make it stop on every floor. The studio is on the ninth floor so it takes forever to go up and down. We ask Auntie Edie if we can go and buy fish and chips and we don't come back for an hour. We play catch in between the parked cars in the street or we just sit and smoke on the fire escape. When one of the twins is sent to find us we give them a quick drag on our ciggies but they don't know how to smoke and they get the filter all wet and soggy.

The only time we stay in the class is when Mr Simpkins arrives. He is an old man with grey hair. But he is very strong because he rides a bicycle everywhere, just like a native. He's always hanging around us children, bringing us silly little presents and asking us for hugs. The older girls tell him to go and jump in the lake but we're too young to do that.

When he dances the Highland Fling he makes everyone laugh, even Auntie Edie who has to stuff her hanky into her mouth. His feet are so long and thin, he can't move them quickly enough around his legs and he ends up looking like a demented grasshopper.

Your arms in Highland dancing are supposed to look like the antlers of the deer but Mr Simpkins' arms go straight up in the air like someone in a gangster film who's just been ordered to stick 'em up. His spectacles move down his nose bit by bit until they are just on the tip of his nose as he looks down at his swords and

Elizabeth and I bet each other bubble gum that they won't stay on till the final bow. But they always do.

The Seann Triubhas is the funniest of all. It's supposed to be a very sad dance because it tells the story of how the English King George forbade the Scots to wear their kilts after he had beaten them in battle. You have to move your legs very gracefully to the side while you balance on the ball of your other foot. Mr Simpkins is always falling over because when he lifts his leg to the side he chucks it out with such force it's as though he hates it and wants to get rid of it.

Mr Simpkins once invited Annie and me to his church fête and Auntie Edie said we had to go. It was an Anglican church and we saw some shocking things. White people were kissing black people. We even saw a white girl sitting on a black boy's lap and feeding him jelly and custard. When we told Mummy and Auntie Edie that evening they said, 'Never again. That's the finish.'

When we dance at the National Eisteddfod in the city hall all the other dancers think Highland dancing is very boring, like Voortrekker dancing. Until Annie comes on and then they all stop and watch. You can't not watch when Annie dances because she's like a young deer leaping through the heather. Jilly gets fed up always coming second to Annie at the Eisteddfod. But that's the Eisteddfod. The judges come from London. At the Highland Games it's different because the judges belong to the South African Official Board of Highland Dancing which means doing it the Scottish way. Jilly does better than Annie at the games because personality doesn't count.

When the judge at the Eisteddfod adjudicates Jilly she says, 'This competitor executes the steps with strength and precision but lacks presentation. Having achieved so high a standard of technique she needs to concentrate more on building a rapport with her audience who, after all, have come to be entertained. Nevertheless, I have no hesitation in awarding her the silver medal.

'When it comes to the gold, however, there can only be one winner and that is the little dark-haired girl. This competitor is a natural, a born dancer. One simply cannot take one's eyes off her. Her positioning is, at times, a little inaccurate but her wonderful smile and personality make up for that. Will she please come forward to receive the gold medal.'

And Annie goes up to the front. Everyone in the city hall is cheering and applauding except the other Highland dancers and their mothers. As she takes her award the judge bends forward and whispers in her ear, 'Keep up the good work. You've got a great future ahead of you.'

The other Highland dancing teachers tell their pupils to copy Annie's smile and ignore her success. And Elsie McKintosh always says, 'These ballet women don't know the first thing about Highland dancing. That girl is just damned lucky what she gets away with. It's nothing but favouritism.'

Every year at the Eisteddfod, Mummy conducts five verse-speaking choirs, one from each of the convents at which she teaches. One of Mummy's choirs always wins. Every year she collects the gold medal and then presents it to the winning convent in their school hall. When our convent wins we three girls always dance at the annual prize-giving.

Reverend Mother stands up and says, 'Miss McKirdy's three daughters will now dance the Highland Fling.' The other parents must wonder about that. Perhaps they think that Miss McKirdy has conceived immaculately like the Virgin Mary. Well, the nuns always say she's a saint.

The faith healer at Hartebeestpoort Dam has worked wonders with Daddy and he is looking fat and happy at the moment. He always carries a bag of striped peppermints wherever he goes. Mummy says it's because he misses the sugar in alcohol.

I like being home from school and lying in bed sucking oranges and reading the love stories in *Woman's Own*. When they describe how 'he grabbed her and held her tight against him', I have to cross my legs and rock backwards and forwards until I gasp and it feels like the walls of my tummy are caving in. I have to keep an ear open in case Mummy comes in to see how I am. I'm so scared she will read my mind and be disgusted. Mummy doesn't like that sort of thing. I know because once she read my horoscope to me and she left out the bit that said I was sexy. Mummy only likes the good bits.

'You are getting more and more impertinent, my girl,' Mummy says to Lena one day, 'and getting more and more slack in your work. You only do what I tell you to do and nothing more. I think you've been with us too long.'

And Lena Mashlunga goes away. The lorry is piled high with furniture. Lena doesn't say goodbye. She sits in the front of the lorry with Axel and the driver.

Axel waves and Mummy says, 'Familiarity always breeds contempt.'

I'm glad Lena's going. I'm too big for a nanny now and I'm sick of her touching my cake.

After Lena comes Charlotte, sweet kind Charlotte. She is a Pondo and her skin is the colour of building sand. Charlotte is very close to being an angel when she's sober but after a few drinks of *skokian*, her homemade brew, she pushes her *doek* over one eye, pulls open her blouse so that her boobs hang out and starts shouting. 'Ag, suga. You make me sick. You rubbish people. Look at my heart. Look at it! It's bleeding. You people make me sick. You make a nonsense in my head. My head is sick, my heart is sick. *Voetsak!* All of you!' Then she falls down the kitchen steps she's

79

always polishing, and lies in a heap in the back yard.

My mother says, 'That's it. That really is it. That girl has got to go. I've got enough on my plate without having to cope with a drunk native when I come home.'

And Daddy says to Mummy, 'I suppose you think you're the only one inconvenienced by all this. I also expect to find my dinner on the table when I come home.' And they start arguing.

I go out and wheel Charlotte like a barrow across the yard to her *kaya*, then I set about getting the food ready. My mother doesn't have a clue about cooking and my sisters aren't much better. I'm the best at doing that sort of thing. When Charlotte's drunk she roasts the chicken in its brown paper wrapper and puts the fruit salad in the oven.

The next morning she somehow manages to sweet-talk her way out of being fired. She doesn't come into the kitchen looking a mess. She comes in looking fresh and clean and busies herself over the breakfast eggs. 'Good morning, my *baas*. My *baas* is looking too happy this morning and I've made my *baas* his favourite poached eggs.'

We have a very silly cocker spaniel called Virginia. Cocker spaniels are silly dogs anyway but Virginia takes the biscuit. She's always jumping up and knocking you over and when she's indoors she barks because she wants to go out, and when she's out she barks because she wants to come in. She gets on our nerves but Charlotte adores her and lets her sleep in her *kaya* at night after Daddy's thrown her out of the house. When Mummy gets to the end of her tether with Virginia she rings up the pound and asks them to come and take the dog away and find her another home. Charlotte hears her saying this and begins wailing and tearing at her clothes. 'This dog is a child of this family. If these men take Virginia then they must take me too.'

And so Virginia stays.

One Thursday afternoon when Charlotte is high as

a kite she falls over a bucket of soaking washing and breaks her leg. It is a complicated break and she has to stay in hospital for some time.

When Charlotte's husband comes to tell Mummy this, Mummy says, 'We're all very sorry to hear about Charlotte.'

'Yes, madam.'

'But you know the master and I work very hard.'

'Yes, madam.'

'And we must have someone reliable.'

'Yes, madam.'

'To look after the house and children.'

'Yes, madam.'

'And Charlotte has been very naughty of late.'

'Yes, madam.'

'And I'm not at all surprised she's ended up the way she has. You see, my boy, I can't manage without a girl.'

'No, madam.'

'When she comes out she'll have to have crutches.'

'Yes, madam.'

'And that will make doing the housework very difficult.' A pause.

'So I think it's better if when Charlotte comes out of hospital she goes home to the Transkei and has a rest and gets properly better.'

'Yes, madam.'

'So please have everything out of her room by tomorrow night so a new girl can move in.'

Daddy says our neighbour, Mrs Weizman, is a bloody parasite because she doesn't do a stroke of work. 'She hangs over her *stoep* every day, all day, laughing and chatting to any idiot who's prepared to listen to her.' She shouts across the street to him when he's watering the garden but he pretends not to hear her over the sound of the hose. Mrs Weizman waves her arms as she speaks. 'Like bloody palm trees,' says Daddy.

My father is a Jack-of-all-trades. As well as being a

musical comedy star and a gramophone salesman, he is also a certificated health inspector and knows a lot about cockroaches and what goes into tomato sauce. He qualified as an electrician but in our house the wiring is all up the pole. You get shocks from the iron, the hairdryer and the radiogram, the washing machine, toaster and kettle and once the cat lost half her tongue biting into a live wire.

Daddy's bosses at the Johannesburg Gramophone Saloons always invite us to all their family barmitzvahs and weddings and we always go. One of his bosses, Max Lipman, says 'you've got to make a big splash' and he does just that. We love the Jewish food and the Jewish jokes although it is no joke when, one Saturday, my mother goes straight to the synagogue after doing her shopping and realizes that under the wooden bench, wrapped in fine brown paper, she has two pounds of sliced ham and five pork pies.

Most Saturdays my mother goes to Gallagher's Bakers in Orange Grove and buys sausage rolls, Chelsea buns and a big Devonshire cream cake. On her way home she stops at the Indian flower-seller and buys bunches of Iceland poppies. When she comes through the back door into the kitchen we shout 'Hello Mother Christmas' and run to help her.

At twelve, I blossom. The pink rat becomes Veronica Lake overnight.

We are all very excited about the trip to Natal. First we are going down to Pietermaritzburg to compete in the Natal Highland Games and then on to Durban for two weeks' holiday. Jilly doesn't want to leave her boyfriend, Terry, but Mummy has issued an ultimatum. 'Either come with us or go and stay with Granny Mac and Auntie Edie.' Jilly says she'll come.

After the cold Transvaal winter and our journey through the Drakensburg mountains where there is snow on the peaks, it is exciting to arrive in the hot, humid climate of Natal where the air is filled with the scent of frangipani and mangoes.

We are staying for the weekend of the Highland Games at the Royal Garden, which is an old-fashioned hotel in the English style. Natal is very British. The hotel is built like a mock castle with turrets and a drawbridge and is set in gardens filled with hibiscus, poinsettia and frangipani. In the distance you can see the Valley of a Thousand Hills and the mud huts of the Zulu people.

Thousands of Indians live in this province because they were imported to work in the sugar-cane fields and now they are traders and waiters and market gardeners. All the waiters in the hotel are Indian and all the cleaners and kitchen boys are Zulu. The Zulus hate the Indians as much as the Afrikaners hate the English.

Of course white girls never think of black boys in that sort of way. But we do look at Indian boys. They are really gorgeous with their perfectly chiselled features and their sexy, sloping eyes. Annie says to be careful because Indians can take advantage. We would never dream of kissing them but it's nice to chaff them. It makes it sexier to know that they can never touch us except when their hands brush past our skin when they're serving us at table. Of course, just like men in kilts, they don't look half so good out of their starched, white uniforms and red turbans.

On the Saturday night, in the city hall, there is a Grand Caledonian ball. Miss McKirdy has bought us three girls identical velvet evening dresses. They have scooped necks, belted waists and flared skirts. Jilly's is sky-blue, Annie's is wine-red and mine is sage-green. Blue and green for the blondes and red for the brunette.

At twelve years old, with a cascade of blond hair tumbling over one eye I look every bit as old as the other two, if not older. Miss McKirdy's daughters are standing together drinking coke laced with brandy when this gorgeous side-drummer from the Natal Mounted Rifles comes up and asks me to dance.

He isn't very good at the Dashing White Sergeant or the Eightsome Reel but when it comes to dancing cheek to cheek he turns my stomach upside down. He is tall and tanned with hair the colour of honey. He smells of Chiclets chewing gum, Silversun tanning lotion and Castle Lager beer and he crushes me to him as the band plays 'Red Sails in the Sunset'.

When we get home to our hotel room Jilly and Annie tell me that I am being a little fool. 'He's bound to find out how old you are when they call out your name in the ten- to thirteen-year-old section,' says Jilly.

'You know how blokes gossip in the beer tent,' says Annie, 'someone's bound to tell him that he's cradle-snatching.'

The next morning, Sunday, he comes round to our hotel to take me for a spin in his red MG sports car. Luckily it's a two-seater so the others can't come. Mummy and Daddy think he's quite charming and don't mind my going out with him. They are so innocent. He isn't the first boy I've French kissed but he is the nicest. His tongue is soft and sweet-tasting and he doesn't try to choke you with it.

I am floating on cloud nine when I get back to the hotel for Sunday lunch. This is served buffet style beside the swimming pool. There is an ox roasting over an open fire and the striped canvas deck-chairs support overweight people balancing plates overflowing with meat and salads.

Irritating young boys are dive-bombing each other in the pool or knocking their sisters off floating rubber loungers. Some of the older chaps are trying to chat us up but they are Afrikaans so we simply ignore them. We call them 'Dutchies' or 'hairybacks' and we won't be seen dead with them.

We are all fair-skinned so we suffer from sunburn every time we go on holiday, turning first bright pink with blisters and then, gradually, a pale, golden colour as the holiday wears on.

On Sunday evening we have to go to the kirking of the chief of the Caledonian Society in the Presbyterian church. The only thing that makes it bearable is that my drummer is sitting in the pew opposite. The wink he gives me during the service assures me that he really is very keen on me. I never know what to say to boys so I hardly ever talk at all. Annie says I'm icy and Jilly says I'm cool. Whatever I am, my drummer likes it. Mummy agrees to let me drive home with him in his sports car but first he takes me to the old pie-cart at the railway station to eat hot dogs with tomato sauce and English mustard.

When we get back to the Royal we sit for a while in the MG in the palm-lined driveway and smooch. He is so gentle when he kisses me and puts his cool hand down the front of my cotton dress. I want him to touch me all over. I want to fall back into a soft cloud, I want to sink into his warm, soft love. That night, after he's gone, I twist and twine in my bed, thinking of him.

Monday is a bank holiday and the final day of the gathering. The first dance of the day is the Sailor's Hornpipe. I love wearing the crisp white uniform with its bell-bottom trousers pressed into seven creases to represent the seven seas where the Royal Navy sails. As usual, our family arrives late so there is only time to get to the platform and dance. Then it's a mad dash to the cloakroom to change into the full Highland outfit for the Strathspey and Reel of Tulloch.

I don't hear the results of the Sailor's Hornpipe but when I take the costume-case back to Mummy on the grandstand, she says, 'Good girl, you won.'

The first time I see my drummer, he is standing outside the beer tent holding a glass and a bottle of Castle lager. He looks straight at me but carries on talking to his mates. Oh God, he must've heard that damn Sailor's Hornpipe result over the loudspeaker announcing me as the winner of the ten years and under thirteen age group. Why do I have to be so stupidly young?

I watch him as he stops to talk to Annie at the platform where she is waiting to dance. She smiles and giggles as she talks to him, over-doing it as usual. Then he strides across the field to join his regiment for the march-past of the massed bands.

A big orange sun is setting over the sugar-cane covered hills as the trophies are being presented. My name is announced. I am the new Junior Highland Dancing Champion of Natal. I go up to the mayor to be presented with my silver trophy, and then walk back to my sisters waiting for me on the grand-stand. Jilly puts her arm around me. My drummer is standing with them. He chucks me under the chin and says, 'Well done, titch.'

Daddy and I are trying to see who can eat the most. He hasn't been drinking for six months now and Mummy is very pleased with him. In fact, we are quite a happy family on holiday together.

Seven courses at lunch today. The Indian waiters think it's a huge joke. They can't believe how much we can eat. Tomato soup, baked fish with lemon sauce, lamb's liver and onions, Madras curry and rice, cold meats and salads, roast chicken and assorted vegetables, bread and butter pudding, strawberry ice-cream and fruit salad.

'Such healthy appetites,' says Mummy, smiling.

Boys, butts and beers, we love,
Boys, butts and beers,
We want to drink and smoke and smooch
And kiss for years and years.

Annie and I lie on our beds in the Fairhaven Hotel and sing to the tune of 'Anchor's Aweigh'. We are crazy about Indian waiters and white rugby players. Come to think of it, rugby players in South Africa can't be anything but white. But we don't even think of that, it just goes without saying.

86

Outside our hotel window we can see the fairy lights of South Beach Parade and hear the ships hooting as they enter Durban harbour. When it gets too hot in our room we cross the road and sit on the children's swings and float in the humid night air and dream of falling in love. Then we walk along the front, past the aquarium and the dodgems and the children's pool with the coloured fountains and order a double-thick malted milk-shake at Dairy Den. It's nice to sit on the rocks and feel the salt sea spray and maybe pick up a couple of guys. Not Afrikaners, of course. Afrikaners are the pits, they're thick in more ways than one and have no manners.

If we're feeling really wild we may hitch-hike along the main North Coast road. The beach at Sunkist is deserted and if the guys are nice, we lie on the sand and smooch. French kissing can be either heaven or hell. If his tongue tastes sweet and he moves it softly and caressingly around your mouth like a moth fluttering around a flame, it's heaven. But if his tongue tastes stale and he batters against your tonsils, it's hell. Either way, it always ends up with his hands trying to get inside your clothes. Convent girls don't mind a little of this, but when it gets too heavy we have to say, 'Stop. Now I mean it, STOP!'

Annie and I never go all the way and that's when boys can turn really nasty and accuse us of being cockteasers. Once two rugby players chucked us out of their car and told us to find our own way home because we wouldn't play ball. 'We wouldn't waste our energy on you two,' they shouted out of the car window as they drove off, 'we've got more important things to do.'

A girl can't win whatever she does. I don't really know what stops us from going the whole hog but it's just unthinkable.

Miss McKirdy is never ill. She just doesn't believe in it. Like Granny Mac, she thinks that most things can

87

be cured by a good dose of opening medicine. She is always giving us Doctor White's pink pills for pale people and Brooklax which looks like chocolate but tastes like poison. Anyone suffering from aches and pains is made to lie in a hot washing soda bath and all eye troubles are treated with Golden Eye ointment. People suffering from biliousness and indigestion are told to take half a teaspoon of bicarbonate of soda in half a cup of hot water. Colds and sore throats are quickly got rid of by gargling with salt water and swallowing honey, whilst skin eruptions are treated with Zambuk, a greeny-brown gunge, or Calamine lotion, which also soothes sunburn.

When the three of us had measles and chicken pox, Mummy turned the big back bedroom into a hospital ward and we had a lot of fun hitting each other with pillows and building wigwams with our bedclothes. I was the only one who had whooping cough and I was sent to Henley with Granny Mac and Auntie to get over it. They told me how Uncle Billy had it 'something awful' when he was a little boy in Scotland and how, before every coughing fit, he would shout, 'The bugger's coming, the bugger's coming,' and then run and hide in the cupboard under the hall stairs.

I am still getting colic attacks even though Granny Mac says it's nothing but tension. Once at Henley it was so bad they had to call the doctor from Meyerton, six miles away, because I was screaming with pain.

Now Annie has started growing black hairs on her face. First Mummy tries pulling them out with tweezers but there are too many for that. Then she makes Annie put on a cream that smells of rotten eggs but that has only made them grow more. Granny Mac, medicine woman of the clan, has offered to help but Mummy says no. Mummy knows that some of Granny Mac's remedies can be dangerous. When she was a teen-ager she had skin troubles and Granny held her down and rubbed some terrible black stuff all over her face.

'Which only made my pimples a million times worse,' says Mummy.

Another time, when she was little, she sat on a pair of scissors and cut her bottom badly. The only thing Granny Mac gave her for that was a good hiding. 'You girls don't know how lucky you are,' says Mummy. 'Your granny didn't handle me with kid gloves. She didn't hand out bouquets. All the same, I have a lot to thank her for. I am the woman I am today because of her.'

Sometimes Granny's cures work. When Jilly was five she fell out of the plum tree and broke her arm. Granny Mac wouldn't let them take her to hospital to have it set because she said it was quite unnecessary. She said she would heal Jilly's arm by massaging warm olive oil into it three times a day. And she did. Apart from a bit of a bump, it healed perfectly in three months. Another time she healed a boil on the back of my foot by putting on a poultice of Sunlight soap and sugar.

Granny believes that washing soda can work miracles. She knew a little girl in Glasgow who had a crooked back and a famous surgeon who lectured at the university there told the girl's mother to make a solution of warm water and washing soda and to squeeze this down her daughter's back with a sponge three times a day for a whole year. When the time was up they went back to see him and he just clicked the spine into perfect shape. 'She was as right as rain after that,' said Granny, 'never had a moment's trouble again and it didn't cost more than a few shillings.' Granny says, 'People only have faith in cures that cost them a fortune. When something is cheap they don't believe it will work and because prayer is free they don't even bother to try that.'

Mummy believes her prayers have been answered when she reads in the *Star* that two sisters from Hungary have taken a suite of rooms in Hillbrow and are opening the first electrolysis clinic in Johannesburg. Their treatment is very expensive but offers 'the safe and permanent removal of unwanted hair'. For the next six years Annie visits the clinic twice a week or three times if Mummy can afford it. The sisters cover her chin and upper lip with needles through which they pass electric current. 'The worst bit,' says Annie, 'is waiting for the shock and knowing it's coming.'

Despite being so naughty, Jilly has done very well in her matric exams, getting distinctions in maths and English. By the time she leaves the convent the nuns are no longer calling her bold and ugly but strong and determined. But that doesn't mean that Mummy has changed her mind. The big argument at present in our house is whether Jilly is going to go to university. Mummy says it's a simple choice. Jilly must give up her steady boyfriend if she wants to go to university and become a teacher. But if she insists on seeing Terry she'll just have to do shorthand and typing at the technical college. Mummy is not prepared to put her through university only to have her get married and chuck the whole lot away.

'At the very least, I expect to get the cost of the fees back and that will mean you teaching for four or five years once you've qualified.' Mummy waited until she was twenty-five before she got married and she expects Jilly to do the same.

Jilly keeps saying that she didn't ask to be born or be sent to a private school. She says she would like to become a teacher but with no strings attached. She cannot swear that she will not get married for seven or eight years but she can promise to pass the exams. Mummy says she is not prepared to discuss the matter any further and the subject is closed.

Daddy thinks that Jilly might meet new friends at the university and would then drop Terry. But Mummy says that is a chance she cannot afford to take. Terry doesn't want Jilly to go to university because he thinks books are a waste of time. 'Who wants to be cooped up swotting when you can be out swimming?' he asks.

His mother is a housewife and she tells Jilly, 'There is nothing more important in life than being a good wife and mother and cooking for your family.' She only says that because she knows that Mummy can't boil an egg. She says Jilly is welcome to come and live with them because in their home she can enjoy plenty of peace and quiet while she is studying to become a shorthand typist.

Jilly stays on in the dutch-gabled house but she and Mummy don't talk to each other. One evening, six months after she's started at the tech, she and Terry are sitting squashed together at the far end of the swing seat out on the verandah. He is holding her hand up and they are gazing down at it. On her finger she is wearing a ring.

Miss McKirdy drives the car straight into the garage and comes in through the back door. As she passes the girl in the kitchen she tells her to serve dinner. It's Wednesday, so it's roast chicken, potatoes, pumpkin and peas. Terry is never invited to eat with us although Jilly often eats at his place. Mummy bangs an empty plate down on Jilly's place but doesn't call her in. Annie and I are very frightened because we can remember another night and another row when Mummy shouted at Daddy, 'Love is sacrifice and service to others.'

And Daddy shouted back, 'For God's sake, woman, your record's got stuck.'

Jilly jumped up and screamed, 'I hate this house and I hate both of you.'

And she smashed her plate down on the table and the food went everywhere. Some of it landed on Daddy's head. Then she ran out of the front door and out of the front gate. I ran after her down the road. My tears were as hot as the tar on my burning feet as I cried, 'Please Jilly, please come back!'

She shook her hair and said, 'No. I'm going to live at Terry's place.'

She did come back but she was gone until very late. Tonight, Mummy knifes the chicken and smashes the peas. We eat in silence. Eventually Daddy gets up and goes out through the fly-screen door onto the verandah. We hear him talking to the two of them. They tell him how much they love each other and what their plans are for the future. Daddy says he can remember what it was like to be young and in love even though it seems a long time ago. 'I can't do anything about your mother but you have my blessing if you want it.'

Mummy rings the bell for the girl to clear away the plates and then starts doing her accounts on the dining-room table. Annie and I stay in the back bedroom. Because we are next door we can hear when Daddy says to Mummy, 'I think they're a sensible young couple.'

'Do you?' she says.

'They're going to save up and buy a house and they'll wait till she's twenty-one to get married. I don't think there's anything to be gained by behaving like this.'

'Well she's made her bed,' Mummy says, 'she must lie in it. Now, as far as I'm concerned the subject is closed.'

Annie isn't prepared to get into Mummy's bad books so she carries on with her homework but I sneak out onto the verandah. I snuggle up to Jilly and she shows me her engagement ring. It's shaped like a bow with a little diamond in the middle. It looks lovely on her soft clean hand. She and I start crying and Terry puts his arm about her shoulders to comfort her. It feels like we are at a funeral. Like someone has died.

Eventually Mummy comes out through the fly-screen door and says, 'So you're engaged!' and sits down stiffly on one of the garden chairs.

Jilly says, 'Do you want to see my ring, Mummy?'

And Mummy says, 'I might as well.' Jilly shows her the silver love-knot. Mummy nods. Then, as it is getting late and rather chilly, Terry goes home and we all go inside and Daddy locks up.

* * *

Annie and I fight all the time. When we're not fighting, we're giggling hysterically and when we're not giggling we're smoking and when we're not smoking we're eating. We go to the Astra Bioscope in Orange Grove nearly every Saturday night if we aren't dancing at a Caledonian function. Our favourite stars are Doris Day, Esther Williams, Jane Powell, Susan Hayward, Rock Hudson, Russ Tamlyn and Tab Hunter. American musicals and war films are our favourites. We especially like the dancing in the musicals and the way in which the guys in the war films are always taking off their shirts.

Although I have my own room I sometimes sleep with Annie because she's like a hot water bottle. At night, in winter, it can get freezing. The cold goes straight through your bones and you can't get warm unless you snuggle up with someone. If you climb into bed with Annie and put your arms around her waist, you are as warm as toast in seconds. It is as though she is on fire inside. We lie in what we call our spoon's position and make up wonderful stories about how we meet and fall in love with film stars. Annie's stories are always the best.

But when summer comes no-one wants Annie because she is so hot and sticky. When she comes to me in the middle of the night and says she's frightened I kick her out of my bed and tell her to try Mummy who may be more sympathetic.

Annie has sympathy for everything, including flies and mosquitoes. She always says, 'They can't help being horrible.'

I say, 'Annie, you are batty. Do you know that? You've got bats in the belfry.'

Annie's daft. One minute she will be laughing her head off and the next she'll be crying and saying she's dying. I'm getting fed up with it. Other people don't understand that it's all an act to get attention. I tell her to stop showing off and to pull herself together and then when she rolls about the floor, gasping and choking and begging for help, I just laugh and step over her.

Dr Fraser has been called so many times and every time he says that Annie is just highly strung. He always says the same thing. 'Palpitations caused by hypertension, that's all, and she certainly won't die from them.'

She does get into some awful panics. She said she couldn't write her geography exam because she couldn't remember anything. Mummy sat up with her right through the night, going over the syllabus and force-feeding the facts into her. 'You'll write this bloody exam if it's the last thing I do,' said Mummy.

She wrote it.

She always was a chatterbox, but now she sounds like a telephone exchange that's got its wires crossed. She jabbers nineteen to the dozen, jumping around from one subject to another. Sometimes you can't follow what she's saying, it's all so jumbled up. And other times she won't speak at all.

Annie's hopeless. She hates booze but when we go out she holds her nose and gulps it down and then brings most of it up again. She says she's looking for 'oblivium'. She's always passing out in the loo and I have to stick her head under the cold tap and slap her face to bring her round. Then somehow I get her home and into bed without Mummy noticing. If she catches us I make up some cock-and-bull story about a hamburger being off or too much sun or some other rubbish.

Annie is pathetic. She never fights longer than the first round and then she backs off and lets me have him. I like big boys. I like them tall and gorgeous. So does Annie, but she never gets them. She always ends up with a fly-half who spends the evening telling her how much he loves his wife and kids. On top of it all she keeps falling for impossible people like the

94

Catholic priest at Marist Brothers College or her best friend's father.

Annie is heartbroken and she has only herself to blame. Her boyfriend is a side-drummer in the Transvaal Scottish and he was really keen on her but she's always running off and giggling with her stupid girlfriends and not paying him enough attention and he's just had enough. Last Saturday night he chucked her and now she's sorry for her behaviour and would give anything to have him back but I think it's too late.

She always manages to do herself down. When guys ring her up she says, 'Wait till you see my gorgeous sister. You'll fall for her like a ton of bricks.' And of course they do. I don't care. I take them if they're nice and if she's stupid enough to offer them. She doesn't seem to mind about being hurt.

Annie is lying in bed with a hot water bottle on her head. I am sitting at the dressing table rolling my hair into curlers.

Suddenly she says, 'There is a man at the window.'

Annie has a fantastic imagination and so I say, 'Don't talk rubbish.'

'It's true,' she says, 'he's staring at me.'

'Where?' I start to giggle.

'His eyes are between the bottom of the Venetian blind and the window sill.'

'You're mad.' I go to the window and yank up the blind and then I start screaming.

Annie leaps out of the bed and we both jump up and down, shouting, 'Daddy! Daddy! Help! Daddy!'

The man just stares at us, moving his head from side to side like a snake watching a couple of mongooses.

We can hear Mummy and Daddy stirring in their bedroom next door and Daddy is saying, 'What the bloody hell is going on in there?'

Suddenly Peeping Tom makes a run for it and so do Annie and I. He leaps over Daddy's Queen Elizabeth rose bush, knocking off the heads as he goes and vaults the spiked garden fence and lands in the passenger seat of a waiting car. Daddy hurls his slippers at the moving car. They miss their target and end up halfway down the street. By now our neighbours are looking through their Venetian blinds in amazement at the bunch of lunatics who live in the dutch-gabled house.

Jilly is hardly ever at home any more. She's got a job as a shorthand typist and at night she is always doing something or out with Terry. On Mondays she goes to her dressmaking class and on Tuesdays and Saturdays she and Terry go to the Drive-In Bioscope out on the Pretoria Road. On Wednesdays she goes to his mother's place for dinner and on Thursdays she stays at home and washes her hair and does her ironing.

Jilly is a perfectionist. When she irons a blouse, she irons it until every single tiny crease is smoothed. She never wears anything that is the slightest bit grubby, or flouncy, or wild, or glittery or common. Her clothes are cotton or pure wool.

On Fridays she goes with Terry to meet some of his friends at the German Beergarden or the Zanzibar Curry House. On Sundays he plays baseball and she scores, and afterwards they go to the clubhouse for supper and drinks.

Annie and I are off to stay with a middle-aged couple in Salisbury, Rhodesia. We met them on holiday in Durban and they are super. Such fun. They don't have children of their own and think youngsters are wonderful. They give us cigarettes and beer and tell us dirty jokes. When they invite us to stay with them we say, 'Great!'

Mummy sees us off from Park station. She bribes the head steward to give us a compartment all to ourselves. As soon as we've stopped waving out the window and the train has gathered speed, we light up. At dinner we drink a lot of beer and giggle because the Afrikaans waiter doesn't have any teeth.

I love being on trains, travelling through the African night. Lying in my bunk between starched white sheets I listen to the music made by the wheels on the tracks. The veld is like a black blanket and the train is a shiny snake crawling over it. It feels dangerous and safe at the same time. When the train stops at a station you can smell the delicious aroma of roasted coffee and hear voices outside the compartment windows, and the sound of milk churns being loaded. It's nice knowing that they're all out there in the cold and I am tucked up in the warm. When the train stops in the middle of nowhere you can hear lots of strange noises and you wonder if it's the sound of a lion or a hyena. You want to check if the window's closed but you're too scared to move.

Salisbury is much smaller than Johannesburg but the streets are wider and lined with jacaranda trees covered with flowers as blue as our hostess's hair. English is the official language, and as we drive through the town we see Union Jacks flying from all the government buildings. In Rhodesia you can buy boxes of fifty cigarettes for pennies and brandy is sold in flagons. Our hostess tells us that we are going to appear on television. South Africa has no television so this will be the first time we see it, let alone appear on it. We are going to dance the Highland Fling on a young people's programme called Teen Time.

One night, before dinner, we are fooling around in the lounge with our host who is like an old cuddly teddy bear and our hostess, who has been in the kitchen, comes in and sees Annie sitting on her husband's lap. She goes completely berserk and starts screaming and calling Annie a whore and a slut and telling her to go and 'shit on her own doorstep'. Her neck and face are all puffed up and pink like a turkey-hen because she's so angry and because she's drunk a lot of gin. She tells us to pack our things and get the hell out of her home. We say we wouldn't dream of staying a moment longer even if she begged us to. Our host just sits in his chair looking like a naughty little boy.

The next thing we know, she's thrown us out into the street with our suitcases half open and spilling sundresses and shorts and sandals onto the pavement. We manage to stop a passing rickshaw and he takes us to the railway station and we are able to catch the milk train back to Johannesburg.

As the train rolls south Annie starts rolling around on the floor of the compartment, having another of her panic attacks. Being with Annie has started to mean nothing but trouble.

I am fourteen years old and I'm giggling in the back row of Sister Lelia's maths class. The more she tells me that I am a disgrace, the more I giggle.

Then my mother arrives to give us an elocution lesson and sister Lelia says, 'Miss McKirdy, I have a terrible thing to report to you. Your daughter has disgraced herself.'

'Oh Sister,' says Mummy, acting appalled, 'I'm sorry to hear that.'

Sister Lelia calls me to the front of the class and tells me to go down on my knees and ask the Blessed Virgin (she doesn't mean Mummy, although she's pointing at her) to forgive me for upsetting my wonderful mother. My skin prickles and blazes and it feels as if a thousand bees are buzzing in my head. I start to cry. 'Crocodile tears,' says Sister.

'I promise I'll never do it again,' I say.

Then I hear my mother's voice, 'Stand in the corridor outside.'

It's a relief to be in the fresh air but I'm terrified Reverend Mother will come along and see me and then I'll be in really serious trouble. Eventually, after forty minutes, the bell goes and my classmates file past. They glance sideways at me from their lowered lids.

'Poor you,' their looks say. 'Poor you, having a mother like that.'

Afterwards Mummy says, 'All that was very unnecessary. But the nuns do get very hot in their habits.'

Jilly is getting married on her twenty-first birthday so it no longer matters if Mummy withholds her consent. I don't think she will ever give her blessing. The service is to be in the Presbyterian church, Orange Grove, which suits both families. It's going to be a big do and Annie and I are to be the bridesmaids.

Jilly has lost a lot of weight and, now that her acne has cleared, looks more than ever like a China doll dressed in her white lace wedding gown. Annie and I are both rather overweight and look even plumper in our Grecian-style white taffeta dresses with tartan sashes. We also wear floppy white picture hats and carry bouquets of carnations and sweet peas tied with tartan ribbon. It is a very Scottish affair. The bridal retinue is piped up and down the aisle of the church and into and out of the reception hall. For Annie and me the most exciting moment of the day is when the fish-tail of Mummy's blue satin dress drops into the lavatory and Auntie Edie has to get out the iron and steam press it.

No boots and streamers are tied to the back of Terry's Opel Kadett because he is very proud and protective of it, and has warned that he will kill anybody who lays a finger on it. As he is a qualified motor mechanic, his mother says that one thing they won't have to worry about is the car breaking down. Mummy says, knowing him, she's not so sure.

Jilly throws her bouquet and then they're off for their honeymoon to the Fairy Glen Hotel on the Wild Coast of Natal.

Daddy is drinking again. At the wedding he said, 'I'll just have half a glass of champagne to drink my daughter's health,' and now he's back on the bottle. He comes home from work and you can see he's had quite a few already, and then he goes into his bedroom to read the evening paper. And when the dinner is put on the table he comes into the dining room but he hardly eats at all. He looks up from under his eyebrows and says nasty things about everyone.

'Not naked? Not completely naked?'

'Completely naked, except for a dressing gown,' says Mummy's friend.

'You'd think a man in his position would set an example,' says Mummy. 'You'd think he would try to be a source of inspiration to young people.'

'Sadly, he's more a source of corruption,' says her friend.

'He appears to be so distinguished when you see him on the stage,' says Mummy.

'Well that is the illusion of the theatre.'

Mummy and her friend are discussing a well-known actor who also runs his own theatre. Mummy is no stranger to the goings-on in the acting world. She once played a leading role in 'The Quaker Girl' for the Operatic and Dramatic society. Apparently the producer on that show was an absolute swine who screamed and shouted at everyone, including the principal singers, until eventually Mummy could take it no longer and let him have it. 'Of course I wanted to cry, but I wasn't going to let him see that,' she told us.

The theatre is 'absolutely no place for Annie' declares Miss McKirdy, putting her cup firmly down on the saucer. 'We don't want her living in a mad world like that.'

Mummy is now considering whether Annie should do a BA degree in speech and drama at Natal University. However, she's unhappy about the fact that the head of the department of speech and drama is an intellectual rather than a theatrical person because if there's one thing Mummy can't abide it's an intellectual. She gets very touchy if the subject of her having failed matric ever crops up. 'Book knowledge is all very well,' she says, 'but it's how you put it across in life that matters.' Mummy doesn't think Annie is cut out for tragedy. 'I think comedy is more her line.'

In the end Mummy decides that Annie will do her Trinity College exams and study English at Wits University which is nice and handy, being near to home. This will still leave her time to serve as Mummy's apprentice, teaching the junior classes at the convents.

Annie is twenty-one and going to Scotland for the second time. She will sail overseas on a Union Castle liner and spend a few weeks by herself in London and on the continent before travelling to Scotland to dance at the Edinburgh Festival. In Glasgow she will stay with Auntie Edie's old school friend, who still lives in Clydebank in the same street they all grew up in. Annie has bought a cine camera to film her trip, especially the eight-day 'Thomas Cook tour of six European countries'. Of course, typically of her, she holds it the wrong way round and only ever succeeds in filming her own eye.

Mummy, Daddy and I are accompanying Annie on the liner from Durban to Cape Town. All four of us are flying from Johannesburg to Durban on the midday flight and a lot of people are coming to say bon voyage. At breakfast Mummy asks Daddy to check the time of the flight. 'For God's sake, Duncan, just get the tickets out and have a look.'

But Daddy refuses. 'Everything is under control,' he says, cutting the top off his boiled egg.

When we get to the terminal it is very quiet and at least twenty porters rush up to take our luggage. The reason for this is because our plane left an hour earlier. No matter what Mummy says to him, Daddy refuses to apologize. Luckily we are rebooked onto the evening plane which leaves at six o'clock. As we are waiting in the terminal building it is announced over the tannoy system that the Prime Minister, Dr Verwoerd, has been shot and wounded at the Rand Easter show.

Immediately after this news a terrible electric storm delays the flight. When we finally climb up the steps of the plane, Daddy turns to Mummy and mutters something about the Ides of March. Mummy tells him to shut up.

The summer in Britain is rainy and Annie finds Clydebank bleak and depressing. Auntie's friend is the kind of old lady who spends her time peeping through lace curtains. She is critical of everything and everybody. She won't even allow Annie to talk to the next door neighbours because she fell out with them during the First World War. Annie gets more and more depressed and she refuses to practise or go to her dancing lessons. She won't even wash or get dressed. Finally she sends a postcard written in pencil which says, 'I am finished.'

Mummy knows that Annie is in a bad way and that she must go and fetch her. Within twenty-four hours she is on a plane. 'Thank God I have my little nest-egg tucked away in the Post Office,' she says.

When she arrives in Clydebank Annie has locked the door of her bedroom and Mummy has the devil's own job getting her to open it. When she finally does, Mummy is shocked at the state Annie is in. She finds her unwashed, hungry and with the blankets pulled over her head. There is only one thing for it and that is to get her back to South Africa fast.

On the plane Mummy orders them both large whiskies, hoping that the alcohol will knock Annie unconscious, but quite the opposite happens. Mummy is out for the count but Annie is as high as a kite, rushing about the aircraft, chatting crazily to the crew who are trying to serve dinner and afterwards to the passengers who are trying to get some sleep. By the time the plane lands at Jan Smuts airport everybody on it is in a state of collapse.

Nobody knows what to do with Annie. She won't stop talking and she won't go to sleep. Daddy is refusing to consider that she might need a psychiatrist. Daddy gets like that. Once we were all being eaten alive by bugs but he refused to have a fumigator's van parked outside our front gate. He just put his foot down flat. In the end we found a company who used plain grey vehicles and he succumbed.

Daddy, Mummy and I are sitting around the dining room table discussing the problem. It is a week since they got back from Scotland and Annie is much worse. 'I cannot understand this,' says Daddy, 'my family have always been completely A1 in the upstairs department.'

'I thought you said an aunt of yours hanged herself on the back of the kitchen door?' says Mummy.

'That is something entirely and altogether different,' says Daddy. 'It was the drink in her case, not the mind.'

'So you admit,' says Mummy, 'that there is something wrong with her mind?'

'Nothing,' says Daddy, 'that can't be sorted out between these four walls.'

'Right,' says Mummy, 'you sort it out because I have had enough. I've used all my savings rescuing her, I've sat up with her for the last seven nights listening to her incoherent babbling and now I have to earn the money to keep this place going. I wash my hands of the whole business.'

With that, she gets up and goes to her room. Daddy and I sit at either end of the table and look at each other. We can hear Annie singing her heart out in the next room.

'It's a nervous breakdown, I'm afraid,' says Dr Fraser. 'She needs sedation and shock treatment.' We are

103

standing on the front verandah of the dutch-gabled house, shivering in the winter chill. 'I'll see if I can get her admitted to a sanatorium, but I'm warning you it'll be expensive.'

'She's cost me so much already,' says Mummy, 'what difference does it make?'

It looks lovely from the outside with ranch-style buildings, trim lawns banked with flowers and an all-weather tennis court. Inside it's a different story. Peeling green paint is coming off the scuffed walls, there are bars on all the windows and in the corridors concrete-faced nurses walk up and down jangling bunches of keys. One of them is leading Mummy and me to Annie's cell in the lock-up section. We can hear someone crying, 'Father, forgive them for they know not what they do.'

'Jesus,' says the nurse.

'Pardon?' says Mummy.

'That's our Jesus Christ. Medical student from Wits.'

The nurse stops at a steel door which looks like a cold-storage unit. He lifts the flap and peers through the peephole. Mummy and I take it in turns to have a look. 'You can see for yourselves that we are doing everything we can.'

Annie is huddled on a mattress in a corner of the cell. She is naked and there are brownish blood marks on her thighs and stomach. Her eyes stare vacantly at the bare walls and her face is covered in black stubble.

Mummy says, 'The girl's got her period. Couldn't someone have given her some sanitary protection? Can't you see what a mess she's in?'

'Inmates must provide their own luxuries,' says the nurse. 'Drop a packet in and we'll see she gets them.'

A cold, winter sun is shining through the trees as we climb into our car. Mummy and I feel terrible leaving Annie in a place like this. Mummy revs the engine and reverses out of the parking bay. One of the staff comes running up to the car and taps on the side window. 'Excuse me,' she says, 'but would I be right in thinking that the girl you were just visiting is one of the famous Highland dancing sisters?'

'Yes,' says Miss McKirdy, 'she's the middle one.'

'Ag, shame,' says the woman, 'I thought I recognized her. She used to be such a pretty kid.'

Because of the cost, Annie is moved from the private clinic to a big public mental hospital. Her young, handsome psychiatrist tells Mummy and me that Annie has an excess of something in her system and this builds up until it causes pressure on the brain. He says it's physiological not psychological and best treated by giving her shock treatment.

Mummy says the psychiatrist agrees with her that Annie's childhood has nothing to do with her illness.

'My girls were all brought up the same. Same discipline, same opportunities, same amount of love. It MUST be physiological because there's nothing wrong with the other two.'

Shock treatment is the thing Annie fears most. She hides under the bed but the nurses drag her out and tie her down on a stretcher.

When they wheel her out afterwards she looks like a rag doll. Her arms and legs are floppy, her head is thrown back, her mouth and eyes open wide.

Mummy hits me from the kitchen, along the passage, into the front sitting-room and out onto the verandah and then all the way back again. I have refused to accompany a visiting Scottish singer to the Hogmanay ball in the city hall. I am sixteen and he is thirty and I think he is the biggest drip I have ever seen.

'I will not tolerate impudence from you. If it's the last thing I do, I'll see to it that you will do as you are told.'

In the end I go. Mummy always wins.

At first Jilly and Terry seem to be the perfect couple. They still call each other Cookie, but now she isn't agreeing with him quite as much as she used to when they were first married. Because Mummy and Daddy are always fighting Jilly is determined that she and Terry won't. She always tries to see his point of view although sometimes it is very different from her own.

Terry likes keeping a gun and a fierce dog, Jilly doesn't want either. Terry thinks the Americans won the war, Jilly thinks it was the British. Terry thinks the Nationalist government is right and he would like to see even stricter pass laws. He says that if his daughter ever married a kaffir he'd shoot them both. Jilly feels we should love one another and do unto others as we would have them do unto us. Terry buys beer by the case, Jilly is teetotal. Terry doesn't think he could run his own company, Jilly believes he could. Terry wants to kiss and hug, Jilly would rather he didn't. Terry still goes to baseball on Sunday, but now Jilly goes to the Christian Science church.

Jilly and Terry and their two little girls live in a pretty house with rose trees and a wishing well in a suburb of Johannesburg called Orange Grove. Jilly teaches Highland dancing to make ends meet.

When the pupils have gone I help Jilly to bath the babies and feed them. It's difficult for her when she's alone, coping with two. The older one has started walking and last week I took her to the convent. We are allowed to bring baby brothers and sisters on break-up day but I am the only girl in matric to have a niece. Jilly dressed her in a frock that she made herself with matching panties and bonnet. The material is beautiful. We got it in the Vrededorp Indian market – fresh white cotton sprinkled with bunches of primroses. On her little feet she wore white cotton socks with proper white leather shoes. Very grown up.

When Morag and Carol are ready for bed, Jilly and I tuck them up in their bedroom, one in the cot and one on the divan. We kiss them goodnight, then Jilly turns off the light and closes the door.

In the kitchen she cooks the dinner while I sit at the table smoking and talking to her. I tell her about my boyfriends and she laughs as she bastes the roast. I like Jilly's cooking, especially her gravy. Terry's mother has taught her to make it properly with flour instead of Bisto.

Then we hear the car arriving and Terry comes in smelling of beer and carrying the *Johannesburg Star* which he throws down on the table. You can tell that Jilly hates the smell of his breath because she turns her head away when he kisses her.

He tugs at my nose and says, 'So duck-tail, what's your problem?' And then he opens the fridge and gets himself a beer and goes through to the lounge to read the paper.

I set the table for dinner. Jilly carries through the food. Terry carves and serves. When the meal is over Jilly and I clear the table and he pops out to 'see a man about a car'. We both know that the man is the Radium beer hall.

About two hours later he comes home again and joins Jilly and me in the lounge where Jilly is sewing and I'm still smoking. I'm old enough to smoke in front of him now but years ago he made me sign a certificate promising never to smoke again. I only signed it because he threatened to tell my parents. It didn't stop me smoking.

When he's drunk enough to be in a good mood he starts teasing me. He ruffles my hair and prods and pokes and tickles and challenges me to arm wrestling. When we're down on the floor he starts doing leg-holds, arm-locks and shoulder-lifts. I never win because he's twice my size. Because Jilly has to stay with the children, Terry drives me home. In the car he grabs my boobs and says, 'We're all part of one family now.'

At parties I drink and smoke and everybody thinks I'm much older than I am. I wear tight skirts and stiletto heels and Mummy never worries where I am. She's always too busy worrying about Annie.

The mental hospital has huge grounds, tennis courts

107

and a swimming pool. Annie is on Largactil and so she can't sit in the sun as the two don't mix. She either lies on her bed with the blankets pulled over her head or she's in the canteen chatting and chain-smoking. She drinks hundreds of cups of tea and cokes but when she's fed up with everything she walks out of the hospital and buys a bottle of gin. Once a garden boy found her dead drunk on his compost heap and an ambulance was sent to pick her up. We've tried not giving her any money but she always manages to sweet-talk a loan out of someone or exchange a couple of her Highland dancing medals for a half-jack of gin.

In her manner of drinking, Annie is completely different to Daddy. She slugs down the whole bottle and throws most of it up again and he drinks on the hour, every hour, twenty-four hours a day. He says there's nothing psychologically wrong with people who drink. It's just a disease. You either get it or you don't.

One Saturday lunchtime Daddy announces that he is retiring without any pension from his job at the gramophone saloon. That leaves me without any hope of going to university. I had wanted to be a lawyer or a social worker but now there's only enough money for me to do the same thing as Jilly, shorthand-typing at the tech.

Jilly is enormous. Everyone says she must be about to produce a baby elephant. She is teaching a great deal now, every day and most nights. Terry spends a lot of time at the Radium beer hall. He says he can't listen to the radio at home because of the noise of the Highland Fling. Jilly says she's quite pleased to get rid of him because he complains about her teaching but not about the money it brings in.

When Jilly is a week overdue, the doctor decides to do an X-ray and the picture shows she is having twins. He says that if nothing happens over the weekend they will induce on Monday. She still has a few Friday pupils to teach and when they've gone she climbs into a hot bath and her water breaks. One baby's head is coming out as Terry gets her into the car and her eight-and-a-half-pound son is born as he gets her out of the car at the nursing home. What would have been her third daughter is dead on delivery.

'It's just as well she didn't make it because pushing her brother out like that would probably have crippled her,' the doctor tells Jilly.

But the nun at the nursing home says, 'Doctors bury their mistakes. That baby was perfect.'

Annie is out. The shock treatment seems to have worked. She has joined the Operatic and Dramatic Society and is also singing at a lot of functions. Her most popular numbers are 'The Scottish Soldier', 'I Believe' and 'Love is a Many Splendoured Thing'. When she sings these songs tears pour down her cheeks. The audience loves it and cries along with her. Annie hates practising her singing in the front room if Auntie Edie is accompanying her. She says Auntie Edie has no feeling for the music and thumps out love songs in just the same way as she thumps out the Irish washerwoman jig.

Little children love Annie. They crowd around her, trying to be near her to talk to her and to touch her. They tell her stories and listen to hers. They put their arms around her and kiss her. They hug her and show her their new teeth. They love her and want to be loved by her. They applaud and cheer when she comes into the classroom and groan and moan when she leaves. They never seem to get on her nerves or tire her. Whenever you see a cloud of dust moving across the hockey field you know it's Annie and the children coming from the playground known as fairyland.

She does marvellous productions which she writes, designs and directs herself. She's never short of pupils but their mothers soon take them away when the

children go home with stories of how their favourite teacher was so drunk that she couldn't stand or
how she didn't turn up at all.

When she goes missing she can nearly always be
found at the back of a bottle store, drinking with the
delivery boys. Or she might take a bus to Hillbrow and
go to the Skyline Hotel and order a bottle of brandy.
If she's lucky some kind person may bring her home.
If not, one of the family is ordered out to track her
down.

Then the old photograph albums come out on the
kitchen table. She can't stop looking in the mirror and
laughing and saying, 'People think I'm wonderful. This
lovely native said he wants to marry me but so does
my psychiatrist. A woman I've never seen before came
up to me in the street and told me I looked just like
Elizabeth Taylor. Everyone thinks I'm wonderful.'

Mummy never comes to watch me dance; she's always
got too much on her plate but, for the South African
championships, she's there. A voice over the tannoy is
calling the dancers for the final of the championship.
Jilly and the kids are very excited. The two older children hug and kiss me and then carry on jumping up
and down in their grandstand seats. I jiggle the baby,
Jilly checks that my kilt's straight and I bounce down
to the oval stadium.

When I get to the platform some of the girls are warming up doing a whole lot of different steps. I panic back
up the tiers of the grandstand. 'They say we've got to
do the Highland Reel instead of the Reel of Tulloch!'

Around us, young black vendors are being hailed
by the Transvaal members of the Scottish clans who
demand that they be fed with crisps, candy floss, hamburgers, toffee apples, hot dogs, ice cold Pepsis and
Eskimo pies.

'What absolute rubbish!' says Mummy.

Mummy read the letter from the South African Board

110

of Control which stipulated the steps and dances to be performed in the championship, so she should know. She's coached twelve dancers for this event and all of us have practised the Reel of Tulloch.

'Please come down! You're so good at sorting people out.'

I've already won the Highland Fling, The Sword Dance and the Shean Triubhas so it all depends on this fourth dance. This year I've won every possible trophy in all of the three South African provinces that hold Highland dancing competitions. The Orange Free State is too calvinistic even for the Scots.

I do know, more or less, how to do the Highland Reel but I could make a complete mess of it, out of nerves. Or stop. You're disqualified if you stop. You can't just make it up, throw your feet around, you've got to know what you're doing.

Mummy's walking as fast as her high heels will let her. Two men stop practising their bagpipes as she passes, taking her in from her coiffed brown hair to her elegant legs. She speaks to the official on platform duty. He's a nervous, red-faced man wearing a kilt with a comb stuck in his sock where his hunting knife should be.

He says, 'I'm terribly sorry, but Elsie McKintosh's pupils are right.' Mummy closes her eyes and breathes deeply. The official adds, 'As far as I know.'

Mummy's two older girls lost the South African championship to Elsie's daughter. Jilly lacked charm and Annie lacked precision on top of which, of course, they were ostracized and victimized. Elsie McKintosh's daughter no longer competes; she is now a junior teacher, assisting Elsie in the same way as Jilly assists our mother.

I am the last hope. This may be our final chance to get our name on the cup. My nearest rival is from Elsie's school. All I need is one point from this round and I've won. If there's a tie I'd be pretty sure to win the dance-off. But what if I don't get the one point?

Mummy's drop-pearl earrings quiver as she swings around and picks her way through the curious, muttering clusters of men in tartan. The official tent is out of bounds. There isn't a sign outside which says so but you know it is. Scorers, judges and members of the gathering committee may pass through its canvas portals but no-one else.

Mummy pulls back the flap and walks in. I don't know what she's saying to them. My mother holds the highest qualifications in Highland dancing in South Africa so I don't suppose they'll argue. A compromise is reached to accommodate Mummy's pupils. The Board of Control agree to alter the rules.

'Thank God she's fixed it!' I think as I dance. As it happens, I only come third but it's enough to win the championship.

'Yes! That was my name! I'm the new South African champion!'

Jilly throws the baby in the air.

The mayoress looks very like the trophy: top-heavy with large ears and a pointy hat. She hands me the enormous trophy and the crowd applaud. I will be the only one of Miss McKirdy's three daughters to have my name inscribed on it.

I'm surrounded by a scrum of photographers. People are shaking my hand, some put their arms around me; it's really something to have Jilly hug me like this.

Everyone is congratulating Mummy and she's wreathed in smiles. The floodlights are coming on all over the stadium and the massed bands are mustering for the march past.

A pushy woman with a shorthand notebook asks me if I would mind answering some questions. It's so dark now she has to strain to see her page of squiggles. 'Have you got a boyfriend? Do you wear anything under your kilt? Don't you get hot dressed in all that gear?' she asks. I answer 'yes' to all three.

An official puffs up to tell me that I haven't collected

all my medals. I say, 'Thank you.' But I won't bother –
I've got hundreds of medals at home.

Jilly stays with the children while Terry weaves off
to look for their new Opel Kadett. He's been in the
beer tent all day. Mummy and I say goodbye and start
searching for our Renault in the carpark. We stumble
from pothole to pothole, grateful for the headlamps
of the other cars which are roaring around playing
dodgems in the dust.

Mummy's scratching in her handbag. 'This time I
haven't lost my keys, I've lost my husband! Darling,
go and get him. I'll watch the suitcase. Hurry, I don't
like standing here alone in the dark.'

Daddy's still in the beer tent, surrounded by men who
are congratulating him on 'his' achievement. They've
been slapping each other's backs and buying rounds
of drinks since Daddy nipped in for a 'quick one' this
morning at ten. A cheer goes up as I look in from behind
the flap of the tent which is for men only. There's no
sign that says so but you just know it is. While I wait
outside Daddy is forced to have at least two for the
road.

I reach up and pick some mimosa blossom off a tree.
I'll take it home and press it in my diary. Today has been
an important day. The night air cools my sunburnt face.
The native boys have started cleaning up the grounds
for a cricket match tomorrow.

Daddy's in trouble with Mummy but I don't mind.
At least, for once, he hasn't been drinking alone. I've
never seen him have such fun. He's looking like he
did in some of his young photographs – a dashing,
handsome man-about-town. Eventually he comes out of
the tent, staggering a little. 'I can manage,' he says when
I go to help him. And he pushes me away. The last thing
he wants is anyone's help, especially his daughter's.
But I'm used to that. You have to guide him without him
noticing. With your shoulder you edge him so that he
veers away from trees, potholes and cars, especially

moving ones. Although, to Daddy, everything's moving.
'Just give me the keys,' says Mummy.

'Perficklickly cable,' says Daddy as Mummy digs into his blazer pocket and pushes him toward the front passenger seat. For a long time nothing is said as Mummy grates the gears and reverses and manoeuvres out of the carpark. Daddy is whistling softly in between his yawns.

'I'm not surprised you're exhausted, Duncan, after the day you've put in,' says Mummy. As we drive along Louis Botha Avenue she lectures Daddy on the subject of selfishness, while Daddy, with equal determination, continues to whistle 'Scotland the Brave'. I sit in the back of the car, crying and clutching my trophy.

The next day, on the front pages of the *Johannesburg Star* there is a picture of me holding up the huge silver trophy under the banner, CHAMPION RETIRES AT SEVENTEEN. I've quit at the top, unbeaten.

'We've given her enough to knock out a horse,' says the psychiatrist. 'She just won't go down. I've never seen anything like it.'

'Jesus,' moans an Afrikaans male nurse. 'I'd rather take what's coming to me in a rugby scrum than try to hold that one down to give her an injection.'

'You should try getting her to take tablets,' says the Sister. 'You'd think we were trying to kill her the way she goes on.'

The sun warms me as the doors of the psychiatric ward open and I go through. Annie is 'committed' and I have signed the papers. Mummy has asked me to do that for her. 'I can't take any more,' she says, as the doors of the ambulance close. As I leave the matron's office Annie flies at me and tries to strangle me. 'Judas,' she screams.

GRAND FAREWELL CONCERT AT THE JOHANNESBURG CITY HALL. The posters are all over town and it's

114

all been organized for me. I am going to Scotland to dance at last. I have officially retired from Highland dancing but this is to be my final fling. Mummy will accompany me on the games circuit and our visit will culminate at the Edinburgh Festival. A Celtic scribe from Pietermaritzburg has written a poem for me.

God speed you now in all you choose
With courage brave and true
And if you win and if you lose
We'll still be proud of you.

The concert is more or less the one our family has been doing for twenty years but tonight I am the centre-piece. Mummy recites some Scottish verses and her *pièce de résistance*, 'Little Miss Muffet', done in various accents: French, German and Scots. Daddy performs the renowned 'Day at the Zoo', a narrative number sung to 'Charlie is My Darling', 'All Through the Night' and 'Rule Britannia'.

And Annie, who's again out, sings. She is radiant and strong.

I believe for every drop of rain that falls
A flower grows
I believe that somewhere in the darkest night
A candle glows
Every time I hear a newborn baby cry
Or touch a leaf, or see the sky
Then I know why I believe.©

My bon voyage is on board the *Pretoria Castle* to Southampton from Durban. Jilly, Terry and the kids are on holiday and they come and wave me off from the quayside. The band plays 'Auld Lang Syne' and streamers are strewn.

I throw up my seven-course dinner the first night out at sea. But my recovery is rapid and over the next three weeks I eat, drink and defend my virginity against a number of would-be plunderers who include an English engineer, a Springbok high jumper and the tall, blond, blue-eyed ship's doctor.

He is so gorgeous that when he wants to give me an injection for a mouth infection, I won't drop my shorts for him. I insist on taking it in the leg. As a result my muscles seize and I am forced to cancel my guest appearance at the ship's concert. The down-and-up step in the Sailor's Hornpipe would be out of the question. However, I do manage to contribute something to the evening by dancing the cha-cha, the twist, the jive, the shake, the penguin, the pepsi and a few smoochy cheek-to-cheeks on the pool deck.

I take the train from Southampton to London. My first impressions of England are the thousands of chimney-pots, the lack of space and how green everything is. In London, I'm booked into the same hotel which Annie stayed in when she came to Britain the second time. It is owned by an ex-opera singer who spends all her time telling me how wonderful Annie is. The night before Mummy is due to arrive at Heathrow Airport I have dreams of death and dying. Daddy always says disasters come in threes. There have been two plane crashes in the past week and when I ring the airport to check on Mummy's plane they tell me it has been delayed. On my way out to the airport I see planes coming in to land at the rate of one a minute so the odds against hers being the one to crash are not exactly high. Still, I'm relieved to greet her as she comes through arrivals with her luggage.

The first thing she tells me is that Granny Mac is dead. I can't believe it. We thought she'd go on forever, especially after she'd recovered from a burst stomach ulcer. Apparently she brought up a bucket of blood sitting in the car after the Sunday lecture at the School of Truth but she still refused to see a doctor. She wasn't going to take off her underclothes for any strange man.

The family insisted and finally a doctor was called. He said she would have to have a transfusion as her life was at stake.

'He's daft,' she said, 'there's nothing the matter with me that a good dose of Epsom Salts won't cure.' And she got better. Within a few months, there she was, Granny Mac, her old self again, hale and hearty and ordering everybody about at the age of ninety-three. She insisted on calling Auntie Edie 'wee Edie' even though 'wee Edie' was into her seventies. Her mind had begun to wander a bit and she would ring Mummy and report that not only was 'wee Edie' drinking and reading filthy books in the back bedroom but she was entertaining businessmen whose laughter Granny could hear when she was trying to take a nap.

This went on for another two years.

'She was cremated yesterday,' says Mummy, 'so everything fitted in just perfectly.'

Mummy suddenly remembers something she has to tell me. We are on the train to Scotland; our cousin is married to a Church of Scotland minister. They live in the manse in a small town which is famous for its missionaries, most of whom went to Africa in the nineteenth century.

'By the way,' says Mum, 'whatever you do, for God's sake don't mention that you went to a convent.'

The manse is a grey stone house. Inside, the wind howls, the carpets squelch and it's summertime. We are to sleep in a room which overlooks large Victorian tombstones in the graveyard adjacent to the manse. The minister is angry because he would have liked to have been a farmer, but now he has to make do with a solitary sheep called Rab.

We sit down at the oak table; the five children cower silently as grace is said and we begin to eat. 'What would you say the educational standards in Africa are like?' the minister asks my mother.

I answer for her. 'Well, we don't know too much

about government education because Jilly and Annie and I all went to a convent. Whoops! Sorry, I forgot I wasn't supposed to say that.'

Our cousin is committing each piece of fish to memory as she serves it. Outside in the churchyard Rab bleats. The children suddenly remember their homework is to revise tablecloths, potatoes and sterling silver forks. Mummy obtains the highest possible qualification in plate passing.

'Oh God, remember Mummy how you used to make us pretend that we believed all that Catholic rubbish just to keep the old penguins happy? And then, how you would say to us when we got home that you thought all that rosary business and penance stuff was so negative compared with the School of Truth which is all about love?'

'The salmon is freshly caught,' says the minister, 'I hope you'll both enjoy it.'

Later Mummy giggles just as she did when I used to imitate the nuns. 'You are a devil,' she says.

The minister turns to me. I have moved in my seat at the breakfast table. 'Can I help you with anything?' he asks.

'I'm looking for the sugar.'

'We take only salt with our porridge in this house.'

'Well, bully for you,' I say, 'but I would like some sugar.'

Four out of the five children stifle smiles. Only Fiona, who is going to be a missionary, chews her salted porridge thirty-two times before swallowing it.

The minister's wife, our cousin, pushes back her high-backed oak chair, plods over to the oak sideboard and returns with the willow-patterned bowl. 'For our guest,' she chirps, placing it immediately in front of my porridge bowl.

Mummy doesn't take any sugar but she has noticed something about our cousin. 'You know,' she says to

118

her, 'you look so very like our Jilly.' And she does
too – the same chiselled nose, the same frank eyes
and the smile that is meant.

But our cousin has Annie's personality – desperate,
neurotic to please, constantly on edge. She really didn't
want to marry this man but everything had been arranged and she felt compelled to go through with it.
After each baby she's had a massive breakdown and
been admitted to a sanatorium.

'Will you grace us with your presence in the kirk
at morning service?' the minister asks. Mum nods, so
I suppose we must go.

Down the street the Orangemen come marching to
the skirl of the pipes, carrying their banners into the
icy kirk and down the centre aisle. I'm sure he doesn't
get a crowd like this every Sunday. Readings from the
gospel are droned by a boy with lamentable acne and
a girl in dire need of blood. Then the minister delivers
his sermon.

Yesterday we saw him among the tombstones. He was
lying in the grass chatting affectionately to Rab who was
running around, kicking up his woolly legs. It was the
first time I'd seen him smile. Then his daughter came
out to tell him there was a parishioner to see him. 'Och,
tell her I'm out,' said the man of God.

And now our reverend relative is thundering against
Rome and the papists. We are dragged through six
hymns.

Then everyone brightens up. The congregation rises
and the organist vamps quite jazzily. Obviously everybody's been looking forward to this annual treat: several
jolly choruses of 'Kick the Pope' punctuated throughout
with booting actions.

At the end of our visit our cousin and her five children hug us shyly. When Mummy reaches up to kiss
the minister, he stops her short with, 'Och! No, no, no.
That sort of thing's nae for me.'

The last place we visit in Scotland is Edinburgh,

119

where I am to compete in the competition at the Festival. I am neck and neck with an American dancer.

Mummy has never been so supportive. Annie won this particular championship when she was thirteen years old. I'm eighteen and much is expected of me because I'm a national champion. I've been coached by a top Scottish teacher who rates my chances very highly. This time the Sword Dance is the last event. It will be the decider. All goes well until the final moments when, with a flourish, I kick my swords right off the stage. I've never done that before, not even in practice. Sympathetic groans. I am totally disqualified. I have to stop and stand there until the other competitors are finished. I look straight ahead, my eyes are stinging. This time Mummy consoles me when I sob. 'These things happen,' she says. 'You can't win everything.'

On my return home I decorate my bedroom and everyone says it looks like something out of *Homes and Gardens.* Ephraim has painted the walls midnight blue to match the new carpet. The bed and Dolly Varden dressing table are covered in white net over cotton, specially made. The curtains are frothy white lace tied with blue velvet ribbon. Auntie Edie gave me some white china bowls from Granny Mac's house and I have filled them with irises and red roses. Clusters of old family pictures cover the walls and white lamps light the room. Mummy's pupils ask if they can peek in at the end of their lessons. I enjoy looking at it through the window myself. I've done that since I was little, doing a room up, filling it with flowers, and then looking at it from the outside as though I were a stranger.

The day after Nelson Mandela is sentenced to life imprisonment I fall helplessly and hopelessly in love.

We are dancing cheek to cheek. The band is playing 'Misty' when it happens. I feel as 'helpless as a kitten up a tree', my knees are weak and I think they'll buckle under me if he doesn't hold me close. The walls of my stomach are collapsing and my heart is hurting with love.

We are at his football club's dinner dance at the Henley-on-Klip Hotel. During the war the soldiers and pilots brought their girlfriends here to dance away the last few hours of their leave and often lives.

He is not what you would describe as a dish but he is nice, and Mummy quite likes him, even though his parents live in the Southern Suburbs. They've sent him to a private school because his father has a good job.

Freddie is a lot of fun to be with because he has a delicious sense of humour. Laughter shoots out of his mouth like water from a burst main, first the initial gush and then subsiding into a few frothy bubbles. Once he starts laughing you have to join in, it's impossible not to. He also has big hazel eyes which twinkle and shine and a nose a bit like a pigeon's. He loves playing soccer, even though he isn't very good. To him the game's the thing, not the goals.

I want him to be mine. I want to land him like a fish with the hook stuck in his throat. I know he cares about me but I want him to find me irresistible. When we sit in his Morris Minor outside the dutch-gabled house and smooch he never gets carried away. He always says, 'I think we should stop now because we've gone far enough.'

I want passion, red hot and ravenous. I want to set him alight and then be consumed by his love. I want to go all the way but he won't.

He's ambitious. He wants to go to the top. His bosses see a big future for him so long as he does what he's told. They transfer him to Durban and send him on a special training course. I rant and rave and threaten suicide. He says he's doing it for us, our future. But I must have him now, I really can't wait. I don't want him to belong to anyone, not even himself.

One night just before dinner he calls to say it's over. He says I don't know how to love someone other than by force. He says all I know about is winning and losing and that I don't know how to dance just for the love of it. He says I've worn him out.

When Mummy serves dinner I feel sick but once I start eating I think, 'What the hell. There are plenty more fish in the sea.'

When Jilly and Terry and the kids come to dinner in the dutch-gabled house it's a nightmare. No-one has even noticed Jilly having her fourth and fifth children, a girl called Sheila and a boy called Grant.

Mummy and Daddy sit at either end of the table with Terry and Jilly on the one side, Annie and me on the other and five children squashed between us. Mummy rings the bell and Jeanie, the new girl, brings the food. As soon as the meal is served Terry starts. 'Stop that with your fork, or I'll give you a crack. Watch out or you'll get the back of my hand. Sit up! Sit down! Don't move. Eat up. Watch out! Take that. Do this. Shut up!'

It isn't possible to have any conversation while this is going on. The kids are cuffed and hit and bullied and bashed until they weep. They are forced to eat by threats and thumps. Eventually Daddy says, 'I think, old chap, we've had enough, don't you?'

And Jilly says, 'Cookie, they are only kids.'

Mummy says he's a bully and Daddy blames it on his German blood. When we say, 'Actually, he's Danish,' Daddy says, 'Close enough.' Annie and I feel like stabbing him with a carving knife.

'Heil Hitler! All hail the Great Dictator!' Annie says when Mummy fetches her from a neighbour's house. She has rung the doorbell and asked for sanctuary. It's four o'clock on a freezing winter's morning.

Then she runs and hides behind their three-piece suite and says, 'I don't want to go back to that prison. I'm chained up in there and Auntie Edie's a lesbian.' My mother apologizes to the neighbours who are always very sympathetic. Then the ambulance arrives.

122

On the phone Mummy says to the psychiatrist, 'It's terribly embarrassing, but you can't help laughing at some of the things she says!'

The psychiatrist says, 'She just needs more shock treatment.'

'I've got to get out of this car!' We're sitting at the traffic lights near King Edward's School, on Louis Botha Avenue. The whole evening has been a disaster. My best friend, Marilyn, rang and asked me to go out with Douggie Jones and his friend from Durban University. She wanted to celebrate. On Wednesday she will finally be divorced from the shit she married when she was eighteen. I was her bridesmaid.

The voice inside me is screaming that something terrible is going to happen. I put my hand on the handle but I don't open the door. They're smooching in the back. My date wants me to go to his place and I want to go home. Now! Say something! I open my mouth but there are no words. They'll laugh at me if I tell them something terrible's going to happen. Oh God, it's too late, the lights have changed and we're moving. I can't jump out when the car's moving. We're approaching Death Bend on Orange Grove Hill now. Maybe I'm just an idiot.

The minute the tyres hit the crash barrier the car is out of control. It spins and somersaults over and over. I dig my stiletto heels into the floorboards and scream at God that I don't want to die. There are a series of undignified thumps and bangs and finally it all ends in a terrible silence.

My first thought is, 'I must be dead,' and my second, 'Fire!' Somehow I find the strength to crawl out from under the mangled mess of the Alpha Romeo which has come to rest on its hood, having sliced clean through one of a set of four traffic lights. Marilyn is lying trapped in the wreckage, head thrown back, a tiny trickle of blood coming from her nose and ears. I try to pull her out but my right arm is dangling from its socket, inside out.

Suddenly there are people, police and an ambulance. A woman is trying to get me to lie down on her fur coat but I don't want to get blood on it. All I can think of is how cross Mummy and Daddy are going to be if I'm late home.

They've got Marilyn out of the wreckage and they're putting us both into the ambulance. We drive slowly. The driver is avoiding every bump. As we come down Hospital Hill and turn into casualty, the ambulance man draws the sheet over my friend's face, just like in a film.

Mummy has always said, 'You have no idea what it's like lying here waiting for you to come home, waiting and waiting for you to waltz in and praying that the hospital doesn't ring and say something awful has happened.'

Oh God, Mummy, I'm so sorry.

Daddy doesn't say sorry to Marilyn's mother when he speaks to her on the telephone. She tells him that Marilyn is dead and all he says is, 'Thank God it wasn't our girl.' He didn't mean to be horrible, he was just upset.

Marilyn's husband got the house and the two little girls. Her parents never really got over it.

Annie gets full of dutch courage when she's drunk. Gradually, as she sobers up, she starts apologizing to Mummy and asking for her forgiveness and saying that she will stay with her forever and take care of her.

Mummy strokes her hair and holds her close and says, 'Of course you will, darling. Where would I be without you. Who would find my glasses for me and make me a lovely cup of tea when I get home?'

Then Annie snuggles up and tells Mummy how she hates the demon drink and how that is going to be the very last time she ever drinks another drop.

In, out, in, out, like a yo-yo. Into the mental hospital to be drugged and shocked, then released to the outside world of Mummy, Daddy, Auntie Edie and the dutch-gabled house. New beginnings, same 'I can't take any more – you'll have to go back to the hospital' endings.

After six months of working in a lawyer's office I decide that secretarial work is not for me. I've never quite mastered the art of shorthand. All those squiggly bits drive me nuts. But if no-one breaks my concentration between taking down dictation and getting it typed up, I'm all right. I just sort of memorize it. My boss is always asking why I change his words. 'Do you think your turn of phrase is superior to mine?' he asks. On top of it all, I can never get my petty cash book to balance, but I love reading the clients' files which I'm not supposed to do. But I'm very good at arranging the flowers in the front office and preparing the trays for lunch.

After I leave I talk my way into setting up a nursery school for Chinese children in downtown Johannesburg. I don't have any qualifications to do this but then you don't need qualifications to teach Chinese children. In no time at all I have them eating with knives and forks and reciting, 'My little dolly is sick, sick, sick,' in what, I'm sure, must be the only Chinese choral verse-speaking choir outside a convent.

In the afternoons I teach dancing. I'm qualified to do that. Jilly and I now run the famous McKirdy dancing school. Auntie Edie is paid to play the piano. Most of the time she spends chatting to the mothers and reading *The Path of Truth*. We have to yell at her, 'OK AUNTIE, PLAY.'

I don't teach the Highland Fling any more. Jilly does that. I teach Irish and Hebridean dancing and the Sailor's Hornpipe. I also teach my pupils to act the emotions portrayed in these dances. The sailor puffs and blows while pretending to pull in the ropes. The Irish washerwoman simulates Celtic fury at an imagined enemy. I exhort my pupils to 'feel it' and 'get into it' and 'make me believe it'.

At night I go dinner-dancing with hockey players, insurance salesmen and traffic cops, but in the end it is a rugby player who takes my virginity on the floor of a flat in Hillbrow. When he's finished I think, 'Was that it?' But when I put on my lipstick in the bathroom, I see a different person looking back at me from the mirror.

My new best friend is called Linda. She is married to a self-made millionaire and they have two daughters, only one is his and one is hers. His child doesn't know that Linda is not her mother because she was only a toddler when her own mother ran away and left her. Linda's own little girl, who is a year younger than her stepsister, also doesn't know that the millionaire isn't her real father. The tycoon is an ex-fighter pilot, short and tough. He enjoys having two blondes at his dinner table so I usually stay on after the children have had their dancing lesson. He is insanely jealous of Linda and she is a bit of a flirt so there are frequent quarrels.

The telephone ringing at three in the morning is the alarm call that alerts me that something is wrong and I wake Daddy and tell him he must take me to their mock tudor mansion in Johannesburg's 'diamond belt' immediately. The house is set in an acre of manicured grounds with the usual swimming pool and tennis court and is protected by the obligatory seven-foot white wall and six-foot black nightwatchman.

I enter the house through the kitchen door where the two women servants are standing stunned and ankle-deep in a sea of smashed plates, cups and saucers. They shake their heads and wipe their wet cheeks on the hems of their checked aprons. The two little girls are sitting at the kitchen table in their pyjamas drinking milk out of plastic mugs.

Cautiously I open the door into the passage, expecting to hear the sound of violence, but instead all I can hear is heavy breathing. I go into the big lounge which is large enough to accommodate forty people standing with glasses of champagne in their hands.

In the pale dawn light it is unrecognizable as a home. It is a demolition site. The antique furniture is splintered into hundreds of bits of mahogany and oak. It's as if a bulldozer has been driven through the room destroying all in its path.

He is leaning up against one wall. She crouches against the skirting board of another. Both are breathing like wounded animals. Both are streaked with each other's blood.

Her nightie is ripped open and a huge chunk of her blond hair is missing. Later she will show me her back and the perfect imprint of teeth marks where he has bitten through her flesh. He is threatening to kill them all. By some miracle I manage to persuade him to let Linda and her little girl come home with me.

'Just don't touch my kid,' he warns dangerously.

Linda packs hurriedly, at the same time explaining to the hysterical child that she is not her real mother.

She says she is never going back to him and, this time, I believe her.

Miss McKirdy has a strange attitude to university education. She seems to think that sending us to a private school is her duty done. She's always made it perfectly clear that anything more than a shorthand-typing course must be paid for out of our own pockets. Except for Annie, of course. She is different.

So with the money I receive for compensation for injuries sustained in the car crash, I enrol at the University of the Witwatersrand and begin studying for a BA degree. Mummy insists that I'll appreciate it more if I pay for it myself. But I don't.

At the convent the nuns made us chant our studies. Therefore if we learnt the song, we passed the exam and we didn't have to even understand what we were saying. 'Spiro-gyra is a filamentous green algae found on the top of slowly moving rivers and lakes.' To this day I do not know what Spiro-gyra is because Reverend Mother, who taught us botany, never showed us any. We were never taught how to think things through for ourselves or even how to look information up in the reference library. So when I get to university I simply drown in a proverbial pond of Spiro-gyra.

Also I don't exactly fit in with the rag-stunting, sports car-driving, predominantly Jewish, first year students at the University of the Witwatersrand. I feel out of it. I try hanging out with the gang at Pop's cafe but I've never been attracted to young boys. When the only schoolboy I ever went out with took me home, I chatted up his dad.

Towards the end of my first year at Wits, I enrol in a three-week drama course organized by a husband-and-wife team whose theatrical productions are currently the talk of Johannesburg, and they offer me the chance to understudy the leading role in the romantic romp, *The Owl and the Pussycat*. The play will open Johannesburg's most up-to-date theatre.

As it is a two-hander and as the leading lady is being imported from England where she is still completing the run of a play in provincial rep, they decide to start rehearsals with me. At the end of that week I am called to a meeting of the directors and management and offered the leading role.

I don't get an easy ride from the Actors Union or from the other professionals in the business who are outraged that an unknown, untrained and inexperienced nobody should be given such a break. But fools barge in where angels fear to tread and I sail through the whole furore blissfully unaware of the storm I've blown up. All thoughts of study fly from my mind as I prepare to launch into a theatrical career, while Miss McKirdy, ever mindful of what might befall her daughter backstage, offers her services as my dresser.

I just love being the centre of attraction. I love being

128

photographed and interviewed and lunched and wined and dined and, more than anything, I love having Mummy fetching and carrying for me.

On the evening of the opening night I arrive at the theatre in the late afternoon. My name is outside in neon but not in lights yet. In the newly-carpeted foyer my face smiles back at me from every framed picture. Jilly and Terry are having complimentary seats, it's her birthday and their anniversary and I've arranged for them to have dinner, somewhere nice, after the show. Daddy doesn't like first nights. He says he'll come later when everything has settled down.

My freshly-painted dressing room looks like a private ward in an expensive nursing home. It is bursting with bouquets and baskets of flowers. A stack of telegrams and cards is piled up on my make-up place whilst a giant stuffed yellow pussycat, a present from my directors, occupies the chair. My dresser, Miss McKirdy, will be here any minute. She's coming straight to the theatre from a rehearsal of her current production, *Joan of Arc*, at a West Rand convent.

I check my costumes and start opening my mail. Most of it is from people I hardly know, acquaintances of my parents or members of the Caledonian Society. I stick them up around my mirror and fill the basin with water for the flowers.

Mummy arrives. She looks pale and drawn as she puts down her bag of books and says, 'Would you believe it. Tonight of all nights!'

I know exactly what's coming, I've been through it all a thousand times. 'She's bad, very bad,' says Mummy. 'They've taken her in.'

'Well, you're staying here tonight,' I say, pointing my finger at the dressing room floor. 'Your duty is here.'

'I know. I know,' says Mummy. 'It's just that—'

'Oh, Mummy,' I whine, sounding like a six-year-old. 'You promised!'

'I know, dear. I know. And I will.'
And she does but her heart isn't in it.

Annie is the star of any mental institution she is put into. Everybody loves her, the patients, the nurses and the cleaning staff. She is so generous.
'Do you like it, my darling? Then have it. No, please, take it – it's yours.' It doesn't matter if it's a lipstick, a ciggie or the coat off her back.
'She's so talented,' says an old Jewish woman who is recovering from a nervous breakdown. 'Such a beautiful voice.' 'She's so kind,' says a young girl with bandaged wrists. 'She's so p-p-pretty,' stutters a shy lad with a hare lip.
'Guess what?' says Annie, as we sit beside her bed in the psychiatric ward of the general hospital. 'I've been chosen to represent South Africa on the moon. Many are called but few are chosen. The training will be intense. Only two of us will be in the rocket, me and my darling doctor. We're in love, you see. He's going to tell his wife and she'll be very upset, of course. But when she sees me, she'll understand.'

Next I am offered the juvenile lead in a British farce. The two leading roles will be played by famous English actors, one of whom will also direct.
The second time I am late for rehearsal the director orders me to apologize individually to each member of the cast. Burning with embarrassment, I move around the room mumbling to one hostile face after another until I get to a man with masses of hair and a pair of large, horn-rimmed glasses, who smiles back at me. His name is Robert. At the coffee break he puts an arm around my shoulder and says, 'Tough way to learn a lesson, but one you'll never forget.'
He is in his late thirties, a converted Catholic and married with four children. In fact, Miss McKirdy teaches two of his daughters at the convent. As rehearsals

progress, so does our friendship. He listens to the saga of my love life and then tells me how his wife serves him chicken five times a week even though he hates it and how she wants him to go back into selling insurance which he left because it was making him ill.

He brings me his writing to read and I cook him lasagne in a friend's flat. Then he tells me that he has fallen in love with me and I answer that the same has happened to me.

Gossip travels fast and his wife starts pitching up at the theatre. On the morning before the play is due to go on tour Robert tells her that their marriage is over and he won't be coming back.

We consummate our relationship in a Durban beach-front hotel. Lying in Robert's arms afterwards, he calls me by his wife's name. 'Well, when you've lived with somebody for thirteen years . . .' his voice trails off.

The next morning he buys me twenty-four beautiful red roses. Robert calls me his 'miracle woman' because, he says, I've raised him from the dead.

He looks like a Jewish intellectual. He has an over-generous mouth and eyes that are vivid blue. Maybe it's the bags under them that make me love him so. I'm mad about bags under men's eyes. They make them look as though they need looking after.

I have never met a man who can send himself up the way Robert does. He tells such wonderful stories about what a rotten soldier and sportsman he was. In this country, where these two groups of men take themselves so very seriously, it is like a breath of fresh air.

On our return from tour Robert finds a bachelor flat and moves in. I know now what it is like to walk into a room full of talking people and be met by silence. I also know that people hate me for taking a man from his wife and children.

Robert and I live in constant fear of attack from his wife and one night, outside the stage-door, it comes. She is waiting in the shadows and as we emerge, hand in hand, she pounces. Her fists move so fast that Robert can't get hold of them. I am pinned against the wall, my sophisticated turban arrangement knocked over one eye. In one hand I hold my beauty case and a bouquet of flowers but make no attempt to defend myself with my free hand, preferring, in my guilt, to let her blows rain down upon me. There is a momentary lull in the fighting as another member of the cast walks by and we all wish him a polite goodnight after which hostilities are immediately resumed. Fortunately for me she is not a strong woman and I survive the assault with nothing more than a slight puffiness around the mouth. There is a great sense of relief as I say to Robert after it is all over, 'Perhaps now we're quits.'

'You've got to tell your mum and dad about us.'
I don't want to get up. I want to stay here forever, in Robert's bed. I want to unzip his skin all the way up the side of him and crawl inside and zip him up again and live there forever. I feel soft all over. I don't want to put my feet on the cold parquet floor. I don't want to put on my prickly clothes.
'This bloody getting up in the middle of the night wouldn't have to happen then. You've got to tell them sometime.'
'I will, I will. Don't nag.'
I'm very good at lying to my parents. They don't know we're having an affair but they do know Robert. They're impressed that he's taken me under his wing. The theatre is, after all, the second oldest profession; they're happy that their daughter is being looked after by someone who knows the ropes.
When I snuggle up to him Robert slows the car down so that he can bite my nose. He's taken such a pounding for leaving his wife and kids yet he's brave enough to be honest, why can't I? He lets me change gears for him.
'Now feel what you've done,' he says.
'No,' I say, 'it'll only make me feel sexy again.'

When we get to the dutch-gabled house Ching, my deaf white cat, will be sitting on the gatepost waiting for me. I will roll down the window for her to spring into my arms. Robert and I will play with her for a few minutes while the car idles. Ching will roll and arch in Robert's lap, sliding her claws down his arm and biting his fingers. We'll try to stretch the moment before Robert and I kiss quickly and I'll leap out of the car and run down the path to the front door. Robert will watch me let myself in and then, as always, there'll be a moment before he drives off.

My cold bed will give me goose-pimples so I'll lie on my side and curl up tight into a foetal position. Throughout what's left of the night I'll be dreaming he's with me and I'll keep waking up thinking he's there.

We turn the corner. 'Jesus, why are the lights on? It's after two. They're always in bed by eleven!'

I think something's happened. A death, a burglary, a murder in the servants' room or, the usual: Annie's gone schizophrenic, manic-depressive walkabout. Someone's looking out through the fly-screen. It's Daddy in his blue striped pyjamas and tartan dressing-gown. This time the problem isn't to do with Annie. In fact, I think I can see her in the room and Mummy too. And Daddy's telling them we're here.

Robert is my sanctuary now. I turn to him. 'Come on.' He pulls the handbrake up and switches off the engine.

Mummy and Annie are in the room and standing on either side of Daddy. All three of them are peering out through the fly-screen door. They are drawing up a line of defence and I am on the outside in the dark, looking in.

I am carrying my shoes, my feet are bare, so that the only sound disturbing the silence of the sleeping suburb is the flip-flop of Robert's sandals on the garden path.

'What time do you call this?' says Daddy as we reach the verandah.

'Duncan, please. Not out there,' says Mummy, retreating into her parlour.

Daddy flicks up the catch on the fly-screen and opens the door. Annie is elated – someone else is copping it for a change. She has gone into the dark passage to hover.

Daddy mutters, 'You're lucky I'm not younger.'

Robert and I flinch, half expecting him to whack us as we pass him.

'Let me handle this,' says Mummy.

She has forgotten what she looks like. Her brown hairnet covers a headful of pink plastic curlers and her face shimmers with Elizabeth Arden's orange skin food. She closes her eyes and places her hand at her throat.

'Robert, according to the hysterical telephone conversation I have just had with your WIFE this evening, my daughter is a home breaker, a slut and a few other names that frankly, I cannot bring myself to mention. Naturally your wife had my firm assurance that these allegations are false and now I want to hear from you that this is so.'

'Don't be silly, Mummy,' I say, 'of course we're having an affair.'

But she drowns me out, 'I AM TALKING TO ROBERT!'

'Then, if you're talking to me talk TO me not AT me. I'm not a classroom of kids.'

'If only I had a gun,' says Daddy.

'Duncan, for God's sake, don't be stupid,' says Mummy.

Annie dashes into the centre of the room and, with her knees pressed up against the coffee table, pronounces, 'I hope you realize you've broken our mother's and father's hearts,' and swoops back to the passage.

Daddy is still staring at Robert. 'I could kill you, taking my daughter's virginity like that.'

Robert gasps mildly and looks down at his flip-flops.

I look at Daddy. Daddy looks at me. And I know that I must say goodbye to him. I must say goodbye to being his baby, cuddling him and calling him 'my

Tubby Tilkins'. He can be such a difficult old shit but I have never been afraid of him, not real fear like I've known with Mummy. He is quick to rant but he is also quick to cry. He gave me my first, very own little patch of garden so I have him to thank for my love of flowers. But now I have to go beyond our backyard. You must let me go now, please let me go. I love you, but please let me go now, Daddy, because the moment has come to grow up. And so I say, 'Daddy, my virginity's been gone for years.'

'Nonsense!' says Mummy for the benefit of any passing nun.

And Daddy snorts as if to say, 'Don't try to defend this vile swine who has besmirched your honour.'

I know this room so well, this room we're standing in. I know every piece of furniture, every swirl in the carpet's pattern and every frond of fern. I can remember each one of Daddy's three smart girls bringing home each one of the trophies, and the cups and the shields that are displayed on the shelves and on the top of the piano. I know whether the engraving bears Jilly's name or Annie's or mine. I can recall the matter-of-factness with which Mummy greeted each victory. I know every ornament on the ledge above the picture rail and every photograph hanging on the walls.

It seems that all my life I've been gazing up at the Indian elephant with the jewelled eyes and hoping that one day I'd hold it in my hands and it'd be mine. It looks exotic. It is black and on its back it carries a burden of many different colours. The elephant always looks cross, perhaps because the burden it carries is too heavy for it. I long to take the weight off its back and set it free so that it can stop being a silly teapot.

Everyone is looking very surprised as I say, 'You know, you two really don't know anything about me. You don't know about my abortion two years ago. You don't know about me crawling down the front path of this house with the blood pouring out of me like a

135

stuck pig, and how I lay in bed thinking, This is it. I'm going to die but actually I think I'd rather do that than have to tell them about this. What on earth do you think I was really doing all those weekends I went away? Robert didn't take my virginity. For God's sake, I'm twenty-three years old. I'm not a baby any more.' Once I've said the word 'abortion' the rest gushes out of me as though it were a burst water main.

Mummy is saying, 'ridiculous!' as though I were some tiresome child making up stories.

Daddy is just staring at me but when Robert asks if I am going with him, Daddy says, 'You're not leaving this house!' I try to say something but he goes on, 'Don't talk to me about men, I know all about them.'

Robert says, 'You should do. Once upon a time you were one.' (He will always regret that remark.)

Mummy says, 'I think everyone should calm down.'

'Oh, go and jump in the lake,' says Robert. 'We're off.'

I follow him. I am burning my boats. I am leaving home. As he strides towards the front door, I am hot on his heels, so hot that I step on his left flip-flop and we both fall arse-over-tip onto the lounge floor with Robert's head inches from the fly-screen and me on top of him.

'Shit,' exclaims Robert, 'cocked up the bloody exit!'

The day after the Night of the Big Fight, the Great Isolation begins. When I return to the dutch-gabled house to pack my bags Mummy comes into my room and sits on the edge of my bed. She says, 'Despite your unfortunate sexual problem, Daddy and I still love you.'

'For God's sake, Mummy,' I shout, 'I'm in love with a man, not a woman or a Scottie dog.'

'A married man with four children,' she retorts quick as a flash.

'And I'm going to live with him.'

136

'You do that and you're on your own. Your father and I wash our hands of you.'

'OK, Mum, just remember this is your choice. You did it to Jilly and now you're doing it to me.'

'You think you know all the answers, don't you? Well this time it's over to you. You make your bed, you lie in it.'

Robert and I flee to Cape Town to make a fresh start – 'the geographical cure'. We are pursuing a dream, going somewhere over the rainbow. We arrive late at night and in the morning he gets me out of bed, walks me to the window, draws open the curtains and orders me to look. There, lying below me, is the azure blue Indian Ocean and nestling between it and the flower-covered mountainside lies the tiny fishing harbour of Kalk Bay. It is built of stone, bleached blond by the Cape sun and filled with bobbing, brightly coloured fishing boats.

Orange and vermilion bougainvillea cascade down the fronts of whitewashed cottages clustered around the harbour. From where I stand, I can see the narrow coast road slithering serpent-like around the base of the mountains. It is paradise. 'I want to live here!' I scream with delight. And we do.

Within a few short months we are pretty fed up with paradise. The coloured fisher folk live in grinding poverty. Their suffering is only alleviated by the constant consumption of cheap alcohol, and the white society is, with few exceptions, racist, parochial and gossip-ridden. Besides, we are stone broke and you can't eat a view.

Having pursued our dream to its conclusion we leave Kalk Bay and try the Atlantic side of the peninsula. We are loaned a beach house by a friend of a friend who, believing Robert to be Jewish, wants to give us a helping hand. We are so poor that we collect cold drink bottles which we take back to the local shop for refunds. The owner of our love-nest is on a trip abroad and we are staying here in exchange for looking after his dog, a professorial airedale called Henry. He also owns the local steakhouse, and so three times a week a van delivers Henry's prime minced Scotch beef which Robert and I use to make hamburgers, shepherd's pies, meatloaves, pasties, Bolognese sauces and stews. Henry shares our food with us and thrives.

He is the bane of the beach, running around kicking sand onto the oiled bodies of the bathers. At first I run after him, calling his name and trying to catch him which only ends up with the angry suntanners calling me names. 'When he does that, pretend you don't know him. Just join in with everyone else when they start complaining about people who don't know how to control their dogs,' advises Robert.

Henry is always bringing his friends home to play. He stands barking at the back door until it is opened for him. Then in he comes followed by a collection of poodles, alsatians, toy poms, spaniels, scotties, mongrels and, on one occasion, a huge white sheep dog. He looks at me as if to say, 'Hi Mom, meet the gang.'

Robert spends hours playing games with Henry. His favourite is throwing a tennis ball at the settee for Henry to retrieve. Although curtained in chintz, the base of the settee is solid. Henry never seems to tire of running smack into it. Each time he strikes his woolly head he turns around and gives Robert a quizzical look and then rolls his eyes heavenward in a classic cartoon 'seeing stars' expression – Henry, the mad professor, brilliant and thick as shit.

When it comes to sex, Henry is a deviant. The minute things start to hot up under the sheets Henry leaps onto the bed and wants to join in. Robert and I aren't having any of that which of course means keeping Henry out of the room, but this proves more difficult than it sounds as there are no doors in the beach cottage. Well, there are doors, but they don't have any hinges and, as we can't afford to buy any, they just lean up against the walls.

It therefore becomes part of our love-making routine for Robert to leap out of bed and heave the bedroom door across the frame to keep Henry out. But if the damn dog can't join us physically, he is determined to join us vocally. Every moan I make is echoed by him. He is a brilliant mimic. As my sexual excitement increases so does his and when I let out my climactical cry, Henry, in perfect pitch on the other side of the unhinged door, choruses, 'Aaaaaaaooooh!'

Beaten and broke, we return to the Transvaal to face the music which turns out to be more melodic than we imagined. Work is offered in abundance and we find a lovely place in which to live.

One Sunday night around nine, the front doorbell rings announcing the arrival of an unexpected visitor, Robert's teenage son, Edward. 'She's thrown me out. She says I'm to come and live with you two.'

He is clutching a suitcase of dirty washing and his photograph album which she has already been at work on, cutting herself out of every family picture. The boy's crime has been to express curiosity as to what I'm really like.

'You're about to find out,' she apparently screamed as she bundled him into her battered Volkswagen Beetle. 'But if she's not to your liking, don't bother to come back.'

Three months after this, I too decide to leave.

'Please come back to me,' Robert pleads. 'I only said I was in two minds about a baby because she said she'd never give me a divorce. But if you're prepared to go ahead without marriage, so am I.'

'I'm prepared.'

'OK, let's make a baby.' That night in each other's arms the moment arrives. Inside me, Robert says, 'Here it comes. Here comes our love-child.'

Every night, on stage, I have a line to say in one of my revue sketches which is, 'I am Lucille, the ball of fire.'

One night a man in the front row shouts back, 'You certainly are a ball, dear.'

Thank God we're getting married at last. I can't hold my tummy in any more. I want Mummy and Daddy to come to the wedding. Three years of the Great Isolation have been hell. After the Night of the Big Fight I've been out of my family and I want to get back in. After the show tonight I'm going to see them. But Jilly says I must tell them the truth.

As I walk down the path of the dutch-gabled house my heart is pounding with fear. I know they'll go mad when I tell them I'm four months' pregnant.

Mummy opens the fly-screen door and says, 'It's very late. Your father's already gone to bed.'

'I told you I could only come after the show but I said I wanted to see both of you. So can you call him, Mum?' She goes through to the front bedroom.

Nothing inside the house has changed except that everything, like Mummy, looks older. Oh please, Daddy, I want you to put your arms around me, and tell me you love me. I don't want to hurt you, I've missed you so much these last three years. Oh God, if only you knew how every night on stage, I've listened for the sound of your cough. I so wanted you to see me succeed. To be proud of your daughter following in your theatrical footsteps. But you were never there. And now all those performances have gone up in a puff of smoke.

Daddy comes in. 'So what's all this about, then?' he says.

'I just came to tell you that Robert and I are getting married on Friday at the School of Truth, and I'd like you to come.'

'About time,' says Daddy.

'I presume he's divorced,' says Mummy.

'He will be tomorrow.'

They look at each other. I take a deep breath and harden my face. 'There is something else you should know. I'm having a baby.'

140

'My God,' says Daddy. 'I always knew something dreadful would happen to you.'

Even the foetus growing in my stomach is becoming tetchy as the constable struggles to read the application for our special marriage licence. Robert and I are getting married tomorrow. I am twenty-six and he is thirty-nine and we are standing at the counter of the Hillbrow police station in Johannesburg.

'Dear God, could you make this pimply cretin of a cop pull his finger out?' I shift from one swollen foot to the other. Robert lights a cigarette.

Please God let there be time to buy my cream shoes. And also let the stalls in Market Street still have apricot-coloured carnations and be open till six. And please take away the pain in my back.

Thank you, God, for Robert getting a divorce at last. And don't let Daddy be rude to Robert tomorrow and let him not have a drink. And let Mummy like our flat.

What is this cop's problem? Dear God, I know he is one of your children and the poor bastard's got a twitch in the leg but if this is a lesson in something, could you make it a quick one. If we don't get our marriage licence soon, I'll have the baby right here.

'What the hell is this bloody cop kicking under this bloody counter?'

Oh my God, there's a man down there. He's been kicking a man.

That's all I need – I've got enough on my plate getting married. Still, I'm just so grateful that the Great Isolation is over. It's wonderful that Mummy and Daddy are coming to the reception. Perhaps everything will start to get back to the way it was before the night of the Big Fight.

It is very dark under the counter. The man's skin is very dark so you notice the whites of his eyes as he looks up at you. He is handcuffed, manacled wrist

141

to ankle and chained to the bottom of the counter, balancing on his haunches in the foetal position.

'Shut up!' snaps the cop, booting him in the kidneys. There isn't any expression of pain on the man's face. In fact, it all seems extremely familiar.

'Shut up!' The policeman kicks the man in the face as if trying to get rid of that stare. They say black people don't feel pain like we do. There was that story about the black guy who came into Baragwanath hospital with a headache, and they found a broken-off dagger stuck in his skull.

And Mr Oats, who runs a building company, says that one of his black workers fell nine stories onto his head. And bounced. I don't think I believe that.

The policeman clicks the end of his ballpoint pen and walks to the other end of the charge office where special marriage licences are kept.

'Excuse me,' I hear myself saying. The policeman turns.

'Yes?'

'Excuse me, but what is that man doing down there?'

'What's it got to do with you?' He is bored. With the marriage licence, with me, with kicking the man, with everything. He pulls something out of a drawer.

'Lady, do you or do you not want this licence?'

Robert speaks now. 'Of course we want the licence. But, my wife . . .' (Robert is used to calling me his wife when dealing with the caretaker, or the woman at the cleaners, or the milkman or anyone else who may have been offended by our living in sin) '. . . my fiancée asked you why this man is down there and I want to know why you're kicking him.'

The policeman walks back to the counter with the special marriage licence in his hand. 'He happens to be a dangerous criminal.'

'Has he been charged?'

I speak again, 'I thought people were supposed to be innocent until proved guilty.'

142

Very little light is allowed into this charge office. High above the back wall there are three small barred windows in a line, six spaces apart. It is hot outside but chilly in here. You wouldn't think so to see the sweat running off the black man's body. Mind you, Robert's sweating too. Sweating is messy like crying. The policeman isn't perspiring, nor am I – I'm just itchy and uncomfortable. And there's a screaming match going on inside me. I want nicotine but I must think of the baby.

Robert is making one of his logical speeches. 'If you have decided that this man is a criminal before he's been sentenced, let alone been tried in an open court, and if, furthermore, it is your considered opinion that he is not only a criminal but a dangerous one to boot, then shouldn't he be in a cell with walls at least five feet thick and a big steel door? Aren't you worried that he might break free of these puny leg-irons and run amuck?' Robert writes radio scripts and has an insurance diploma.

'Look, if you're going to carry on like this, you can just forget about this licence,' says the cop, his bare arm brushing against his holster which is strapped to his ribcage.

Robert says, 'We demand to see your commanding officer.'

'OK.' The cop shrugs and puts the marriage licence down out of our reach. He walks through and speaks to another constable in the next room. Well, at least he's stopped kicking for the moment.

Another policeman now saunters around the charge office counter through a door and up some rather elegant wooden stairs. This police station was a beautiful house in the days when Johannesburg was a small mining town. Perhaps the commanding officer is in what used to be the drawing room. In that case Robert and I are now in what was the kitchen.

Robert nudges me. He has opened a brand new box of

143

king-size Virginias. With an involuntary gesture which has become as natural as a flower turning towards light, I reach for one. The policeman is slouched over the counter, leaning on his left elbow. He is neither uncomfortable, nor embarrassed. Every now and then he fixes us with an amused glance. Then he looks upwards at the ceiling and at the veteran fan, its blades lazily cutting the air. Then another glance at us, and a very slow nodding turn towards the bilingual posters on the nicotine covered wall. Everything official in this country is written in Afrikaans and then English. He is looking anywhere but at the man on the floor. In time with the tapping of his ballpoint pen on the counter, our thoughts chorus with his.

'You people. You people make me sick.'

We hear footsteps on the floor above the charge office. At last! Could it be the commanding officer? No, it's the other constable, the one who went upstairs. With the help of the balustrade he swings down the last five wooden stairs and mimes a rugby pass to his colleague. The other cop pretends to catch the ball. They smile. You can see their bad teeth.

The station commander marches into the charge office. He looks very overworked. Well, he's not the only one, I've got a couple of things to do myself. Somehow I have to find the energy to get through five solo spots and three dance numbers tonight. And tomorrow there's this little matter of my wedding.

Robert stands up and moves to the counter. The station commander drums his fingers on the wood. 'What seems to be the trouble here?' he asks. Thank God, at least he seems to be able to speak reasonable English.

'We want to know why that man is down there.'

'Lady, if we decide that down there is a safe place to keep him, then he must stay there. The cells are all full just now. Look, don't worry about this, we know what

144

we're doing. Now. You came in for a licence. Do you want it?'

'Yes, we do want the licence,' says Robert, 'and we also want something done about this man.'

The station commander chuckles warmly.

'Listen, don't you worry about him. That's our job, not yours. You just worry about your licence. Do you still want it or do you want to discuss this boy down here?'

I say, 'Yes, we've said we want the licence. And we want to be sure that this man is not going to be kicked any more.'

'Look why don't you just take your licence and go quietly and have yourselves a nice wedding. Because, if you don't, I can promise you, you will be in big trouble. What you're doing here is obstructing police officers in their duty. That's serious. Now I'm going to say this just one more time. This Bantu is in the custody of the police. WE are the police. WE make the decisions around here. And WE don't like troublemakers. OK?'

'Is there a more senior officer in this building that I can speak to?' asks Robert.

'No, I am it.'

Robert turns to me and shrugs.

Even if we went to our city councillor who sent us to his provincial councillor who helped us get to our member of parliament and even if he arranged a meeting with the Minister of Justice, who made an appointment for us with the Prime Minister, the answer would be the same. You can't win with these guys. They can sling you into prison for no reason at all.

I once saw a white woman arrested in John Orr's for shoplifting. She was screaming like a wild animal as they dragged her into the lift. Why doesn't the man scream? Why doesn't HE talk to the cop? Why doesn't HE tell the cop to stop kicking him? Why does he leave it all up to us to do the complaining?

But blacks don't get upset like that. When they get

145

arrested, they get slung into vans, and there's no fuss, no arguing. No threatening to sue. They even sing and dance. Imagine being thrown into the back of a police van, and then into the cells, and then the courts and then prison. But they're used to it, there's no disgrace attached to it like there would be for one of us.

I can hear Mummy say, 'How could you do such a thing! How could you disgrace us all like that!'

We turn back to the counter. 'OK' – I think I'm the one who says it – 'give us the damn thing.'

The station commander flaps our application form at the constable. The constable fills in the licence like someone who has broken his good arm and is learning to write with the other one.

'Congratulations!' says the commander and returns to his office upstairs.

Outside the police station we walk back the same way we came. The path runs between two gardens. The palm trees are still waving their arms in the warm air, the kikuyu grass, tended by convicts, still looks immaculate, the borders of regimented lobelia and primula are still perfect, the car is still the old Cortina we arrived in, it is still parked where we left it and the box of tissues is still squashed under the glove compartment. Over the roof of the car I look at Robert to see if he still looks the same. He does.

We smile at one another like two schoolkids who think they've got away without paying their busfare.

We are married the following day in the School of Truth. It is Friday the thirteenth. The wedding march plays on a tape recorder at the back of the tiny church which makes us giggle. There are only a handful of people present, mostly actors, all killing themselves laughing.

I wear a cream trouser suit and a floppy straw hat. The trousers have an elasticated waistband to accommodate my expanding belly.

I want to have my baby at St Mary's maternity

hospital because it's staffed by nuns. They have such a good reputation and I feel at home with nuns. Well, at least they're familiar to me. Jilly had all five of her children at St Mary's.

Close to the end of my pregnancy I spend the whole morning in the radio studio recording three weeks' episodes of a serial in which I play the leading role. The producer wants to get them safely 'in the can' before I pop. After lunch Robert and I visit my Jewish gynaecologist. He is a hero, a crown prince to Johannesburg women who are obsessed with obstetrics. He is handsome, brilliant and known to everyone as Mr Goldfinger. The nuns at St Mary's adore him and he adores St Mary's because it overlooks his golf club.

He examines me and announces that the baby will be born over the weekend. Robert and I rush out and buy nappies and bottles, plus, of course, all the infant paraphernalia listed on the nursing home form.

I cannot sleep that night. The pain in the small of my back is agonizing. The only relief I get is when I'm down on my hands and knees shampooing the sitting-room carpet. I'm like a cat, cleaning and cleaning in preparation for my kitten.

At six in the morning I wake Robert and tell him I think I'm in labour. He rings the nursing home and they tell him to bring me in around eight. In the bathroom, I put my arms around Robert and tell him that I don't want to have the baby. He laughs and says, 'What goes in must come out.'

There are two or three other mothers-to-be in the labour ward. We smoke and drink machine tea in plastic cups as we chat and moan. By one o'clock I'm on the delivery table, legs up and open, head twisting in pain.

'Breathe. Breathe!' orders the Sister. 'You haven't drunk anything, have you?'

'No . . . Sister.' Oh God, the tea in the plastic cup. Will someone tell on me? I wish I had a bottle of

Oudemeester brandy. I'd down the lot like Annie does, anything for 'oblivium'.

'Stop that.'

'Sorry, Sister.'

'Come on girl, push.'

The eyes of the nuns are looking alarmed above their masks.

'Just going to snip a little.'

The gynaecologist kisses my forehead. He has managed to have lunch before taking charge of the proceedings. Through the pain haze I can hear the sound of knives and forks clicking and hungrily breathe in the tantalizing smell of fried fish and chips which the doctors are eating next door.

I gasp as he eases his hand deep inside me. It wouldn't be Scottish to scream. Besides Jilly would never have screamed and I must live up to her standards. 'You're so brave. She's so brave.' He keeps talking.

He won't use a forceps unless there's no other way. 'There now, there now.' He's manoeuvring the oh-so-close-to-coming-out head with firmness and delicacy.

'Help the doctor!' barks the nun.

'Don't shout at her, Sister,' says my hero. 'She's such a champion.'

Robert is watching this on closed-circuit television next door. Suddenly the screen goes blank.

'It's stuck,' says Mr Goldfinger. 'Don't you worry, you brave, brave girl. It's just overshot the mark but we'll get it out.'

Frankly I couldn't care less what they do with the bloody thing. The baby has overshot the opening and its shoulders are lodged where its head should be.

A God Almighty, Mind-searing, monumental, Jesus Christ pain makes me feel as though my womb has split apart. A moment more, and he's drawn it down and pulled it out, out and up and into the air. It's over.

'Now,' says my doctor, 'whose daughter can this be?'

I turn my head away and close my eyes.

'Look at your baby! The doctor's holding her up for you to see.'

I don't want to look. I'm too tired. Too damn tired and too damn sore to care. 'You're a very unnatural girl if you don't want to look at your baby,' hisses the nun. The guilt gets to me and I open my eyes. I see a miniature version of me, a crinkly, squashed up, baby pink rat. My own *petit rattus*.

And I know that it will never, ever be just me again.

When the visiting hour begins I am sitting up, wearing my new Victorian nightie. I've put on mascara and blusher and coral pink lipstick. Down below I'm still raw and bleeding. I feel like a gum that has had a tooth wrenched from it, but that's under the bedclothes.

Robert arrives. He is chuffed and very relieved. A nun brings in our Louisa. She's been washed and has soft blond down on her cheeks. It's so strange but I know this person well, this mummy wrapped in white viyella. Because Robert's already had four kids he knows exactly how to pick her up and cuddle her. I watch how he does it. She's happy being held by him. He hugs me with the other arm.

I whisper to him, 'The woman over there asked me the date of our marriage and I couldn't tell her because I couldn't do the maths.'

The door opens and in comes Sydney Naidoo, the *maître d'* of our favourite restaurant. Sydney does a good job of looking impressed with what Robert and I have brought into the world. We are pretty impressed with what Sydney has brought into the ward: a massive silver platter of never-to-be-forgotten yum-yums. Giant prawns, caviar, smoked salmon, palm hearts, parma ham, anchovies, fat white asparagus and giant black olives.

'You can't have any,' says Robert to our love-child, watching me stuff handfuls into my mouth.

149

The baby farts.

'That's my girl!'

Mummy's got too much on her plate, of course, so Daddy comes alone the next day to visit me. He doesn't say a word about my baby. I phone Mummy from the hospital. 'I'm heartbroken. He didn't even comment.'

She says, 'You know your father – he can be very insensitive.'

And Auntie Edie really upsets me when she says, 'Och, don't you worry, you'll see she'll turn out to be quite a nice wee baby.'

'Never mind,' I tell Louisa as I feed her, 'you'll be a beautiful woman.'

Her birth weight is average and Jilly advises me, 'Don't bother with all that weighing business. You can tell if a baby's happy and satisfied. Forget the scales and trust your own judgement.' Jilly knows about these things but I don't, and when Louisa's weight drops drastically I panic and call in a paediatrician.

Sol Weitzelman has some unusual ideas. First of all, he doesn't communicate with adults, he only speaks to babies. Mothers are left to eavesdrop outside the nursery door and then carry out the written instructions left by him on the little one's pillow. These are to feed the child mashed sardines and avocado pear, sweet potato and paw-paw. Porridge and broth are absolutely forbidden because they are not eaten by the inhabitants of the South Sea Islands, on whose diet the doctor's feeding philosophies are based. It does cross my mind that Granny Mac and her lot didn't do too badly on oatmeal and barley but I am not about to argue with Johannesburg's number one paediatrician. Added to the loss of weight, Louisa is now projectile vomiting which means that the wall in the kitchen is almost permanently covered in a bile green emission of Polynesian staples.

One Sunday I leave her with Mummy in the dutch-gabled house while Robert and I do a day's filming

150

outside Pretoria. When I collect her later that night Mummy reports that the baby was unable to keep down more than a teaspoon of sweet potato. 'If you don't take matters into your own hands,' she warns, 'you won't have a child to feed.'

When I discuss the subject with Robert on the way home, he simply says, 'You do what you think's best.' Later that night, alone and sick with worry, I walk up and down the stripped pine floor of our hallway. 'Please Granny Mac, medicine woman of the clan, help me!' I cry out.

Then I go into the kitchen and begin boiling up a pot of thin gruel. 'When people come out of concentration camps,' I think to myself, 'they are fed tiny amounts of simple food twenty-four hours a day. This is what I will do with Louisa.'

On receiving the note informing him that his services are no longer required, the doctor breaks his rule of silence and telephones me to discuss my decision. He more or less says, 'Be it on your head,' to which I reply, 'I just have to trust my own instincts.'

My decision proves right and it isn't long before we are the proud parents of a plump *petit rattus*.

Daddy is sitting up in bed looking remarkably pink-cheeked for someone with inoperable cancer. His snow-white hair is clean and combed. Robert and I are sitting on either side of his bed in what used to be the front bedroom, the room we were all born in. It is now Daddy's room. On the bedside table is a small bottle of baby food for his supper. It's all he can keep down these days. There is also a bottle of scotch and a glass. The doctor has told Mummy that there is to be no more fighting about Daddy's drinking; no more smashing of bottles or pouring the contents down the sink. 'He'll live and die an alcoholic so let him enjoy it.'

Mummy has reluctantly agreed and, once a week, purchases a bottle of the cheapest stuff available. This he calls his 'official scotch'. But Daddy has never stinted on his whisky. And so Joseph Kabendo, the garden boy, is sent with a note and enough money to buy a decent supply of the very best. The good stuff Daddy keeps in his wardrobe concealed in various coat pockets. Ever since I can remember there's been a bottle hidden somewhere in Daddy's wardrobe.

I kiss him and Robert gently slaps his shoulder. 'Hello, old chap.' They exchange smiles. The two men have been getting on really well lately. 'Funny chap,' Daddy still says about Robert. 'An enigma. He writes some good radio plays though.'

Daddy's tartan dressing gown is laid on the end of the bed; his tartan slippers have been neatly placed together on the floor. He is wearing his old blue-striped pyjamas. 'I've had a wonderful day,' he says.

I've never heard him say that before. He looks like he's been somewhere really interesting. Someone must've taken him out. 'Where've you been?' I ask him.

'Scotland,' says Daddy. 'I've been lying here reviewing my life. It's been like a cavalcade going past.' He shows us with his hand. 'Like that. A procession of people and things that I've known there and here. My old aunties, my gloves, my ship, my dickey-box, then coming here to South Africa. You know, on my first holiday in Durban even the soles of my feet got burnt. I'd forgotten. And today, remembering it all . . . mainly good bits, some not so good, I lived through it all again.'

He looks at us for a moment. 'I'm talking about the Great War here. Kids today don't know what war is. We were in convoy and the bastards got the ship alongside us. They got her smack in the guts.' He punches his hand. 'Spot on. You could imagine them lining her up and then, bang, they fired that damned torpedo. I was up on deck doing my watch and the lads on our sister ship were down below eating breakfast. It wasn't so much that they ran to the portholes – they were falling past them. Staring faces piled up, piles of eyes, all popping. You just wanted to laugh. It was so damned quick. Sometimes I'm not sure if I ever really saw it. The ship went down like a brick. One minute she was there, the next there was just empty sea. What a waste, what a bloody waste. Why don't we have a drink?' he says, suddenly changing the subject. 'Would you chaps like a drink with me?'

Robert and I look at each other in amazement. The offer is unique. I sit on the edge of the bed stroking his hand.

'I think I'd have drunk too, Daddy,' I say, 'to blur the memory of those young faces.' More than half a century has passed since it happened and yet you can tell how haunted he remains by the memory of that horrific image. And how it still makes him very, very angry. Robert fills three glasses with what's left of the 'official' scotch and adds a dash of water to each glass from the basin in the corner.

'Cheers,' we say.

'Your good health,' says Daddy.

'Were you dreaming?' asks Robert.

'No,' says Daddy. 'I was very much awake and it was all very clear.'

I finish my drink and go off to see Mummy who's playing with Louisa. Robert comes into the lounge and calls me. It's time for us to go and do the show. Every Sunday night at a lakeside restaurant we perform one of Robert's one-act plays. We're not sure how permission was ever granted for a show on a Sunday but the restaurateur does play golf with three cabinet ministers.

When we fetch Louisa after the show we'll ring the bell and Mummy will hand Robert the carry-cot through the fly-screen door. Daddy will be asleep. His light will be out.

Tonight when Robert comes into the lounge he says, 'Go and kiss your dad goodbye. Make it a really big one.'

'Do you think so?' I ask, feeling suddenly cold.

'Yes,' says Robert. 'He and I have finished the last of his secret supply.'

The next morning at about eleven o'clock I am called out of the radio studio. Auntie Edie is on the phone. She's been looking after Daddy while Mummy is out teaching. He seems to have made his peace with her too.

'You'd better come,' she says. 'Your father's gone.'

Everyone's very understanding but we still have to finish the recording. Fortunately Robert and I are working together so we have each other on the drive out to the dutch-gabled house.

At the fly-screen door Auntie says, 'He was listening to you on the radio and died as he got out of bed to go to the bathroom. Your voice must have been the last thing he heard.'

We go straight to Daddy's bedroom. He is lying on his bed in the same blue-striped pyjamas. There is a gash on his forehead but no blood. Robert ushers Auntie out of the room and closes the door leaving me alone with my dead parent.

Daddy looks happy. Something is amusing him. I lift him into my arms. He is surprisingly light. All the weight has left him. I kiss his cheeks, the top of his head. I stroke the soft white hair and tell him how much I love him. I have never been able to be so close; to kiss his face or talk to him like this, or to just hug and hug and hug. It's such a treat.

Outside Auntie Edie is saying to Robert, 'I think she's been in there long enough.'

And I hear him reply, 'She'll stay in there until she's ready to come out.'

Jilly and the children arrive and then Mummy.

As Mummy's Renault turns into the driveway, Jilly's five children rush out through the fly-screen door and across the lawn to meet her. They can't wait to tell their Granny about the main event of the day. They leap about and wave their arms chanting, 'Grandpa's dead, Grandpa's dead, Grandpa's dead.'

I can't recall a happier funeral. The sun is streaming in through the windows of the crematorium; the tartan ribbons on the floral tributes blow in the breeze.

'My God, I envy you,' I think. 'You're out of it now.' It immediately strikes me as a strange thought for someone newly married with a baby.

As we walk out of the crematorium Mummy says, 'I'm glad I stuck it out for forty-one years. At least I can say I saw it through to the bitter end.'

Annie's latest escapade involves buying a bottle of gin, going into the Ladies' cloakroom at OK Bazaars, locking herself in the loo, swigging down the entire contents and passing out. She is discovered at closing time and I am dispatched to rescue her. When I get her back to the dutch-gabled house, Mummy and I dump her, in a semi-conscious state, into a hot bath and set about cleaning up the mess she's made of herself. We've just about done the job when, with an enormous belch, she throws up what's left of the bottle of gin. Somehow we manage to haul her up from this cesspool of faeces and vomit and, after hosing her down with a hot shower, beach her like an injured whale on the cold tiles of the bathroom floor. Things haven't turned out quite as expected for South Africa's Shirley Temple.

Because we don't have a full-time servant I take Louisa to the radio studios with me in a carry-cot. But I'm sure it isn't too good for her. Actors aren't always baby haters but they are chain-smokers.

Then a friend says, 'You may not be very keen on the idea of having a male nanny but wait till you meet Ishmael.' An appointment is arranged and Ishmael duly arrives at our home, clad from top to toe in lilac. He is five-foot, ten-inches tall and one can see the

155

muscles rippling through the pastel nylon of his shirt. He has spent fifteen years working underground in the gold-mines of the Transvaal and his biceps are as hard as the rock he has hewn.

Ishmael has the most cross-eyed eyes I have ever seen. When he tries to focus, they move laterally as well as up and down like berries on a fruit machine.

He rings the front doorbell. Ishmael only ever comes to the front door. I say, 'You must be Ishmael.'

'That ith correct.' He also has a bewitching lisp. There are lashings of showbiz about him. In fact, he oozes star quality. There is no way I'm going to continue this interview without Robert.

At first Robert is irritable, being dragged away from his writing, but soon he, too, is under Ishmael's spell.

'My name is Ithmael Bantu Lewithi, but you can call me Ith.'

For all of us it is love at first squint. He goes straight to the pram which is on the verandah under the shade of the bougainvillea.

'Ith thith my baby?' He picks her up and cradles her in his huge arms, 'Hello Nunu,' he says, smiling down at her. From then on, and for the rest of her childhood, Louisa will be known by that name. Nunu, the little insect.

As he rocks her she coos and gazes lovingly into his beaming black face – for him and for our entire family a Chinese communal bed of adoration.

And then he says, 'I can also do flower arrangements.' Can he start tomorrow? He can.

Ishmael doesn't have a pass which is tricky, to say the least, because he can be arrested at any minute of the day or night and anywhere, even on our own property. We can face stiff fines as well as the inconvenience, but what the hell, we think, we'll sort it out, somehow, later. The mere thought of facing South African bureaucracy is enough to make one ill. So of course, we never do sort it out.

Ishmael does a little light housework, but his main task is looking after Louisa and most of the time he's diligent. Almost nothing can distract him except the tinkle of an ice-cream vendor's bell. He has a penchant for young ice-cream boys. Every once in a while Robert and I return home to find, outside our garden gate, an abandoned ice-cream cart – a bicycle with a refrigerated side-car filled with Tutti-fruttis, Eskimo pies and popsicles.

In the kitchen Ish is entertaining, in every sense of the word. Wearing his saucily-tied, white mini-apron, he places his guest on the pine bench in the breakfast alcove and uses the rest of the kitchen as his acting area.

One night Robert arrives home and, as he comes through the front door, he shouts, 'Where are you darling?'

And from the kitchen comes the reply, 'I'm in the kitchen, master.'

About two months after Ish has started work, Robert and I are out at our respective radio studios when the police raid. The army-style police trucks roar and rumble around the white suburbs with two white constables sitting in front and black plain-clothes policemen hanging on behind the locked doors. They are known as the ghost squad. The modus operandi is surprise attack: while the two white policemen sit in the van the black ones charge into houses and gardens, leaping over walls and fences and make their arrests swiftly, efficiently and violently.

They grab Ishmael and are about to handcuff him and haul him into the truck when he pulls himself free. Even though there are two of them, they appear to think twice before taking him on and he walks calmly away. The white constable suddenly appears at the bottom of the steps. 'Hey, where the hell do you think you're going?' he shouts.

Ishmael's voice is very quiet but firm. 'To fetch my baby.'

157

'What's he say he's going to fetch?'

'My baby,' says Ishmael, loudly and clearly over his shoulder. He picks Nunu up out of her pram parked under the peach tree and holding her firmly but gently he walks towards them. When he reaches the white constable he straightens his arms, across which the soft bundle lies, serene and trusting, and offers up his wrists ready for the handcuffs.

'You can't bring that in the van.'

'*Baas*, I am responsible for this child. If I go to jail, this child goes with me.'

A nicotine-stained finger wags warningly, 'Today is your lucky day, my boy. This time, hey. Just this time I'll let you off.'

There is, of course, no reason at all, and yet of course there are a thousand reasons why a white baby cannot be taken into a van full of black people. The South African police are not that stupid.

It is now clear that something has to be done about Ishmael's papers. Officially he doesn't exist. One afternoon I sit down at the telephone with a list of numbers. Bantu Affairs department, section K to M, refers me to Western Transvaal Department of Registration for alien bantu persons. Males – Mondays, Wednesdays and Fridays; females – Tuesdays and Thursdays. The clerk at that number refers me to the Western Deep Bantu Affairs department, Unregistered Persons department who refers me to Records Section K to P which brings me to the Krugersdorp Registration of Bantu Births and Deaths and then, finally, to persons born prior to 1954.

'That office no longer exists,' I am told.

'Do you mean it's closed down?'

'It's burnt down.'

'Do you mean there aren't any records?'

'That's right.'

'So how's a person supposed to get registered?'

'A Bantu must take his papers to the registration office.'

'But what I'm trying to tell you is he doesn't have any papers.'

'Then he must apply.'

'But in order to apply there has to be a record of him and there's no record of him.'

'There IS a record of him.'

'Oh. Where?'

'In the Krugersdorp Department of Bantu Births and Deaths prior to 1954.'

'But you told me that that particular office burnt down.'

'That's right.'

'So what the hell is the point of applying.'

'Listen lady, don't get stroppy with me. I'm only trying to do my job.'

Robert arrives home and discovers me sitting in the entrance hall with tears plopping off my cheeks and forming a black stain on my blouse. I am still staring at the phone wondering for the millionth time in my life where to turn for help in this bloody country.

A week before this the prime minister of South Africa had made a 'watershed' speech, calling for co-operation between all races and promising change within six months. So Robert tells Ish and me, 'Listen you chaps, I've got a plan, I know what I'm going to do.'

He then composes a letter to the Prime Minister, the Right Honourable John Vorster, in which he explains that because the office housing the recorded details of our valued servant, Ishmael Bantu Lewisi, has been destroyed by fire and no longer exists it would appear that the authorities are trying to imply that the man himself no longer exists. Robert goes on to tell the PM that he broadcasts a weekly programme on the external service of the SABC and how he intends to tell the world the story of the man who through absolutely no fault of his own is being denied the official documentation which will not only give him identity but according to the 'law of the land' will allow him to work legally in the province of his birth.

Chortling with delight, Ish immediately sets out to post the letter. Three days later, at seven forty-five in the morning, the phone rings. If the phone rings at seven forty-five it is usually Robert's ex-wife nagging about her maintenance cheque or somebody desperately short of an actor or somebody desperately short of a script. Or it's Mummy telling us that Annie has gone alcoholic AWOL.

The voice I hear is a no-nonsense male voice with a kind of Afrikaans accent that deeply resents the English language. An Afrikaans voice on the telephone at seven forty-five can only bode trouble and my heart starts pounding. 'That's right,' I say, confirming that he has the correct number and wishing that he hadn't.

'I understand that you have an Ishmael Bantu Lewisi in your employ.'

'Ye-es.'

'I'm phoning on behalf of the Minister of Bantu Affairs who has had your letter passed onto him by the Prime Minister whom you apparently wrote to?'

'Ye-es.'

'The minister says that this Bantu must report to the Bantu Affairs department this morning.'

'Ah . . . well, you see, we're both . . .'

'Lady, permit me to finish.'

'Sorry.' That's a big failing of mine, never letting people finish.

'Eighth floor. Appropriate papers will be issued to him forthwith.'

'How long will it take?'

'I said forthwith! They're ready now. The minister wants this thing wrapped up with immediate effect.'

Instead of pinching myself, I become practical.

'But you see we're both working. Neither of us can possibly get him to the Bantu Affairs department today.'

'You sure?'

'I'm positive.'

'I'll ring you back.'

Robert and I have hardly had time to share half a Rothman's and a decision not to have a breakfast Scotch when the phone rings again.

'Listen, we're sending an official car for MISTER Lewisi at ten o'clock.' Nero rescues one Christian from a slow death and lays on a courtesy chariot. I put the phone down and tell Robert. We tell Ish. Ish hugs Robert, Robert hugs me, I hug Ish. Then we all three jump up and down, hugging.

We will take Louisa with us to the studio in her pram.

At ten o'clock precisely a big, black shiny car draws up outside our front gate, complete with white driver. Ishmael Bantu Lewisi, clad in lilac, climbs into the back and they're off to the Bantu Affairs department in Mooi Street.

On any given day over six hundred black people can be seen queuing along the street and around the block. Ish has to push past two rows of black people before walking into the building and taking the lift to the eight floor where a white official is waiting for him. He is waving a special pass book at Ish. The white man gestures to the ink pad. Ish presses his thumb down onto it and thumbprints his passbook. HIS passbook. Having lived and breathed for over half a century, Ishmael Bantu Lewisi finally officially exists but only as long as he hangs onto this special passbook. There is no other record of him.

Ish takes the lift down again, he walks out of the building, passing between the same two black people who have not moved an inch forward in the queue. He gets into the back of the shiny black car and at eleven thirty-five is deposited back at our front gate. He skips up the garden path. Reborn!

Christmas comes and we are enjoying a particularly happy Boxing Day or as Jilly's boy, Gordon, calls it, Punching Day. Ish is entertaining our family party with his specially adapted version of *Swan Lake*. Robert and I have seen him perform this before but now a more lavish production is being presented to a wider audience.

To conceal the orchestra, as it were, Ish places his rickety record player behind the white wall which masks his *kaya* from our back patio. When the music swells he makes his entrance, hands above his head, in third position, tippy-toeing onto the patio, his huge biceps and massive thighs glistening with sweat. He is dressed in a grubby salmon-pink tutu with a tiara of tinsel on his head and a pair of toe-popping 'tackies' on his feet.

As the music progresses we watch with amazement as this fifty-year-old, cross-eyed, muscle-bound black miner transmutes into a flying flamingo. Then one Sunday, when he should have been off having a good time, Ishmael is sitting morosely outside his room.

I ask, 'Ish, what's this? You don't usually stay at home on a Sunday.'

'No. Today I am tired and I'm resting.'

I know Ish too well to accept this obvious lie. 'Ishmael, has something happened to your passbook?'

If he could go bright red he would. The ludo eyes roll in every direction. He doesn't answer.

'Ish, you haven't sold it, have you?'

'Mmmmmmmm . . .'

'Ish? You haven't given it to anybody, have you?'

'Mmmmmmmm . . .' He exudes guilt.

'Ish, what have you done with your passbook?'

'I washed it.'

I stare at the geraniums in their baskets, hanging from the lower branches of the avocado pear tree. Doves coo. In the distance an aeroplane flies over. Our neighbour's Alsatian, straining against its restrictive chain, howls and whines and is finally silent. The afternoon sun

162

reflects in the kitchen windows, making me squint almost as badly as Ishmael. 'Oh, Ish!' I shake my head from side to side. He nods his up and down. After the dream of getting the pass comes the nightmare of washing it away. I want to be sure, I want to see it for myself.

'Show me.'

He shuffles off to his room and returns with a plastic holder in which he has, all too late, placed the flaky, faded pages. As I look at it I think that Ish has always managed without a pass. Somehow. He's gone to prison, paid the fines and no doubt he will manage again. Perhaps, deep inside him, he feels that the passbook is making him a slave and subconciously he's washed his shackles away.

Ish finally parts company with us after another and much more serious ice-cream boy incident. One day Robert returns from the studios earlier than expected to find three-year-old Louisa wandering around the house on her own. Ish is nowhere in sight. Two hours later he swings merrily back through the front gate and is confronted by Robert. Looking after a small child has proved incompatible with the ice-cream life.

He's a hard act to follow. Dora, our new 'girl', has worked for twenty-eight years for a Jewish family who have emigrated.

'You vant I should lay the table?' she asks in a thick Yiddish accent.

She exhorts Louisa to, 'Eat, eat.'

Dora makes fried fish the Jewish way. She explains the secret. 'Christian fried fish is egg, then flour. Jewish fried fish is flour then egg.' She boasts to her friends, 'Ven I get upset, my madam always says, "Dora, keep cool, don't panic, ve'll make a plan," and ve alvays do.'

When Dora's house in the township is burnt down by thugs we organize a Sunday benefit. Wine, food and cabaret is offered to our theatre friends in return

163

for donations in cash and kind. Everyone wants Dora to sing and she obliges – off key and out of tune. On top of it all she is the only black person I have ever known to have no rhythm. An actor at the back of the crowd shouts, 'Thanks love, but don't call us, we'll call you.'

'Best actress of the year, 1973,' says the announcer. I made up my mind that I would win this award within seven years and time is running out. This is my third nomination.

He calls my name. I'm not sure they'll know how to take my speech. I'm trying to avoid saying, 'I'm amazed! I'm stunned! I'm overwhelmed!' So I simply say, 'I think my mother's very lucky to have a daughter like me.' When I arrive back at our table, bearing the award, Robert is almost as proud as he was the day Louisa was born.

He and I are enjoying great professional success, writing, acting, filming, working together on reviews and running our own theatre company. Our pictures are constantly in the papers. We are quoted and congratulated and applauded. We have a lovely home and an adorable baby girl, a new car with a sunroof and a host of theatrical friends. We give parties and are invited to them. We are in with the in-crowd.

Robert's new stage play, in which we both appear, is a sell-out. It could run for months and months and months. But as it's a piece about his first marriage, we are finding it rather a strain to perform.

Also there's all the other work: radio serials, radio commercials, sitcoms, sketch shows, and plays. Despite all this, every night, when we come home, Robert has to do extra writing to keep up with his maintenance payments and me.

I wake up at four o'clock one morning. Robert is standing next to the bed. I look at him through a drowsy, drunken haze. Why is he standing on one leg? When he sees my eyes are open, he asks, 'Darling, do you know if I'm putting these trousers on or taking them off?'

I am a greedy girl. For the amount I eat, it's amazing I don't get fat. It has to be good food. I like the look of food, lots of colour and crunch. That makes me happy.

I should be satisfied with what's on my plate. But I worry that there's not going to be enough. That worry comes from deep inside me. I can't enjoy what I'm eating because I'm worried that there won't be enough left to eat when I've finished what I've got. So I pile my plate high, but then I feel ugly and greedy because I've got such a piled-up plate. I eat very fast. I think how ugly I must look: blown-out cheeks and eyes sliding from side to side. I'm ashamed of my plate and I'm ashamed of myself, but I can't stop. I can have a huge meal and I'm still hungry.

I think of piggy people. I also think of poor people. When I come out of a restaurant and I'm surrounded by kids with outstretched hands, I give them some change but not everything in my purse. I put myself first, you see, not like Mummy. She says, 'Putting oneself last is the answer to all one's problems. Sacrifice is love in action.'

That makes me feel worse, it makes me fill my plate more because I think, 'I'll never be able to give more than I receive. I don't have it in me.'

I think I'm quite a cold person. I drink to feel warm. It makes me laugh. It's not that I can't laugh without drinking, but I like the kicking-my-shoes-up-to-the-ceiling laugh it gives me. I drink very fast. I drink at home – that's my best place, drinking at home with Robert. And then we fall straight into bed.

I don't like to start drinking unless I know that there is more booze available than I can drink. Sufficient is not enough. A full cupboard of booze is real security. I might drink no more than half a bottle. I can make that decision there and then, as long as I've got a back-up supply.

If we go out and people are mean with pouring me drinks, panic sets in. I do envy people who can have a drink and then say, 'No more, thanks.' I can't. Even when I'm not going to be denied more I still feel the need to line up three or four glasses behind a palm tree.

I don't have the early morning brandy and the coffee that Robert has – he needs that to get going at the typewriter. I have my brandy and coffee at ten in the radio studio. Well, we all do.

Then definitely no more till someone shouts, 'Has it passed midday, folks?'

'It's half-past eleven. Good enough.'

Then there's a whip around and a messenger is dispatched. It will take him until twelve to come back with a two litre bottle because he has to queue on the non-white side of the bottle store.

Then it's 'Mugs away'.

'*Gezundheid!*' '*Skol!*' 'Cheers!'

It's red or white cheap Cape wine. Good value for the price but God knows what it's doing to our insides. A couple of glasses and then we all pour out of the studio and into the Spanish restaurant next door. Lunch kicks off with a couple of gin and tonics. Then there's wine with the meal and a usual brandy in the cappuccino afterwards. The afternoon is spent sobering up in another studio.

'Oh,' says everyone, every time the African woman brings in more coffee, 'You're a treasure. You've saved our lives.' And of course everybody is chain-smoking and taking headache pills.

Come sundown and the whole process starts again either at our home or someone else's. Now it's brandy mixed with coke or ginger-ale. Three hefty ones before the meal, then wine with the meal, as much as we want. The hardships of the early part of our relationship are over. We're successful now, making lots of lolly. 'Oh, let's finish off this bottle and then we can open another.'

After the meal there's usually a couple of nightcaps: brandy with coffee or whisky, neat.

There are always lots of discussions between Robert and me about how all this has got to stop, particularly when a hangover is so bad we can hardly drag ourselves to work. But a good long steam in the shower usually gets rid of the fumes and clears the head sufficiently to face the day. And at ten o'clock the brandy in the coffee helps.

We have an account at the bottle store. It's usually me that rings. 'Hello, it's that wicked drunken actress again. How're things with you? . . . Oh, couldn't be better. Listen, we're expecting a big cheque any day now . . . Oh, you're a darling. And I haven't forgotten your tickets. Any Monday night. Just let me know. Now, the poison. Let's have a bottle of brandy, a bottle of gin, bottle of Scotch. Oh, wait a minute, we're having people for dinner so you'd better make that two brandies. Half a dozen dry white Riesling and, just in case, a rosé. Oh yes, and half a dozen Cabernet. You know, I think we'd better have some vodka. For people who don't want to taste what they're drinking. And what are the nice liqueurs? One of each of those, please. Oh, and the usual cokes, tonics, sodas, ginger-ale, and we'd better have some tomato juice just in case. Oh no, not a case! Just in case! Well now, I think that's that then. Yes, well, no unfortunately it's not a musical but it does have funny bits. Oh hang on, it's Saturday today, isn't it? Mmmm. Two dozen beers as well. Thanks, cheers. Within half-an-hour would be great. Bye.'

The van draws up and the delivery boys carry it into the house. This ritual takes place every week. Alcohol brings me to a place of security, I suppose. Peace.

Because the fumes dull the pain, they smooth the jagged edges. Alcohol helps me to receive and give affection. When I'm pissed I find it easier to hug and kiss and to be hugged and kissed. Like food, I use alcohol to fill me up with something. I've seen alcoholics carry a bottle with as much care as a mother carrying her child.

I always have to be slightly drunk when I have sex. Concealment seems necessary. Dark lighting, a darkened awareness. I feel I cannot even think about sex without a drink. It's as though sobriety might expose some truth that I'd rather not know about.

When it comes to men I think they are rather like cauliflowers. You can pick them up and put them down endlessly and still not be sure you've got the best one.

I smoke about forty cigarettes a day. I don't think anybody ever really likes smoking; I certainly don't. I was sixteen when Daddy finally caught me smoking. He was very angry. 'There are a few things in my life I'd rather not have done,' he shouted, 'and smoking is one of them.'

I always buy cartons of three hundred and I get really excited when I see rows and rows of fat white cigarettes. I smoke without discipline, first thing in the morning, last thing at night, during meals, in the bath, on mike and whilst feeding the baby. Well, the jingle for my brand goes, 'The one cigarette that really satisfies . . .'

The more I smoke the more guilty I feel, but after a few drinks I think, 'What the hell. I'm a smoker. A drinking smoker. A smoking drinker. I'm not hurting anyone except me.'

Theatrical party-going has become a lot more frenetic. I start a craze for jumping, fully dressed, into swimming pools. Apart from the obvious attention-getting element of this I'm looking for some real stimulation. All this standing around with glasses in our hands, discussing our anti-government review sketches which no-one in authority ever sees is getting a bit boring.

'Come on, have another one. Stop getting heavy.'

Everyone's drinking heavily. Everyone's seeking 'oblivium'.

When her psychiatrist thinks she's well enough, Mummy collects Annie and her battered blue suitcase and they drive out through the hospital gates planning her future. Annie talks of getting a job and going to live in Cape Town but Mummy always says, 'Don't talk absolute rubbish, darling. You can't look after yourself in Johannesburg, how on earth are you going to do it in Cape Town?'

Jilly and I always say, 'Let her go, Mummy. Let her see for herself just how tough life really is in the real world.'

But Mummy always says, 'It is my duty as her mother to take care of her. I can't stand by and watch her destroy herself.'

Annie is known to all the black nannies in our suburb. They pick her up when she falls, they wash the vomit from her jumper and they tell her to forget the money she owes them. Mummy never lets her forget.

'I'll stand by this girl because she is my responsibility and it is my duty. I have given her my life. She can never give me back the years of grief. My heart is unmendable, broken into a thousand pieces. She is my cross and my Gethsemane.'

Annie has made yet another bungled attempt to kill herself by swallowing a powerful cocktail of pills. This attempt, like all the others before it, ends not in the 'oblivium' she seeks but in a painful stomach pump-out in the casualty ward of the General Hospital. 'Sometimes,' I say to Robert, 'I feel like inviting her to end it all by drinking the entire contents of our liquor cabinet. At least she'd die happy.'

Louisa likes the park, so Dora tells me. She loves the bridges over the ornamental river and the swings. It's very convenient because it's just over the road from our home, but I have too much on my plate to take her there.

Still, once the patio's paid for, I'll have more time.

The other day Dora told me about a rather elegant old woman who'd been watching Louisa in the park and then called her over. 'Come here, little girl. Let me see your dress. I love the embroidery. Who did that? Your mummy? Come, sit down here beside me. That's right.' Louisa climbed up onto the 'whites-only' bench while Dora knelt on the grass beside them. When she asks Louisa where her parents are, the three-year-old crosses her legs and says, 'Well, you see my Daddy's a typist and my Mummy goes out at night.'

Terry and Jilly hardly see each other any more. She is always rushing past him to get through her punishing timetable. In order to fit it all in, she has to start studying her Bible and the writings of Mary Baker Eddy at four in the morning. Being a Christian Scientist takes a lot of time and dedication.

She doesn't have a live-in servant like most white people in South Africa. She doesn't approve of one person having to clean up after another but, quite honestly, I'm not sure she can even afford one.

After studying Science and Health, she does the housework and washing before going to her morning job in a lawyer's office. At one o'clock in the afternoon she drives out from the city to various convents in the suburbs to teach Highland dancing for the remainder of the day. The children take it in turns to cook the evening meal as she only gets home after seven in the evening.

After dinner she either teaches again, or goes to a meeting of the South African Highland Dancing Board of Control, the Dancing Association of the Transvaal or the Royal Scottish Gathering Dance Step Group. Jilly is a model committee member, committed, clear-headed and calm.

At the weekend there is little respite. She teaches all day Saturday, from seven in the morning till seven at night after which she usually does her accounts and invoices.

Sundays is when she catches up on all the other bits and pieces like ironing, knitting on her machine, cleaning cupboards, mending clothes or working in the garden. She's constantly racing against the clock, trying to get it all done in time.

But the harder Jilly tries, the more chaotic it all becomes. Her eldest daughter, Morag, is on a student exchange to the United States where she is suffering from an enormous bout of homesickness and requires constant moral support from her mother. Her second daughter, Carol, the one for whom she had such high hopes as a ballerina, has taken to secretly eating vast quantities of junk food and has ballooned into teenage obesity. She and her father are forever at each other's throats and Jilly is almost at her wit's end with both of them.

The surviving twin, Gordon, won't settle. He runs away from home, from school, from any kind of control. At fourteen he runs away from the strict boarding institution to which Jilly has sent him, spending his days in the veld and returning at night, unbeknown to the family, to sleep in the cellar under their house. When he is finally caught, Jilly and Morag frog-march him back to the school where he asks to be allowed to wash and brush up before seeing the headmaster. When he hasn't emerged from the lavatory after half-an-hour they force the door and are faced with an open window. Several days later he is returned home by the police but he remains unrepentant and laughs off his dad's punishment and his mother's concern. What worries Jilly most is that he has taken to stealing from her purse and dishonesty is something she cannot abide.

Her third daughter, Sheila, is a reserved girl who presents a calm exterior and, like her mother, keeps her emotions under wraps.

171

It is over her education that Jilly has to stand up and fight Mummy yet again. Having kept up the family tradition by sending her three daughters to the convent where Miss McKirdy is still getting a special rate (three grand-daughters for the price of one) Jilly suddenly decides that she is unwilling to have Sheila, now a committed Christian Scientist, suffer the same double standards that were imposed on her. They are both uncomfortable with Catholicism, finding its belief system irreconcilable with the teachings of Mary Baker Eddy and after much soul-searching it is decided that Sheila will leave the convent and enrol at the local non-denominational government school.

Jilly's 'baby', seven-year-old Grant, is her love-child. Conceived in a last attempt to make the marriage work, he is the only one of her children who wasn't a 'mistake'. He is the 'card' of the family – funny, warm and affectionate and forever hugging and kissing his mother and everyone else. Occasionally, the two of them enjoy a visit to the local steakhouse.

Terry continues to drink and drive until finally the law catches up with him and he is arrested and charged. This results in him receiving a heavy fine and losing his job, leaving her as the breadwinner of the family.

No matter what she earns, she owes. She can never make enough to pay for it all. Despite her husband being a motor mechanic, her car is always breaking down. But then, so are her shoes.

Through it all, she nods and smiles and tries to track down the truth, to find the answer, to understand.

Some o' them have kilts and stockings
Some o' them have none at all.

Auntie Edie starts jiggling Louisa on her knee from the time she is a wee thing. Naturally, as soon as she can walk, Auntie Edie has her doing a bow and is telling her to get her foot up on her leg. Some days Louisa

172

is left at the dutch-gabled house and Auntie Edie has her practising all afternoon. She comes home exhausted. Mummy and Auntie don't believe in letting her play: 'Waste of time' they call it.

How can a three-year-old stand up to them? She's such a sweet child, she just wants to please.

'Isn't she an angel,' I say to Robert. He looks into the rear-view mirror. Louisa is standing at the back of the Cortina, opening and closing the ashtray. I hope that one's clean.

'She's just a bag of nonsense,' says Robert. She puts her arms around his neck and kisses him. 'Don't you try to butter me up!' Her hand moves up towards his glasses. He catches her fat little wrist. 'You know what happens to bags of rubbish.'

'In the compost heap,' says Louisa.

Our yellow and white Cortina convertible corners smoothly into Derby Road. Robert hasn't put the sunroof down because all that Cape wine we've been drinking has made us headachy. When we draw up at the big brass number 37, Robert will hoot. The wall enclosing our newly-bought house is seven feet high and cost a couple of grand. Our servant, Dora, will run out of the kitchen, smiling and waving, and unlock the wrought-iron gates. Dora will take Louisa to bath and feed her, leaving me free to do my own thing.

First I will go into the garden and breathe the sweet scent of honeysuckle and jasmine and gardenia. My horticulturist friend, who is Louisa's godmother, has always told me, 'Never water plants in the heat of the day, it might singe the foliage.' So when the sun goes down, I will give them a long drink and wash their tired, dusty leaves.

And I'll look at the trees, the ones I planted, and wonder if I'll ever see them grow to their full height. Still . . . ' 'Tis better to have loved and lost than never to have loved at all.' I'd always dreamed of opening my bedroom window and looking out at a Weeping

173

Mulberry, a Pussy Willow and a Yesterday, Today and Tomorrow, and now I've got them.

Granny Mac always said you can't buy good soil at a garden centre, not lush, fertile soil. You have to make that yourself. You have to dig in the leaf mould and the compost, and then you have to turn it, tend it, nurture it. Only then can you grow saplings that have strong roots, saplings that will flourish. Because then you will have rich, deep sub-soil, not just the shallow, thin top-soil you buy in bags.

I am so blessed, I have an adoring husband, a darling child, a super home. And success. What more could I want?

I spend every Saturday afternoon rotating the furniture and objects in my home. Sometimes I sneak in the odd Wednesday as well, just to put in the finishing touches, like moving the antique brass jam pot from the solarium to the breakfast room. I also change whole rooms. The breakfast room, the solarium and the back porch have all been at one time the dining-room and the sitting-room has been the dining-room, twice. But that proved no more successful than extending the sitting-room into the dining-room because so much stuff had to go into the garage that Robert wasn't able to park the car in there.

I go into the sitting-room which is now the dining-room. Yesterday I thought it might grow on me. But no, it definitely doesn't work. Damn, and I've just ordered those new cupboards.

I move to the dining-room which is now the sitting-room, and try out my newly-upholstered settee. No, not quite happy with it yet. I have a permanent account at an upholsterers, a splendid coloured man who takes no more than a couple of days to replace the heavy velvet cushions with chintzy cotton numbers. Mind you, there's nothing I like so much as a complete redo, when I give myself permission to attack the lot. Curtains, carpets, upholstery, wall colour and

174

pictures are all up for grabs. In no time at all, the *King Solomon's Mines* look, jangly-brass-zebra-stripes-sultry-lighting, disappears and is replaced with light country equivalents in cream and salmon, topped off with a plethora of pot-pourri.

Careful not to disturb the rainbow of scatter cushions, I sit and consult my colour charts. I'm still using Ephraim, the Swazi painter, when he's not in jail for pass offences. He continues to make his home in the toolshed in the yard at the back of the dutch-gabled house. Now, of course, with Daddy gone, he doesn't have an agent.

Ephraim is able to do an average-sized room in a matter of hours. Robert can pop home from the studio and what was Coffee-Mocha at breakfast can be, by lunchtime, Red Pepper or Shrimp Pink. No room has escaped these colour changes except the kitchen, which is merely touched up but is forever Brilliant White. The passage is the easiest of all the rooms with which to experiment with shades. Since moving into the house, Ephraim and I have been carrying out a search for the perfect passage colour. Unfortunately, that is where Robert writes, at a very long trestle table, so there's the added palaver of covering up his typewriter and papers with sheets. Ephraim has to break his own record brushing on the gloss paint before Robert gets back but that doesn't stop him complaining even though it takes only a day or so to dry and the smell isn't too bad if you put bowls of sliced onion everywhere.

Once Robert came back early, without warning, and caught us at it. He was furious. Being a Taurean, he dislikes change in his environment.

Possibly my favourite thing in the whole world is pottering. When it comes to relaxation there is nothing like a good, long potter. Ideally, pottering should take place when everyone is out but it can be done at any time so long as one's concentration isn't broken. Then many blissful hours can be spent rearranging

175

the cushions or fiddling with the terrarium, putting a plant in, taking one out.

Clocks, sea-shells, pressed flowers, sweet bowls, lamps, brass candlesticks, brass bowls, brass plaques with Arabic writing, brass bomb-shells from World War One, overflowing fruit bowls, baskets filled with butternut, gem squash, pumpkins and gourds, an array of lighters, semi-precious stones, dozens of ashtrays, an assortment of decanters, ornamental coffee-pots, dried grasses, marble eggs, ceramic animals, framed photographs, vases, a chunk of fool's gold, the miniature Shakespeares, the samovar and the cats made of coal. All are moved, and moved again.

On the walls there are masses of paintings dashed off by me to cover the holes made by my constant changes. I use mainly oils from by birthday box, a pressie from Robert. I scarcely ever use a brush, preferring the simplicity of palette and fingers. My impressionist pink and green floral scenes are in our pretty Victorian-style bedroom while in Louisa's room, laughing children, coloured red and black, pink and yellow, hold hands against a blue sky. In the room occupied by Robert's son, Edward, when he's home from boarding school, there hangs a muddy grey mess intended to depict a storm at sea.

In pride of place, above the mantelpiece in the sitting-room (I say sitting-room now instead of lounge because the head of the English service of the South African Broadcasting Corporation told me that lounges are only found in railway stations) used to hang my *pièce de résistance*, a pile-up of pineapples, mangoes and pumpkins spattered all over with bougainvillea blossoms. For some reason Robert was extremely fond of this particular work, saying that it reminded him of me. Sadly, it is now obliterated as a result of a particularly passionate pottering session. Forever in pursuit of that extra something, I got out my oils to enrich the reds, enhance the pinks, enliven the yellows and enorange the orange but before I knew what was happening I had created a landscape of sun-splashed rocks, split by a winding passageway which becomes ever darker the deeper one goes, until finally one is lost in the murk. When Robert came in, having just popped out to the local shop for the evening paper, he thought he was in another house.

He asked, 'What happened to my lovely picture?'

To which I replied, 'Oh it's gone. Sorry about that.'

We come to a stop in our Cortina beside our newly-painted wall. As we get out, I notice red wine stains on my cream trouser suit. 'Shit!' I think, 'Another write-off.'

Robert locks the car now because it's got a radio in it. Dora comes out of the front door stooping quickly to pick up one of Louisa's sandals. We watch her through the bars of the wrought-iron gate. Dora turns the big key in the old-fashioned lock and opens the gate. We go in, first me, then Louisa, then Robert. The gate swings shut. Dora does the locking up. Louisa is playing with her father.

'You know what we do with rubbish,' he says absently, picking her up. 'We turn it upside down.' I can tell he hasn't stopped pondering my question. I wasn't ready for it either and I'd shivered when I asked it. As we drove up to the high walls of our home I'd said, 'How do you fancy England in the spring?'

A lot of people are emigrating from South Africa to England in 1975. Not us. We are going on what we have convinced ourselves is a holiday. Louisa and I will meet Robert's family and Robert is going to consult a National Health doctor about the condition which is crippling his right hand. He is finding it extremely difficult to type or shake hands or hold the wheel of a car.

But most important of all we are taking Robert's new stage play with us because a top London management has shown considerable interest in it.

177

We sell our house. We tell each other we'll buy a new one when we come back. We tell Dora we'll bring her heather from Scotland, white because that's the luckiest. Dora claps her hands and Louisa yells with delight.

We can't take the dog with us to Britain, of course, not even an adorable red-bearded mutt like Abo. Dieter, a German opera singer, gave him to us when he returned to his boyfriend and *Die Zauberflote* in Dresden. And now we are about to leave, Dieter has come back. Offers of great tenor roles in Johannesburg have proved more attractive than the chorus in Koln. Perfect timing – he can dog-sit.

We are told that clothes in London are much more expensive than they are in South Africa, so I waste no time at all in buying a vast quantity of apparel for Louisa and myself.

Robert has been known to go to work in his carpet slippers. He never notices if his sweaters are inside out or if there's tomato sauce on his shirt. Once he drove to work on his motorbike with a wooden clothes hanger attached to the back of his collar. I am spending at such a rate he thinks he'd better get something for himself before all the money from the house is gone. His main purchase is a jacket which we buy from the kind of shop where you press your nose up against the window and then walk on. The top drawer sales-man is brilliant at matching garment to person. After a brief chat he returns with a checked cashmere number for Robert to try on. It is love at first sight. The cut squares off his shoulders, the back kick-pleat, even the buttons are flattering, simple and elegant. As light as a feather but as warm as toast.

Our house and garden furniture go into storage while we're away. All the plants go to my friend, the horticulturist, who will keep an eye on them – on a temporary basis.

We cancel all our life insurance policies. We'll

178

renew them as soon as we return. We leave the Cortina convertible in a friend's garage. She likes the idea of a spare car for when her other two are being serviced. She promises to start it up a couple of times while we are away.

All our characters in our various radio soap operas are put on ice. They either contract contagious diseases or have nervous breakdowns or just go on holiday. The gardener goes to work for Mummy on the days he used to work for us.

And Robert sends his ex-wife a couple of post-dated cheques.

The family can't make it to the airport but there are plenty of friends and colleagues to give us a big send-off. I am handed lists of perfumes and cosmetics to buy and Robert is taking requests for banned magazines. The announcement comes through first in Afrikaans and I think to myself, 'If I never hear that bloody language again it'll be too soon.' Then in English, 'British Airways regret to announce the departure of flight BA 355 for Nairobi and London has been delayed. The new departure time is 06.00 hours tomorrow.'

Robert strides to the British Airways counter.

The woman there says, 'We suggest you go home, sir, and come back tomorrow.'

Robert says, 'We don't have a home. We've sold it.'

She says, 'We'll find you a suite in the Airport Hotel.'

People had been planning to throw streamers and sing 'Auld Lang Syne' for us and the press are there to take a few pictures. Sadly, it's all rather anti-climactic. Finally, all but one of our friends drifts off, a very grand English actor-laddie named Charles. He remains to dine with us because British Airways are picking up the tab for three persons and Louisa is too tired to eat.

As always happens with Charles, we laugh and drink too much. Finally he leaves and we take off our new clothes and lay them carefully on the bed. We doze in armchairs so as not to miss the wake-up call. I

179

don't remove my make-up, just splash my face and put on more mascara and lipstick.

I nearly faint as we board the plane. An air hostess catches my arm. I keep telling myself not to fall. 'I love your outfit,' she whispers into my right ear.

'Don't collapse,' says the voice inside me. 'And don't look back.'

Somehow I manage to hold it all together.

Part Three

It is pissing down with rain as we step off the plane at Heathrow. Everyone stares at me in my ensemble of palest cream. Clearly no-one in their right minds would wear such an outfit on a day like this. We spend the night at the Savoy Hotel and I order a steak sandwich at three o'clock in the morning. It is wheeled in on a huge round table, covered with a floor-length, starched white cloth. Robert estimates the cost to be a pound a bite.

The next day we hire a car and drive down to meet his parents in Kent. For generations, Robert's family have been farm workers. His father has now risen to the position of farm manager after more than forty-five years of hard labour.

I get out of the car and pick my way through the puddles up to the back door of the farmhouse. Robert is dealing with the three new leather suitcases and the six pieces of matching hand luggage. He has already carried Louisa in so that her frills won't get muddy.

I hug Robert's mother and father. 'I'm so thrilled to meet you,' I say. 'Robert's told me so much about you.'

Robert's family come originally from Suffolk. There are ten children in his father's family and eleven in his mother's. Several sisters have married several brothers so it's a close-knit family in more ways than one. None of them has received anything more than a very basic education.

Back in 1941 when the teacher in the village school told her class that no-one from that school had ever gone on to Grammar school, Robert put up his hand and said, 'Miss, I want to be the first.'

And he was.

But instead of receiving congratulations from his family he was met with remarks like, 'Who do you think you are?' His father went out of his way to belittle his studies and, in one instance, actually defaced his French book.

For nearly two years now Robert has been suffering from a condition known as Dupuytren's contracture which, in layman's language, means a shortening and hardening of the tendons. He is convinced that the red lumpiness in his right hand is caused by gripping the handlebars of his motorbike but I believe it to be the physical manifestation of his anger at having to spend so many hours of his precious time writing rubbishy radio serials to pay his ex-wife's maintenance. The stretch of his fingers is now so restricted he can hardly open his hand at all with the 'pinkie' being the worst offender. It gets in the way of performing the simplest of tasks, even picking up a glass. Worse still, when shaking hands, its peculiar bent positioning often results in complete strangers wondering if he is giving some secret sign to indicate membership of the masons or the *Broederbond*. Through the kind intervention of one of our English actor friends, Robert has an appointment to see a Harley Street specialist who recommends amputation and his name is put on the National Health waiting list. If you want a hedge to thicken, you cut the top bits off, I think to myself.

In the meantime, the three of us head north of the border in a hired car. Scotland, in the glorious summer of 1975, is like home from home. One balmy night in early June as Robert and I sit on the patio of our hotel, sipping wine and watching the sun set over Oban, we make our decision not to return to South Africa. 'What the hell,' we say, 'let's burn our boats and make a new life here in England.'

Two months after our arrival, just as our funds are

beginning to run out, I land a season of repertory in a picturesque theatre in East Sussex. Some of the members of the cast are living, gipsy-style, in caravans parked in the surrounding grounds. When they suggest we join them we're tickled pink at the idea of living like strolling players. Whilst I rehearse, Robert traverses the English countryside looking for more permanent accommodation.

The Rent Act has just become law and people are wary of letting property for fear of never getting tenants out again but he manages to find us a little cottage in the depths of the Kentish countryside. Built in the sixteenth century, it is situated amongst apple orchards and fields of fat, woolly sheep.

Here I am introduced to the eccentric ways of the English gentry. Having grown up in the nouveau-riche world of Johannesburg, I am completely taken aback to find that our neighbours, a middle-aged couple digging their garden in torn pullovers and old trousers, are in fact a real-life lord and lady. And they are completely taken aback when I invite them to dinner. Apparently it normally takes ten years for something as outrageous as this to happen in an English village. I've achieved it in three weeks.

What I find a lot harder is adjusting to domestic life in England. I have never ironed a shirt. I have never washed up after a party (I'd kiss everybody goodbye and fall into bed leaving the mess for someone else to clean up in the morning). I have never painted a door or used a shovel. I don't know how to light a fire and I am thirty years old. Now I am doing the work that Lena and Jane and Joseph and Ephraim and Charlotte and Ishmael and Dora have always done.

I am bathing my own child and preparing her food. I'm standing in bus queues and carrying my own shopping. On my first big shop at a British supermarket, I stand at the checkout, gazing around, waiting for someone else to pack the groceries and carry them out to my car. 'Excuse me, madam,' says the cashier, 'other people are waiting.'

Louisa and I celebrate our first English Christmas in front of the inglenook in which blazes a fire of delicious-smelling applewood while the bells ring out from the tower of the Norman church next door to our cottage. As Robert and I are both nursing hangovers from a champagne-filled Christmas Eve, Louisa takes herself off to the morning service where she sits alone in the front pew gazing up at the young rector with her big blue eyes. On New Year's day 1976 I telephone South Africa and speak to Mummy, Auntie Edie and Annie. They are well but missing us. We are missing them too!

After several weeks of calm, life suddenly goes berserk. Suddenly, in one week, everything happens. Robert goes into hospital to have the operation on his hand, and his play, which has been taken up by the London production company, goes into rehearsal. I am cast in a brand new farce which is to rehearse in London prior to setting out on a long national tour.

February is freezing. The snow lies thick on the ground and I have to be up and away by seven each morning. A twelve mile drive, skidding over black ice, brings me to the railway station and the vagaries of British Rail. If I am lucky I get to the rehearsal room by ten-thirty. Sometimes I manage to call in at the hospital with clean pyjamas and a bunch of grapes.

Robert shows me the severed stump where once his little finger had been. Through the gauze you can see raw flesh and bone. It's going to take a long time for that wound to heal.

When I get home at night, which is usually about eight o'clock, I collect Louisa from our titled neighbour, who has become a real friend. She not only takes care of Louisa all day but often finds time in her own busy schedule to make us a delicious supper.

The farce opens in a grey industrial town in the north

184

of England. In South Africa, touring meant luxuriating in a beach-front hotel, sun-bathing by day and doing a bit of acting by night. So it comes as something of a surprise to find my first British theatrical digs are in a semi-detached council house, occupying a back bedroom overlooking a patch of frozen brussel sprout stalks.

Where I had been used to dining out on lobster thermidor after the show I now find myself boiling an egg in my landlady's kitchen before retiring for the night between pink floral nylon sheets. As I lie in bed dipping my toast into my egg, I count the orange and green swirls in the wallpaper and the red and black feathers in the carpet. The tears silently roll down my cheeks as I think of the life I have chosen to leave behind.

Of course the awfulness of my accommodation is hardly a good enough excuse for going out and committing adultery, but it's the only one I can offer. The thought of a comfortable night between cotton sheets in the playwright's hotel bedroom is more than I can resist. Of course it only ends in tears. I've never been any good at adultery.

'Can you hear me, Mummy,' I shout. 'I'm so worried about you.' Telephoning South Africa from the public phone backstage at the Theatre Royal, Bournemouth, isn't easy.

'Why dear, what's wrong?'

'The riots. Are you all all right?'

'Of course we are. What riots, dear?'

'The Soweto riots. There've been so many people killed.'

'Oh really? I wouldn't know about that. I've been up to my ears in *Iolanthe*.'

To a large extent we survive on other people's charity. We are lent houses to live in, given furniture to use and loaned money to pay our debts.

After a summer season in Brighton the farce is at last 'coming in' to the West End. As commuting between the countryside and the city would require anything up to five hours' travelling each day, we decide to move to London where we are lucky to be loaned, rent free, a beautiful house in Kensington which the owner, the ex-mother-in-law of a friend, wants occupied until such time as it is sold.

The only job Robert can get which leaves him enough time for his writing is in a betting shop in the High Street. However, our combined income from my treading the boards and his writing up on them is hardly enough to support us in anything like the style of life to which we had become accustomed in South Africa.

The cashier in the betting shop is being threatened with eviction from her council flat if she doesn't get rid of her dog. As we're missing Abo, Robert volunteers to take it. Somehow we'll manage to feed it. But we can't. We try every brand of pet food known to dog but the wretched animal sniffs and walks away. In five days, the dog's only sustenance has been a pathetic nibble on a broken tennis biscuit.

Then, on the fifth day, just after putting the hoover away in the cupboard, I notice little bits of chewed paper on my newly vacuumed stairs.

I pick up several of them before I realize what they are. Bits of a five-pound note, the only money I possess till payday. It seems the bloody animal has, at last, found something it enjoys eating.

Screaming, I bring the culprit down in a rugby tackle on the bedroom floor but he wriggles out of my grasp and crawls under the bed. I yank him out by the tail, pin him down with my knee, prize open his mouth and remove the soggy remains of the queen's head.

Just then the phone rings and I answer it in an hysterical state. After calming me down, my friend informs me that the salvaged sogs are still legal tender and that the sum of five pounds must still be paid to the bearer on demand as promised by the Bank of England. I sob all the way to the bank. My masticated money is preserved between two pink Kleenex tissues. The teller listens to my tale. He is amazed, especially by my inability to keep a stiff upper lip about so trivial an amount. He informs me that I will have to write to the Bank giving full details and, of course, enclosing the evidence.

'How long will that take?' I ask.

'Anything up to three months,' he says, looking down at his paying-in slips, paper clips and stamps.

'But it's all the money I've got!'

'Sorry, but there's nothing more I can do.' And he hands me back the chewed remnants. I move aside from the bullet-proof glass.

Passing along the queue on my way out a silver-haired woman takes my arm sympathetically. 'You poor girl! What a terrible story,' she says. 'Tell me, what breed of dog is it?'

'Just a mongrel,' I reply.

'Oh dear,' she says, 'that makes it even worse.'

When you work in the theatre, putting on make-up at eight-thirty in the morning is the equivalent of a bank manager having a gin and tonic for breakfast so I am sitting at the kitchen table looking pretty pasty-faced. Robert and I are off the fags as we just can't afford them anymore. Our home has been a smokeless zone for about three months now. We hear the postman at the door and Robert goes through to collect the mail. He comes back looking a lot more ashen than when he left. In his shaking hand is a blue airmail letter. There is only one person who can arouse emotion in him like that.

'What's she calling me now?' I ask. But Robert collapses into a chair and hands me the letter.

I am shaking now, too. The sight of her handwriting makes me want to vomit. The letter announces the imminent arrival at Heathrow airport of Robert's teenage children, Laura and David. Their mother expresses her desire, in no uncertain terms, that the entire responsibility for these two young people should henceforth rest with their male parent and his current companion.

Like an alcoholic, sliding backwards down the twelve steps to addiction, I say to Robert, 'I'll be back in a moment. I'm just off to the corner shop to buy some cigarettes.'

'Get me a packet too,' he says, putting the kettle on for tea.

My play is due to close the following Saturday and in two weeks we must vacate this house because it has been sold. Our family has, of this moment, expanded to five, and we have neither income nor accommodation. It never occurs to us to go to social security or the local council for help. Well, Mummy always said, 'You make your bed, you lie on it.'

Ever since seeing a copy of *The Lady* magazine soon after our arrival in England, I have longed to apply for a job as a cook or a cowhand or a housekeeper or a nanny. I've conjured up pictures of flagstone kitchens, bustling and steamy with lamb stews simmering in copper cooking pots on cosy hearths. I've imagined myself quaffing mugfuls of mulled wine in front of roaring fires whilst listening to apple-cheeked yokels recounting adventures of country life *à la* Thomas Hardy.

From the days of standing at the gates of Granny Mac's little weekend cottage, and looking across the veld to the servants' *kayas*, I have wanted to be one of them. They always seem to be having such a good time.

I retrace my steps to the corner shop and buy a copy of *The Lady*. We look through the 'couples required' column. There are two advertisements offering three-bedroomed accommodation in return for 'domestic service'.

It is a very bleak day, the kind that makes you think that you'll never get to the end of winter. The year

188

is 1977. We are in an old Austin Cambridge. Louisa, who is now five, is in the back. We are driving down an English country lane, en route to a life-changing interview, only we don't know it at the time. We do, however, recognize a giggly, desperate feeling. It's the adrenalin pumping through the veins.

We are about to meet the Right Honourable and the Right Honourable Missus in their sixteenth-century manor house. Robert wants the part of the chauffeur and I want to play the kitchenmaid.

Robert is avoiding puddles. A chauffeur's car should be immaculate.

We spent all of yesterday washing and polishing our car – even the seats and the steering wheel. Hard work. Poor Robert's hand is still sore even though the operation is almost a year ago. I love washing really dirty cars. The Duchess is a fifties' car we bought for three hundred quid when we were richer. She was advertised as a private sale, only one owner, but when Robert phoned him to say we'd take the car, a different man answered.

'Look here, are you a couple of bloody dealers?' Robert asked him bluntly.

'Indeed we are not,' replied the man grandly. 'I am Mr Walsh's next door neighbour. Last evening on his return from showing you the car, Mr Walsh collapsed and died. Heart failure!'

Poor man! His last act on earth was to make sure his beloved car would be going to a good home.

'She's a grand old lady,' says Robert, patting the wooden dashboard, and I agree. A duchess.

'Duchess Dora,' says Louisa from the back seat. And our banger is baptised.

The manor house is almost as big as a castle. It must be a sanatorium or something. You wouldn't be able to see it at all in the summer because the leaves of the trees would hide it.

'That can't be it.'

189

Robert squints to where I'm pointing.

'That's it all right,' he says. 'Quite something, eh?'

'Louisa, look! Up there on the hill. Can you see it? My god, there's even a lake.'

'Cows,' says Louisa.

'And cows.'

'Who lives there?' she asks.

'Not poor people, that's for sure,' says Robert.

'That,' I say, 'makes Jo'burg money look silly.'

Robert parks on the gravol in the horse-shoe shaped driveway. It's that moment before going on stage. Robert gives us our final notes.

'Louisa, when we get inside, sit very quietly on Mummy's lap. And you,' he tweaks my nose, 'don't say a thing.' We've agreed that Robert will do the talking. I will speak only when spoken to and, on no account, must I call anyone 'darling'.

We get out of Duchess Dora and crunch across the gravel. The air's so cold that we look as though we're smoking although both of us have left our cigarettes in the car.

The door of the manor house is rather like the way the Duke of Edinburgh walks, hands behind its back, unafraid of assault. A brave and essentially British front door. There is nothing so tasteless as a security lock in sight. The crunch of our feet on the gravel has alerted the dogs and from deep within the house there is a great deal of pompous woofing. Before Robert can ring the bell the door handle turns and the sound, like a good vowel, is well-rounded and rich.

There are three people in the hall, two are being ushered out and the third is the owner of the house, the Right Honourable himself. You can recognize him immediately. Clear pink skin, avuncular, portly, fine silver hair, slightly faded but expensive tweedy clothes in the green range.

He is politely ushering the other two people out. He seems to suspect that they are of the mouse family, so he is making sure that they scuttle towards their Mini instead of his pantry. We hadn't noticed another car but we see it now. It's parked nervously behind a tree. After some mutual muttering they scurry away and the Right Honourable turns to us.

'So good of you to come. Spot on timing, too. Come on in and defrost.'

We wipe our feet on the mat outside but we feel we need to wipe them again on the mat inside before taking them across the highly polished wooden floor.

'Oh don't bother, there's been so much toing and froing today. A little more mud won't make any difference. Through here.'

Danger moment. I'm gawking and it's well nigh impossible not to gush. A gross of genies could fly on the carpet. The table could seat Henry the Eighth and all his in-laws. The two sweeping staircases are of burnished oak and the minstrel gallery is big enough for one of Mummy's combined convent choirs. But what I covet most of all are the thickets of azaleas in big, brass bowls, strategically placed on commodes, antique chests and inlaid walnut tables. Because I'm looking backwards, I almost bump into Robert as we turn the corner and then practically trip up Louisa. I bend to offer a supportive hand.

'We thought it'd be more conducive in the snug,' says the Honourable. 'Dear, here they are.'

And there she is – the Right Honourable Mrs. Tall, fiftyish and very well-preserved. Sensible hair, expensively styled in the rich brown range. Sensible suit of pure new wool in the light blue range. Angular, pearled and grand, she observes us like Queen Victoria looking at three urine samples.

'Take a pew, take a pew, take a pew,' says the Right Honourable.

'Did it take you long to drive down from London?' asks the Right Honourable Mrs. Robert immediately catches a whiff of loaded question.

191

'Cruising at fifty with light traffic,' looking at his watch, 'one hour twenty-seven exactly.'

I smile demurely and lower my unmade-up eye-lashes. The equivalent, I hope, of applause on the village green for a well-played cover drive.

'They've got an Austin Cambridge, dear,' says RH. 'I like those cars. Solid, good, reliable old things. Very good.'

'They don't make them like that any more,' says Robert, playing this one straight down the wicket.

'Have you ever chauffeured before?' asks Mrs RH.

'No.'

'Have you any references?'

'No,' says Robert again.

Louisa is on my lap, mother and child. Margarine wouldn't melt in our mouths. RH is looking at my legs. I shift my bottom on the wine-red velvet, uncross my ankles and, pointing my toes, place both high heels tightly together. RH splutters.

'Not . . . not . . . not that references necessarily matter . . .'

'Then what brings you down here?' asks Mrs RH.

Robert composed the speech yesterday afternoon while we were polishing the car and I directed him in it last night. 'Be simple, be real, search for your lines as though saying them for the first time.'

'How best to answer that . . . well, I was . . . born and brought up in the country. Suffolk actually. But . . . I've spent my adult life in . . . cities. I write a bit. And really, more than anything, I'd like my wife and daughter to get away from the er . . . smoke and fumes and well, get a bit of oxygen into their lungs.'

'Quite!' says RH. 'Exactly! Good!'

I don't agree. I thought he dragged a bit. He must speed up now or he's lost them.

'I love driving. I'm not a man who likes stuffy offices. I'm not afraid of hard work but as the advertisement

192

mentioned negotiable hours, I liked the idea of having a fair amount of time off for my writing.'

RH seems happy with this, 'Good, good, good – excellent!'

Ye-es, much better, I say to myself. Robert really drove the thought through to the end of the line in that last speech. And with the right hint of toughness, too. I must say, he does have a lovely quality.

Mrs RH is speaking, 'The chauffeur's duties consist of cleaning and maintaining the cars. There are three of them and, of course, the Range Rover.'

RH explains, 'That's oil, water, tyres, polishing and so on.'

'Keeping all petrol and oil accounts,' continues Mrs RH, 'for the whole household and the gardeners.'

'Mowers,' explains RH who has been folding and unfolding something. 'Big ones, you know, like little tractors. Yes.'

'And maintaining the swimming pool.'

'In the summer months,' says RH. 'Hardly ever used, but still. Oh, and it's heated so . . . temperature maintenance and all that, you know. Not difficult. Bloody nuisance. Still.'

'And, if you were taken on,' she looks at me, 'you would be required for the usual household chores. The job is not a fulltime one so you should have lots of spare time. Thank you both so much for coming down.' We are dismissed.

'Do we have your phone number?' asks RH.

'I have it,' says Mrs RH. The oak door is opened and we're stepping into the cold air. I resist throwing my arms around RH and kissing him. I once did that to a bank manager. He gave us the overdraft but it took years to pay off.

'Domestic service isn't easy, you know,' says RH as he bids us farewell and ushers in the next couple.

There is one essential item which Robert does not possess. And perhaps he wasn't asked to produce it because it is assumed that without this accoutrement nobody would even contemplate applying for the job of chauffeur. He doesn't have a British driver's licence.

I am making a lentil curry, my favourite recipe from Delia Smith's *Frugal Food*, when Robert arrives home. He finished late at the betting shop today. The phone rings. Robert answers.

'Hello, yes, yes. Oh, thank you. Yes. Yes . . . Yes . . . Oh, probably the day before, I think. Yes. Yes. Thank you vory much. Goodbye.'

He comes into the kitchen and sits on a packing case. 'We got it.'

A famous actor once said, 'The best part about acting is getting the role, after that, it's downhill all the way.'

The next morning I telephone the Right Honourable Missus.

'Hello. This is the chauffeur's wife. Just ringing about our house. Do you happen to know what colour the walls are at the moment?'

'I have absolutely no idea,' says the Right Honourable Missus, 'but they're bound to be something innocuous.'

'That's exactly what I was afraid of,' I reply.

From the moment we arrive at the cottage I throw myself into interior decorating. I paint the house myself, in subtle tones, ranging from buttermilk in the bedroom to chocolate brown in the bathroom. A rural theme is evident throughout, especially in the kitchen where locally picked grasses decorate the top of the plate cupboard and a chipped dish hangs over the mantelpiece. Robert isn't able to help because of his hand, the skin of the little finger is closing over but it still looks very pink and raw. Plunging it into a bucket of icy water first thing every morning is proving painful.

The night before Robert's two children are due to arrive from South Africa, I think my heart will break. Their coming means that our little family will never again be just the Three Bears. But once they arrive I try to make them feel welcome with flowers and cards.

My life at this moment is a mixture of playing housey-housey and doing a play. So long as I keep acting I'm all right but some days the part just isn't good enough. I am having great difficulty relating to my stepchildren. I don't like their touch or their smell. I don't want to kiss them or hug them. I really don't want them here at all. I have a little crying cave amongst the trees at the bottom of the garden. Most days I go to this quiet spot to have a weep. It is too painful to think about the theatre or to tell our friends where we are. It seems as if my life has been put on hold, as if I'm living in some kind of halfway house.

Of course, my letters home to the dutch-gabled house in Johannesburg describe our life in the English countryside as being one of domestic bliss set amidst buttercupp'd meadows and hedgerow'd lanes.

Emblazoned on the pale-blue aerograms that Auntie Edie sends in reply are colourful depictions of exotic flowers like the Strelitzia Reginae or Bird Flower and the flame-red orchid, known as the Pride of Table Mountain. Inside, in her large, childlike handwriting she writes:

It was nice to hear from you. So glad you are happy. Your mother and I are well. Annie is out of hospital and looking lovely. The doctors are very pleased with her.

Your mother is very busy. She is doing three different productions of 'The Pirates of Penzance' at three different convents. Jilly and the girls are getting ready for the Royal Scottish gathering. Morag won her section at the Vereeniging gathering last weekend. She dances very nicely.

Fancy Louisa winning the egg-and-spoon race. She is a clever girl. It's nice the two children are settling down. England will be very different to Johannesburg.

The weather is very hot here. We were down at Henley on Sunday and the cosmos were out all along

*the road. They looked very pretty. Mr Murray came
in and asked how you were. Two of his boys are in
the army now.*

*The theatre in Johannesburg is very busy – lots
of shows. Your actress friends are working all the
time. Our television is really getting going now. We
have some interesting programmes, especially on the
English nights.*

*Your mother and I watch the news at six every
night, one night it is in English and one night,
Afrikaans. The rugby season has just begun.*

*I am sitting here, waiting for Jilly to fetch me and
take me to her dancing class. Freddie, the cat, is
well. He is a naughty boy, always rubbing himself
against my legs and nearly tripping me up. Tell
Louisa, I am sending her a postal order to buy
something nice. I hope to get it off next week. I
am enclosing some affirmations for you.*

*THE TIDE OF DESTINY HAS TURNED AND ALL
GOOD THINGS NOW COME TO ME.*

*PEACE IS THE PEARL OF GREAT PRICE THAT
ALL MANKIND IS SEEKING.*

Every good wish,
Auntie Edie

The two children try their best to adapt to a totally
different lifestyle. The contrast between a northern
Johannesburg suburb and a cold cottage in rural
England must be enormous. They are unspoiled and
friendly enough and both have nice manners. Louisa
and David settle into an easy friendship despite the
fact that at thirteen he is seven years her senior.
The brain tumour he suffered as a toddler has left
him emotionally and mentally immature. Laura, who
turned seventeen on her last birthday, is motherly
and protective towards him.

Robert rises at seven, when it's still dark, makes
himself a cup of tea and then goes to the big house

to wash and polish the cars in readiness for the Right Honourables. The two older children go to their comprehensive school on the bus and I walk Louisa, who is now six, to the local primary school. The road winds through misty conifers, making it all seem quite unreal and *Brigadoon*-ish: a sort of waking dream or a terrible nightmare, depending on my mood.

The surreal quality of the whole experience seems to be further enhanced by the fact that I continue to don silk scarves and drown myself in Chanel No.5 before setting out each morning to play the role of a kitchenmaid. Over my arm I carry a simple wicker basket in which are placed my pink rubber washing-up gloves and a pair of secateurs.

Amongst the supporting cast in this country drama are Carlos, the Spanish butler, his wife, Maria the cook, the housekeeper, a fulltime housemaid, a head gardener, two assistants and the girl who looks after the horses.

At last spring comes to Blankshire. The daffodils have managed to push their way through the frozen ground and the trees dance all day in their new green ballet frocks. I decide that, as the sun is shining, I will hang our heavy viyella sheets, a hand-down from my mother-in-law, out to dry. I think there is nothing so sordid as wet washing. Granny Mac always said it was the damp washing draped around Glasgow tenement kitchens that gave them all tuberculosis.

No sooner are my sheets up on the line than it starts to snow and I have to get them back into the kitchen. Two minutes later the sun comes out again and I haul them back out and up onto the line. No sooner have I done that than it starts to snow again. Twice more I perform this ridiculous ritual. I am now as schizophrenic as the weather, laughing one moment, crying the next. Suddenly I arrive at a decision. Lifting the lid off the big black dustbin outside the kitchen door, I dump the whole bloody lot into it.

197

'You stupid, ignorant cow!' Robert throws down his chamois leather and shouts at the disappearing back of the Right Honourable Missus. She is on her way through the courtyard to the stables, dressed in her riding gear. 'For Christ's sake, woman, if someone has the good grace to say good morning to you, can't you have the decency to reply?' It is a moment of history. The ancient bricks tremble, rocked to their foundations.

Icily she rounds on him, 'You are fired.'

'And that's another thing,' he says unable to stop as the flood of suppressed emotion now bursts its restricting gates, 'you know my name. Why don't you bloody well call me by it? What gives you the right to ignore me or anyone else for that matter. I'm not just your chauffeur you know, I'm also a human being.'

Sweeping him with a glacial stare she strides past him, back into the house.

Robert picks up his chamois. He is shaking from head to foot. 'Shit, I've really blown it.' A hundred years ago this could've meant deportation, and we could all have ended up in Australia.

Robert looks more than a trifle peaky as he walks into the kitchen. 'I think you'd better pour us both a scotch.'

'A scotch?' I say. 'At ten to ten?' Even for us, this is going a little far. 'My God, what's happened?'

'I've been fired.'

'Fired! But I've just painted this house!' I scream. I mean labour like that is irremovable. All that brown and beige and muffin, you can't take it with you, off the walls. And what about all the memories in the paint, the news items that go with each section of wall? That stretch of muffin is linked with Elvis Presley's death. And that bit of beige with the IRA siege. Not to mention my mother-in-law, looking at my newly-finished, chocolate-brown bathroom and saying, 'It'll be nice when you've given it a coat of paint. 'In three short months I've managed to change this place from 'innocuous' into 'me'.

The telephone rings and like a zombie, I go to answer it. The voice on the other end informs me that it belongs to the Right Honourable and that he is ringing in connection with the 'beastly business that has just taken place in the courtyard'. He goes on to say that he considers the whole matter a damned shame and one that we should all put our heads together to resolve. He really is one hell of a nice guy. Relief sweeps through my numbed body as I reach out to caress the country clover on the entrance hall wall.

'It's a jolly silly business and I think we must try and sort it out.' I get the feeling that by 'we' he means he and I should take charge of the situation with the sense and sensibility that the other two seem to have lost. There is hope. He is intervening. The situation may yet be salvaged.

Then he says, 'Why don't the two of you come up at six, have a drink, and let's sort this whole wretched business out.' I get the feeling he recognizes the emotions that have led to this outburst and that he nurses a secret admiration for Robert's succinctness in putting the silly bitch in her place.

'Yes, lovely,' I say, 'see you at six.'

Perspiring somewhat beneath our respective colognes, we climb into Duchess Dora for the short journey from the cottage to the main house. We both feel the need to grab onto every vestige of dignity. The old Austin Cambridge swings her plum-coloured chassis up the horseshoe drive and stops outside the huge oak doors. The gravel crunching under our feet alerts the labradors lying in wait behind them and there is the usual confusion of humans and animals as the defences are opened. The dogs, to her undoubted annoyance, adore Robert. She is hovering under the minstrel gallery as RH takes our coats, hangs them in the hall and gestures for us to follow. Not into the snug, as we had expected, but into the drawing room which is large enough to hold two hundred guests. In the early evening light of late April, we can see down to the lake through the magnificent floor-to-ceiling windows. The scene beyond them is a Constable painting come to life. Landscaped trees and swathes of daffodils are arranged in perfect perspective around the grazing cattle.

Inside the room there is a walk-in fireplace, ancestral oils (hunting scenes and portraits) and a polished oak floor covered in Chinese rugs. Settees are arranged in clusters. Mrs RH is perched on the edge of one which dominates the room, a big brocaded bugger in antique gold. I think I always give away my working-class ancestry by the sheer energy of my admiration. 'Gosh, that's lovely,' I say. 'That IS lovely. That is gorgeous! That is simply unbelievably stunning. I mean, one doesn't often see one like that, do you?' My grammar is drowning along with me.

Like a knight of Old England, RH leaps to my aid. Preceded by his Jermyn Street brogues, he cavalry twills himself across the vast distance of the room to ring for our drinks.

She snaps her black and gold only-holds-five cigarette case shut and brands her cigarette with a laser-like flame until one can almost hear the poor thing yelping. Robert and I take this as a sign to light up too. There is relief all round when RH returns from his trek and I decide to launch into the weather.

'Don't you just love it when things start to warm up a little? I mean the cold really seems to get to me somehow. Maybe that's because of where I come from, South Africa.'

'Is that so?' as she exhales through her nostrils.

'Oh yes. The Transvaal is actually famous for its climate,' I say in my best mother-teaches-speech-and-drama-at-six-convents-and-I've-played-the-West-End accent. My mind is searching frantically for my next line of dialogue when the drawing-room door is pushed open and in glides the Spanish butler, carrying the drinks' tray. As soon as he sees us he stops dead in his tracks. 'What they doing here? I no serve them, they servants.'

And with that, he thunks the tray down on the drinks table.

'Thank you, Carlos, I'll attend to it,' says the gallant RH, quickly ushering the peeved Spaniard out of the room.

Oh God what a mess!

We ask for whisky and, looking at the size of the decanter, it's difficult not to add, 'And large, please.' Then we attempt to settle back into the Siberian wastes of the settee.

She jettisons ash from her Balkan sobranie, her finger fluttering over it like a butterfly on barbed wire, and orders gin and ginger. RH yodels across the drawing room to us. 'Would you like so-da?'

'Lovely, yes,' we project back.

RH blasts one of the scotches ferociously with a hand-held syphon. I wave frantically to stop him liquidating the other.

'Just a dash and, no, no ice, thank you.'

'The way I see it . . .' she begins.

It's so interesting how people let you know their strongest sense. Some start a sentence with, 'I'm trying to put my finger on it', or, 'Hit me with it'. Others do a more than average amount of sniffing and saying, 'Fishy', or 'I smell a rat'. She is a bit like me in that she is an 'I see it', or 'Get the picture', sort of person. Robert, on the other hand, is a 'It sounds to me', or 'Listen, dammit, listen!' kind of chap.

She goes on, 'It's not that one's saying one couldn't see you running this entire estate, do you see?'

I gulp my drink. I'd expected a lecture on bad manners and lack of breeding. Not this. She bashes straight on. 'The point is you didn't apply for the manager's job. You applied for the chauffeur's job. And chauffeurs, I'm sorry to say, are not managers. Do you see?'

We both nod – we can hardly not see.

'Therefore I shall treat you as a chauffeur, not as a manager. That is my prerogative.'

'How about treating me as a human being?' counters Robert.

Oh God, eviction. Homelessness. I frantically inflate the survival dinghy. 'I can see your point, I really can,' I say desperately. And then I am forced to add, 'But I can see Robert's too.'

RH grasps the moment. 'You're absolutely right. They've both got a point.'

'You see, Robert,' she says, with a hint of bonhomie – the gin and ginger is doing its job – 'I do know your Christian name, but it is traditional in service to address a person by his surname only.' She wants to say minion, but daren't. 'When you two came into service, you should've found out about these things.'

This time I really can see her point.

'I think we're all going to get along splendidly,' says RH back with fresh drinks.

Peace, for the moment, has broken out in Blankshire.

The laughter and revving of engines from the working men's club across the road from our cottage keeps us awake at night. The happy sounds of camaraderie highlight our own isolation. The other employees at the big house frequent the club. It's the only place of entertainment, apart from the local pub, for miles. We have never been invited because nobody knows what to make of our well-modulated voices and fancy accents.

Finally it is Robert who breaks through the social barrier. No doubt the incident in the courtyard has something to do with it. In the country, walls have ears.

One day, not long after the fracas in the courtyard, the head gardener picks up an almost full can of oil and says to Robert, 'If you're finished with this I'll get rid of it for you, shall I?'

'Yes,' says Robert, realizing that the code has, at last, been cracked. 'Yes, please do.' That afternoon when we return to the cottage there is a huge cardboard box lying on the doorstep. It is filled with the choicest vegetables from her ladyship's garden. It even contains a few pieces of fruit from her ladyship's greenhouse. We dance a jig around the cardboard box in celebration of our acceptance by the workers. The very next day we receive an invitation to the working men's club. Things are looking up.

I too am starting to make a name for myself by challenging Carlos's rules and regulations. Especially the one about pouring leftover wine down the sink. His wife sides with me, no doubt pissed off by being ordered around by a miniature General Franco. But before I have time to fan the flames of the second Spanish Civil war, Mrs RH pays me a personal visit.

She suggests I leave the big house and instead go to work for her son and heir, his wife and newborn baby in their weekend cottage beside the swimming pool. An interview is duly arranged and a favourable salary and hours negotiated, in return for which I will prepare for their coming, be on call throughout the weekend and clean up after they've gone.

The alarm fails to go off and we wake twenty minutes late. I immediately blame Robert. I am a great blamer: 'Attack First' is my motto. Not I'm late, not it's late, not we're late, but YOU'RE late.

'So for God's sake, hurry up now.'

Screaming at the children, I throw on my dressing-gown en route to the bathroom. I am hit by the pong. There is nothing guaranteed to turn your stomach like cat shit first thing in the morning. Since leaving London, our cat has gone doolally and has taken to doing things in the bath at night. It's a woman's lot to clean up shit. Without thinking, I remove the mess with toilet paper and swill the bath out with Dettol. I've managed to get the whole operation down to about two minutes flat.

Fag lit, kettle on, same match for both. Got to make some savings. Grab a slice of toast and marmalade while casting a quick eye over the mail. Letters to the children from their mother are read behind closed doors. Letters going the other way are posted secretly. Jilly's letters are highly detailed reports, almost time-tables, never do they carry any emotional content. But I love receiving them. At a quick glance the one today tells me that:

At approximately 2.15 p.m. on the 16th of May, Gordon was knocked off his bike by a Happy Snax delivery van on the corner of 9th Avenue and Mimosa Road about 200 yards from the Mobil garage. He had to have twelve stitches in his left underarm approx. two inches above the elbow. He was completely unconscious for just over twenty-two hours. The Christian Science healer's clear thinking and comprehension of Scientific Principle resulted in Gordon's complete recovery.

At the Krugersdorp gathering last Saturday, Morag came first in the Fling and Sword Dance and second in the Seann Triubhas. She lost marks in the balance step because her 4th Intermediate aerial position was slightly too high. We are working on it. She is a very sincere girl and tries very hard. Sheila won the Junior Championship.

Carol has lost approx. ten pounds in weight and Grant got 4 As, 2 Bs, and a C in his Easter exams. He is still doing his paper round and helps Auntie and Mummy on a Saturday morning with their shopping.

Working in a country house sounds interesting. The garden must be beautiful. Tons of love,
Jilly

I light my second cigarette. 'I'm sick to death of this smoking. Just listen to this cough. Disgusting. Now I've told you children this before and I'm going to tell you again. If there's one thing I regret in my life it's having started smoking.'

Before I can really get into my stride, Robert says, 'I'm off. Hurry up, Louisa, and I'll drop you at school. Save Mummy the walk.' He goes upstairs to throw on old trousers, shirt and jacket.

The children rush to get dressed too. I shout from the bathroom, 'Look at this bloody basin! You children really piss me off with your toothpaste. Why can't you just put it in your bloody mouths instead of painting the walls with it.'

The two older ones dash to get the bus. Then I clear the table, wash the dishes, zap around with the hoover, can't leave a mess, leap into the bath, quick soap all over and rinse off. Just like my mother. Then I brush my teeth, adopting a *Calamity Jane* pose, foot up on the side of the bath. When that's done I dress. Something nice. Snappy. Everything perfect. No matter what the rush. Slap on some make-up, lots of eyes and always a squizz of perfume. Mummy always says I look as though I've just stepped out of a bandbox. It's not always easy but I do try.

Once I've turned into the long, shady driveway with the gravel crunching beneath my feet, I can start to relax. Whew! Trees all round, bunnies, flowering shrubs. I walk past the main house and into the courtyard where Robert is polishing the cars. He doesn't wash the cars every day although there's always some mud to be got off. He certainly does have to polish every day because she runs her finger over the bodywork before getting into the car.

Robert drives RH up to London three times a week. He waits in the car while RH does his business and then they go to the town flat in Cadogan Square for lunch. RH sits in the dining-room and Robert sits in the kitchen. They eat the same food only Robert doesn't get a peach. On the way home they discuss the merits of Bach and Beethoven. Both have a passion for Stravinsky.

If the Honourables care about their cars, their son certainly doesn't. He races around the country roads as though he's at Le Mans, hitting potholes at full speed and clipping the sides off hedges. Once he misjudged the width of a narrow gate and just drove on, taking the gate with him and gouging out the side of his brand new car.

As I enter the courtyard Robert looks up. 'Hello love. Everything all right?'

'Everything's fine,' I say. No, it bloody well isn't, I think as I stomp past him with crunching clarity. In my head the chatter is going like the clappers. You simply don't understand what I'm going through. But what can I expect from a man? Actually, mate, I'm going through this whole damned business because of you, because of your ex-wife and because of your children.

I unlock the door to the son and heir's flat and go inside. The first thing I do is open the fridge and see what they've left. Our whole family can sometimes get a meal out of their left-overs. There might be some roast lamb or some chicken. There might be ice-cream, or strawberries or maybe some asparagus. I stare at the chaos of unmade beds, overflowing ashtrays and papers strewn about the floor.

My mother always told our servants, 'Start by washing the breakfast things and making the beds and then you're free to get on with anything else,' and I must say it's an excellent method.

The sitting-room is furnished in soft creams – cream pile carpet, big comfortable cream settees, cream fabric wallpaper and delicious silk cushions in shades from apricot to burgundy, and some lovely paintings and *objets d'art*. Oh, how I want it all to be mine.

Suddenly I go at it like a lunatic. I pick up the papers. I plump up the cushions, I empty the ashtrays. I get right into the corners, behind everything. I move the furniture. I push, I pull, I heave, I shove.

When the sitting room is done, I go upstairs to their bedroom en suite. Again, it is all creamy comfort. Beautiful bed-linen from France, soft and matching. As the bedroom overlooks the swimming pool, I look out and see Robert sunning himself against the change room wall. He is having a little doze. Perhaps he's indulging in his favourite fantasy which is to fill a watering can with bleach and mark out a huge hammer and sickle on the front lawn.

To lighten the mood I take on the role of South African housewife shouting at her garden boy. 'Hey, Phineas, you lazy so-and-so, get on with your work or I'll report you to the boss.'

Robert takes on his character instantly. 'Yees medam, sorree medam. Straight away, medam.'

Then, lowering my voice and winking broadly, I say, 'Hey, Phineas, fancy a quickie?'

'Oh medam!'

'See me at lunchtime then,' I say, popping my head back inside.

I make the beds. Then I open daughter-in-law's cupboard and have a look to see what new clothes she has brought down. I hold them up against me and let my fingers run over the expensive-feeling fabric. I look at myself in the wardrobe mirror and covet some more.

It doesn't take long to do the nursery and the nanny's room. She's a full-time professional, Irish and terribly glamorous. She says she likes the job because she enjoys sitting around in parks all day, but she is hoping to land a job in America and marry a millionaire.

Then through to the bathroom to Jif the bath and Harpic the loo. The bathroom suite is in olive-green and shows every mark. I hate cleaning the loo and scum around the bath. It's yuk work. Talk about out damned spot, out I say!

I am manic as I embrace the toilet bowl and, brush in hand, poke and prod to release the nasties around the rim. Then a good wipe of the handle. People forget that the first place your hand goes after you've wiped your bottom is there. Then I put down the lavatory seat and fluff up the cover. This toilet is now so clean I don't want anyone to use it, ever again.

As I pick up the towels from the floor, big luxurious ones, the kind I dream of having, and the assortment of dirty socks and knickers lying around, I remember my mother saying that no-one should ever have to bend down and pick up things for another human being. Before taking the dirty washing down to the machine in the kitchen, I do a quick clean of the basin. There are always little clusters of bluish-grey muck around the bottoms of taps which a cloth won't budge. 'You fuckers are not going to beat me!' I cry as I jab them with a hairpin and then swish them away with clean water.

Finally I get new soap and toilet rolls out of a Mrs Danvers type cupboard. The soap they use is a French tobacco-coloured sandalwood smelling of spice and incense. I like the opulent look of a big new bar of soap. I take a bar home for myself. What the hell. I have few pleasures left in life and one of them is soap.

I'm just closing the door when I think how nice some honeysuckle would look in a slender vase on the loo top. I sprint out and snip a spray or two. Oh yes! Very Japanese.

It's now about twelve-thirty. 'Time for that gin and tonic,' I say to myself. I'm feeling quite chirpy now. There's nothing like a good hard scrub in the crapper to cheer a person up.

I kick open the kitchen door, grab a tumbler from the cupboard and the bottle of gin from the work surface below. Just under half a glass, a triple. I don't give a damn! Oh, honestly, I'll buy them another bottle or I'll do what the servants in South Africa do: fill the bottle with tonic. Alcoholics do that too.

Open the fridge door. A nice bit of cheese and two cold roast potatoes. I eat these as I watch *Married Couples* and have a couple of smokes.

Right! Must get on. Must, must, must get on! Command the legs: Rise! Command the hand. Put out the cigarette! Command the brain. Get out the hoover!

I get myself in a hell of a muddle with the cord. I'm not thinking clearly, which is not surprising after that triple gin. Quick going over the carpets, quick swipe at the banisters – I'm really bored now. So I think I'll go and nick some flowers from the garden. As I set off for the shrubbery, the boom-titty-booming of my heart tells me that I'm getting turned on by the danger.

For those of you perhaps not totally familiar with the marguerite, it is one of nature's simplest flowers. It has a sunny, yellow centre where the bees come to collect the pollen and surrounding this is a circle of perfectly proportioned white petals.

One sunny day in South Africa Robert picked a marguerite and gave it to me. I took it from him, smiling and sniffing prettily. The flower has no perfume, but not wishing to ruin the romantic moment I kissed the sunny yellow centre and began to melt towards him. In seconds my eyes had become puffed up red slits emitting a sticky gunge and my lips transmuted into a pink lump not unlike a piece of pig's liver. The marguerite is still my favourite flower but now I leave it unkissed.

I know the marguerite patch well, just under the garden wall where the sun can reach their beaming faces. I pick a bunch every other day. If I'm caught I'll say they're for the heir's flat. The blood rushes to my head and my eyes go glassy. I breathe heavily. The secateurs seem to have a life of their own. Oh God! The excitement! It's like an art expert raiding the Louvre or a jeweller let loose in Cartier. I wade in amongst the welcoming flowers. Their heads are bobbing at thigh height. 'Pluck me, pluck me,' they beg as they thrust themselves between the blades of the secateurs. I lift at least twenty of the beauties into my arms. 'All right, all right, I love you all, darlings. Darlings.'

'Oh it's you, is it!' My brain immediately glaciates

as I recognize the voice and then the body in front of me. From the Gucci courts to the Charles of the Ritz eyebrows it is Her, Madam of the Big House, Reader of *Horse and Hound*, Sitter on the Tory Council, Lady-Greet-you-when-she-chooses, Supreme Hirer and Firer and Last Person on this Earth I want to see.

My arms drop open in terror. Leaves and flowers dive for cover on the ground.

Following her grilled salmon-watercress-cracker-or-two-excellent-Roquefort-half-a-bottle of Chablis-lunch, she has taken the quartet of Labradors to the stables for a leisurely stroll. On the way back she has doubtless noted the absence of her garden staff who are no doubt ensconced at the village watering hole. Already a trifle hot under the collar, she has now caught me green-handed, *in flagrante depicto*. The walking stick in her hand jabs and stabs the air. She points to the brown stalks of marguerites whose top halves have been plucked by me over the weeks. Even I am shocked at the amount I have taken. The massacre is appalling. I bite my lip and begin to cry. That takes her by surprise. I thought it might. For her to go on now would be like beating a baby lamb. Even she stops short of that. Gasping, 'Don't ever do that again,' she exits stage left followed by the hounds.

It has started raining as I turn into our cottage gate. God, Britain is a stupid little island. Louisa runs out to meet me and I nearly crush her to death as I say, 'Hello my angel. Let me kiss you darling. Oh, I love the smell of you. Are the others home?'

'Not yet.'

'Good. Maybe we can have a few moments together before Daddy gets here. We've still got to go to the laundrette. I've got mountains of washing to do. Damn, there's Daddy in Duchess Dora now. Oh well, let's just get it over with. Come and give me a hand.' Together we lug three huge plastic bags full of our dirty washing out to the car and I slam the boot shut.

We drive off. Oh God, I hate these silences. We've always talked before but now we seem to be growing further and further apart. We can't go on like this, so I say, 'Quite a funny thing happened today. She caught me pinching daisies.'

'I thought you'd stopped that stupid flower stealing business.'

'Oh it was just a few leaves, for God's sake.'

'I thought you just said it was daisies.'

Robert likes to argue about words. He has a knack for stopping an argument dead in its tracks by asking you to define the meaning of a word and why you're using it. It's a delaying tactic and usually results in the real issue getting lost along the way. I'm getting good at sidestepping the trap.

'Did you see her?' I persist.

'Yes, before I came home.'

'Did she say anything?'

'Nope.'

'You don't seem very interested.'

'What do you want me to say? God! What an amazing story!'

'No, I don't want you to say anything like that at all.'

'Then what do you want?'

'I want us to be happy again, like we once were, don't you?'

'I can't say I'm particularly unhappy.'

'Oh God, don't say that.'

'Why?'

'Because that's what you said about being married to HER. That you were neither happy nor unhappy. For God's sake, man, why do you always settle for second best?'

Ignoring this he says, 'We will get out of this mess.'

'When?'

'I don't know when, but we will.'

'Then you'll have to do something about your bloody ex-wife. Confront her, stand up to her!'

211

A laugh, mirthless. 'God, you are so predictable. Always got to blame someone else.'

'Listen mate, I didn't get us into this.'

'Fine, I stand charged. Now what do you want me to do?'

'BLOODY GET US OUT OF IT.'

'Stop overreacting – you are such a drama queen.'

'I AM NOT A DRAMA QUEEN! I just happen to be going slowly and steadily mad.'

'Going?' This said very quietly.

'That's it,' I scream. 'Stop the car.'

Hand patting my knee. 'Come on now, don't be a silly billy. You're only exhausting yourself.'

'Too damn right. I am exhausted from looking after your kids and being a bloody servant. I feel like a beast of burden.'

'I think we're all exhausted.'

'Sure, lifting five pints of beer is a very exhausting business.'

Robert lets that one go by and we drive on in silence. It's a damn nuisance not having a washing machine. Added to that the laundrette is so far away from the car park.

'I'll drop you outside. Can you manage the bags?'

'As though you care,' I say close to tears. I don't want to steal flowers. I want to be given bouquets.

Please excuse the red pen. I bought it thinking it was blue. Thank you for your letter which Mummy brought with her to the hospital on Sunday. England sounds like fun, lots of moo cows and bunny rabbits, I bet. Louisa, I loved the picture of the dormouse you sent me. I have him on my locker. I call him Twinkles. I often look at him. The other patients like him too.

Our winter is beginning but so far it is quite mild. My favourite season is spring. I love blossoms and flowers, especially mimosa blossoms.

I haven't seen Jilly for a very long time. She always

has so much on her plate. Mummy comes to see me
every weekend. She is the most wonderful mother
in the world. I don't know what I would do without
her.

   Hugs and kisses to you all,
   Annie

Sunday lunch is the saving grace of the week. Gin
and tonic in the pub while the joint's cooking. Then
back home for roast lamb, potatoes, carrots, peas and
cauliflower cheese. A doze after reading the papers
then a walk with the family down by the river. I shall
remember to my dying day the sight of Louisa, her hair
a halo of gold, running through a summer meadow,
arms outstretched aeroplane style, clasping a bunch of
buttercups in her hand.

   Another thing I shall remember for ever is the day
I pick my own, home-grown vegetables. I have dug,
planted, weeded and watered this virgin garden. Days
and days of chopping, cutting and pulling. Then watching the little heads popping through. I've worried about
the rain, the sun and the wind. I feel as though it is my
creation. Which is how God must feel when everything
is going nicely.

   I harvest my crop of baby peas, baby beans, baby
carrots and baby potatoes. Before pulling each carrot
out, I think, 'I wonder what you'll be like?' They all
start out as identical seeds in the same soil and develop
so very differently. That's the exciting bit.

   Our friend Charles is the only thespian to visit us
in the cottage. He's tickled pink at the idea of my
being a housemaid. 'Come on,' he says, 'put on your
frilly apron and get up those library steps and let's
have a peek at your knickers.'

   Our other visitor is Hans who we also first met in
South Africa. He is German and the managing director
of an international company based not far from where
we live. Hans loathes English food and so always

213

arrives after dinner bearing a bottle of Remy Martin.

In midsummer, two South African friends arrive to visit. They park their hired caravan in our garden. Although we are pleased to see them there is a sense of shame at what has happened to us. We've lost our footing and have thumped and bumped our way down to the bottom of the tree.

We write on behalf of our client who has instructed us to claim an amount of R3000 from you in respect of alimony owed to her by you, accrued from September 1975. If this sum is not received by us within fourteen days, we shall instruct solicitors in the United Kingdom to proceed against you in this matter.

At five o'clock one Thursday afternoon towards the end of July I am down on my knees washing the kitchen floor in the son and heir's cottage. I am giving it my special treatment: hot, soapy suds and abrasive sponge followed by lots of clean water to remove every possible trace of dirt. When I'm satisfied that the white tiles are entirely without blemish I rigorously apply myself to putting on the shine. Tile by tile I polish then buff my way across the pristine floor. I am just sitting back on my haunches, admiring my handiwork when the door flies open and in charge four muddy Labradors followed by their owner, the Right Honourable Mrs. It has been pouring with rain and they have all been out for a walk in the woods. Like blood spurting from a cut artery mud shoots in all directions. She hands me a note for her son and exits with the beasts in tow.

Up on my memory screen flashes the image of the photograph taken on the day I won the Best Actress of Year Award.

A strategy for survival begins to take shape in my mind.

The Right Honourables have an estate in Scotland and the chauffeur and his wife are required to be in attendance for the whole of the annual grouse shoot. A week before the date of departure I walk up to the big house and knock on the study door.

'Come in.'

'May I have a word please?'

'Ye-es.'

'Awfully sorry,' I say, 'but I think you should know that I won't be going to Scotland.'

'Really.' The face hardens and so does my resolve.

'It's just that I'm filming. And unfortunately the dates clash.'

It is the most aback I have ever seen her taken. I have treated her condition of service as though it were an invitation which might be refused.

'It might just be of interest to you,' she says, 'and you might consider passing this information on to your husband, the lodge in which he will be accommodated is a good fifteen miles from the village shop and as his duties will leave him practically no time for shopping and cooking, catering for himself will prove extremely difficult. The possibility of being fed from our kitchen is entirely out of the question so he will have to fend for himself. And of course it goes without saying that when we return at the end of September I will have to review the entire situation. Your attitude, my dear, is simply not acceptable.'

I bet what's really infuriating her is that we are in the twentieth century and she can't have me put in the stocks. Poor Robert, she really will crucify him now.

As luck will have it, three days after this encounter I am offered a television commercial. I ring the son and heir's wife at their Chelsea home to say I won't be 'doing' for them the following weekend. 'I'm filming, you see!' I don't go quite as far as calling her 'darling' or 'lovey' but the tone is probably in my voice.

'Gosh, filming!' she exclaims. 'That sounds fun. Oh, don't worry about a thing. We can muddle through, for goodness sake. Are we ever likely to see it?'

215

How people's attitude changes when you are doing something glamorous. A short respite from domestic life, in all its senses, is beginning to make me feel quite heady.

Robert has departed for Scotland with a good supply of baked beans and tinned soup, Laura is visiting her grandparents in Kent and Hans has invited Louisa, David and me for Sunday afternoon tea and dinner. I decide to dress in a cream silk blouse, tight black skirt and stilettos. Trying to walk in the skirt is rather like trying to manoeuvre a frigate in a yacht basin. To protect my stiletto heels from the mud outside our kitchen door I adopt a tippy-toe Japanese shuffle. Wiggling and wriggling, I manage to hoist myself into the driver's seat of a somewhat disapproving Duchess Dora.

We arrive a little late for afternoon tea. Louisa and David have been chattering away in the back seat, blissfully unaware of the sizzling siren in the front.

Hans has lived for some years with an intimidatingly gorgeous woman who speaks six languages and whose golden mane has the sort of sun streaks in it that you get from going to places like Mexico and Madagascar. She, too, is away, in some sophisticated spa, opening an exhibition of her paintings.

Hans comes out of his mock Tudor mansion to greet us and as I watch him stroll across the gravel drive, his six-foot-four frame moving gracefully beneath his exquisitely tailored European clothes, I am turned on by the idea that behind his soft, smiling brown eyes exists a powerful, authoritative chief executive of an international company. The Boss.

He greets the children first, twirling Louisa up in the air. She giggles shyly and buries her face in his shoulder. 'And now a big kiss for Mama who is looking oh, so *wunderbar!*'

Jesus, what's happening to the two of us. We have known each other for a very long time but he has never held me like this. Letting go, falling into a cloud and knowing the cloud will support you, safe. Feeling so small, with him so strong.

Seven years before this I had fallen in love with Robert who sent himself up rotten, but one is hungry for different things at different times and right now I am starving.

Robert's duties in Scotland consist of driving hampers, hardware and house guests to and from the shoot. Mrs RH has remained faithful to her promise and has made the gamekeeper and his wife, the cook, swear on St Andrew's cross not to give him so much as a roast potato. His only friend is one of the house guests who is anti-blood sports and prefers to sit in the Landrover with Robert and get pissed. After a while the Scots team thaw a little and he is invited to their lodge to share a dram or two, but no food.

Most evenings after work he drives into the village for a steak and kidney pie and chips at the pub and stays till well after closing time. One night towards the end of his Scottish stint the Landrover hiccups on a bend, lurches off the road and collapses into a freezing Scottish burn. Robert emerges through the left hand window unharmed and squiffily negotiates the final five miles to home base.

The next morning he is up at the crack of dawn and goes into the kitchen to phone the garage. Upstairs, the Honourable Missus is abed, with her face covered in lashings of some miracle night cream purchased to protect the patrician jaw and neckline from the prosaicness of ageing. Around her head she wears a specially designed chinstrap which loops up and over her hear-you-when-she-pleases ears.

The phone is on a party line. Consequently, any ringing or dialling in the kitchen will simultaneously set the bell a-tinkling in her boudoir. Even though Robert tries his hardest to telephone the garage with a stealthy, fairy-light finger, he nevertheless succeeds in alerting

217

the Honourable Missus who has nothing better to do than recline in bed and allow the beauty aids to have their way with her. She picks up the phone and hears the gamekeeper say, 'Oh, hello Bob. How are you, pal? Heard about your little upset with the Landrover last night. The whisky's the same as you drink down south, it's just the water you want to watch out for.'

On the venerable visage of the chin-strapped, eaves-dropping Honourable Missus, Lancome's *Crème de Nuit* visibly blanches.

'I wouldn't be in your shoes,' continues Frazer. 'Is the thing a bloody write-off, then?'

Upstairs, the Honourable Missus leaps from her bed and, forgetful of her gown, swoops down the stairs clad only in her blue silk nightdress. The kitchen door is flung open and behind him he hears, 'This time you ARE fired. And that is final.'

Swinging around, Robert's jaw drops open in shock at the sight of the apoplectic barefoot contessa. Crying tears of laughter he splutters, 'Jesus, have you any idea how funny you look?'

Thus endeth Robert's career as a chauffeur.

Back home I am experiencing a fruit salad of emotion. My feelings for Hans, Robert and everyone else, not to mention England, have been thrown together and mixed up and I simply don't know what to do. That is until a writ arrives demanding ten months' back payment of alimony and then I telephone Mummy and ask her to send two air tickets. Like a migratory bird, I have decided to take my young and head south for the summer.

Robert arrives back in Blankshire on the train and has hardly had time to have a cup of tea when I start convincing him of the wisdom of my newly thought up scheme.

'You will never be free of her until you are free of me. It's me she's after, not you. She'll keep up this barrage of legal stuff until kingdom come. Why don't we play her at her own game and tell her we've split up. And we will – for a short time. My mom has offered to send tickets for Louisa and me to fly home and once I'm there she really will believe that we've broken up – you know what a village that place is. Then after say, six months, I'll come back and we can get together again, but secretly. We'll be the Three Bears again, just like we used to be.'

Robert surrenders.

We call the children together and tell them that we have decided to split up. (Privately, I tell Louisa that it isn't true.) Laura decides to stay on in England and get a job. David wants to go home to his mother in South Africa. Robert leaves Blankshire for London to stay in a friend's flat. I remain at the cottage to tie up the loose ends. Hans drives Louisa and me to the airport where we are met by Robert.

At the departure barrier I kiss both men. They stand together smiling, Robert in his checked cashmere jacket now very much the worse for wear and Hans in his navy blue designer wool suit.

As Louisa and I wave goodbye, tears streaming down our faces, she squeezes my hand and says, 'Don't worry, Mummy, I'll look after you.'

Part Four

As Louisa and I step off the plane at Jan Smuts airport, I notice two things. The police are armed and the earth is red. Green, democratic England seems a long way away.

Mummy and Annie are waiting for us to come through customs. Annie is looking very pretty. Her eyes are clear and her hair has been washed and curled. She has been out of the mental hospital for some time. Mummy says, 'Well, now you've got all that out of your system, you can settle down at home and Louisa can go to the convent.'

The Renault is looking badly bruised. Mummy has had so many contretemps with 'boys on bikes' that the insurance people are refusing to pay out. Her driving is a nightmare. She climbs up the steering wheel peering under its rim and revving the engine cruelly. For ages now Terry has refused to repair her car. 'She drives with her foot on the clutch the whole time,' he says, 'so of course the bloody thing keeps going.'

The dry Transvaal landscape looks sickeningly familiar as we hiccup through suburb after suburb of golden brick houses with their obligatory swimming pools. It is two-and-a-half years since I left South Africa but now it seems as though I've never been away. My heart sinks further as I read the bilingual roadsigns, giving Afrikaans precedence over English. Mummy fills me in on the latest convent and family news while, in the back, Louisa and Annie sit chatting happily about Freddie the cat and the neighbour's budgies.

When we arrive at Jilly's house, the kids run out to

221

meet us and there is hugging and kissing all round. Jilly, clean and pretty as ever, wafts her familiar Blue Grass scent as she carries tea and biscuits out onto the verandah. Once settled, I tell them' what a terrible time I've been through, and how I plan to make Robert's ex-wife believe that it's all over between us. Mummy and Annie are sympathetic. Jilly is less so. She hates deception of any kind and thinks that there must be a more truthful way of resolving our problems. She is such a typical Libran, always trying to see everyone's point of view. Besides which, she and Robert have always been fond of each other. They are quite similar in many ways, especially in their dislike of overt emotion.

Terry stops by the house to say, 'Howzit ducktail?' and I am shocked at how bald and bloated he has become. In the last year he has suffered a major heart attack and has had sixty stitches in his face as a result of falling over the end of the bed. It isn't long before the conversation takes a political turn and he and Mummy trot out the same old arguments. 'You people in Britain want to tell us how to run our country, but we live here and we know what it's like. If it wasn't for the white man there wouldn't be a South Africa. If it was left to the natives there'd be no gold-mines, no nothing. All they want to do is sit in the sun and cook the occasional pot of mealie meal. We'd be overrun by them – they breed like flies. If it wasn't for apartheid there'd be chaos.'

Oh God, I feel as though I'm caught in a time-warp, nothing, but nothing has changed. Jilly and Terry have been in the depths of a cold war for years now. She has become as fanatically committed to Christian Science and Highland dancing as he is to drinking. She continues to drive herself relentlessly, trying to run the half-hour in twenty minutes, as Daddy would've said.

After tea we drive to the dutch-gabled house. Apart from the roof having been painted and the four palm trees having grown taller, nothing else has really changed. Big Jeanie, their 'girl', and Auntie Edie are waiting out on the verandah to greet us. Auntie Edie is still her old smelly self but somehow this non-smoking, teetotaling virgin, now well over eighty, seems to have discovered a secret reservoir of youth and vitality.

When I thank her for the love and support she has given me throughout the past two-and-a-half years she smiles shyly and says, 'Och, it was nothing'. But without those weekly letters and the birthday cards and postal orders sent from 'your mother and me' with the instruction to buy something nice, life would have been a lot harder. I have come to see that Auntie Edie is strong in the detail of loving.

Big Jeanie is fatter than ever and complaining bitterly about how much her back hurts and how many *tsotsies* there are in the township. When I tell her that I have been working as a servant in England, she roars with laughter and shakes her head.

Annie has been using my old bedroom but she agrees to move in with Mummy so that Louisa and I can have the double room. Once I've got my cushions, bed linen and furniture out of storage I'll have it looking like something out of *Ideal Homes* in no time at all.

Subconsciously in need of recharging my run-down batteries with solar energy, I lie in the scorching sun for hours, burning my skin to a blistered frazzle.

The familiarization process continues with a trip to Solly Kramer's Wine Warehouse where, like a child let loose in a chocolate factory, I run up and down the endless aisles unable to decide which Chenin Blanc or Riesling to buy with the money Auntie Edie has given me. Since a bottle of wine costs about the same as a can of Coke in England, I settle on two five-litre flagons of Stellendal which hopefully can be concealed from Annie at the back of my wardrobe. They won't be cold but at least I'll be able to have a drink.

At the first possible opportunity I drive down to Granny Mac's stone cottage at Henley-on-Klip. As soon as we leave behind the built-up suburbs of Johannesburg, the veld stretches out as far as the eye can see and I am suddenly overwhelmed with love for this land. The sheer space makes me cry. It's as though my soul has burst its bars and is once again free to soar in the cloudless blue sky. I am brought down to earth with a bump when we stop to buy biltong and cigarettes at Salojees store and I am surrounded by runny-nosed, starving piccanins begging for food with outstretched hands. But not even this can stop me kneeling down and kissing the red earth of Africa as I step from the car when we arrive at the house.

Mr Murray, our next door neighbour, hails me from across the barbed-wire fence, welcoming me home to the land of my birth. As we chat in the warm sunshine, he informs me that three of his sons are now in the army and that he would willingly see all four of his sons dead and die himself before he would give up one inch of this country to the blacks.

It's not nature's fault that South Africa is a bloody mess.

The press make much of my return and I am interviewed on radio and in the newspapers. Although no actual mention of separation is made, the articles carry more than a strong suggestion of it.

It isn't long before I am offered the female lead in a two-handed comedy. The director has been imported from England and so has my co-star, a handsome hunk who on meeting me makes it abundantly clear that he is hugely homosexual. No luck there! We start rehearsing the play which is a frothy piece about a truck driver and a virgin falling in love.

Friends introduce me to several attractive young men who seem only too happy to do my bidding, treating me with a mixture of deference and desire. Wherever I go, I am fêted and fussed over. I feel young, alive and free again. Memories of arguments with Robert and washing other people's floors are fading fast in the strong South African sunlight.

The play opens to excellent notices and the 'House Full' sign goes up every night. Success brings my confidence flooding back and a fat pay-packet adds to my feeling of well-being. Even after contributing generously to the family coffers there is still plenty of money for Louisa and me to have new clothes and anything else we want. In fact, I'm enjoying myself so much that there isn't time to think about anything but *la dolce vita*.

Robert's letters and telephone calls are full of the difficulty he's having in finding a job and how he has eaten nothing but potatoes for weeks. I find this all rather tiresome as he has only himself to look after and he doesn't seem able to do even that. My resolve hardens.

Louisa is attending the convent. She is in Sister Angelica's class but Sister is recuperating from a nervous breakdown at a home on the south coast. She is also learning Highland dancing with Jilly and elocution with Miss McKirdy. I am driving Auntie Edie's old Hillman Minx which is much sought after by petrol pump attendants who are always asking to buy it. In England it would be a collector's piece.

Most afternoons, I pick Louisa up from the convent, usually accompanied by a handsome young actor who has become my favourite beau. Louisa is not happy about this relationship and one afternoon, as the three of us are having tea, she says in her sweetest little voice, 'My mummy snores when she sleeps, you know.'

Auntie tells me that she cries at night when I've gone to the theatre. She says she is missing her dad.

When his three-month stint is up, my co-star returns to England and a replacement is sent out. From the moment I set eyes on Dash there is something about the tall, athletic blond with the permed hair and gold earring that I strongly dislike. He is very much the foot-on-the-rung young actor, bent on pushing his way to the top of a crowded ladder. He exudes an arrogance which drives me mad and, what is even more unsettling, an animal magnetism that grips me in the groin. At first I refuse his invites to dinner and then one night he turns upstage and winks at me and the walls of my stomach collapse. I find myself agreeing to have a drink with him after the show.

Later that night, sitting at the bar, the first thing we discover is that we are both born under the sign of Scorpio. Then he goes on to tell me how he was born in Wales, adopted as a tiny baby, spent his early childhood in the West Indies and returned to England to attend an expensive public school. There he captained the cricket, rugby and swimming teams but left without any academic qualifications. At eighteen, he married and when the marriage ended he moved to London and studied to become an actor. Over the years he has had a number of affairs but is at present living alone in a small flat in Hampstead.

His green eyes light up when I ask him if he knows who his real mother and father were and he replies, 'Oh yes! A prostitute and a portrait painter.'

He asks me about Robert and I tell him that I believe the marriage to be over.

'Do you think you'll every marry again?' he asks.

I laugh and reply, 'Give me a break' but the realization comes to me with a certainty that makes me feel quite sick as I think 'Jesus! I just know I'm going to marry you.' It is as though a sentence has been passed on me which I know I must serve. (Father, take this cup away from me, I do not want to drink its poison.)

Needless to say, forbidden fruit has always proved irresistibly appetizing to me and it isn't long before the love story between the truck driver and the yellow-haired pussycat spills over into real life. A week later, I tell Robert over the telephone that I have found some-one new. 'I think I'll stick my head in the gas oven,' he says.

'No you won't,' I reply, 'you'll write a play about it.'

The atmosphere in the dutch-gabled house is tense. Annie has gone back into the mental hospital. She collapsed two days before my opening night. Mummy and I are at daggers drawn. She disapproves of my behaviour in general and Dash in particular. Because of this, much of my time is spent at the Hillbrow flat he has rented. He is a potent lover, dominant and satisfying. On one memorable occasion we make love against the background of an electric storm. The cracks of thunder and forks of lightning detonating the sky serve only to heighten our passion. However, it does worry me that when I crawl out of his warm bed in the early hours of the morning he doesn't seem to notice that I've gone and in my hurt and anger I drive like a lunatic screaming, 'Fuck! Fuck! Fuck!' all the way home.

I always try to be back in the double bed with Louisa by the time she wakes at seven, and then pleading late working hours, I leave Auntie Edie to oversee her having breakfast and getting dressed for school.

One morning Auntie draws my attention to the fact that Louisa has developed hard red lumps on her upper eyelids. We put on lashings of Golden Eye ointment and even try one of Granny Mac's remedies, a good rubbing with my golden wedding ring, but to no effect. An appointment is made with a top eye specialist who informs me that she is suffering from a chronic condition of the tear ducts and replies when I ask what the treatment is, 'Well, there is no cure for this condition. She will just have to use eyedrops for the rest of her life and the inside of her lids will need scraping every six months.'

'I can't condemn her to that,' I hear myself saying, 'so, if you don't mind, I think I'll just take the matter to God.'

The medical man is visibly taken aback by my remark. 'Well of course, it's entirely up to you,' he says, 'but I urge you to consider carefully. It's your child's wellbeing that's at stake here.'

On Jilly's recommendation I consult a Christian Science practitioner. Over the telephone he says, 'Those lumps are tears that your little girl feels unable to shed. What is she so unhappy about?'

'I have decided to separate from her father,' I reply.

'Are you angry with him?' he asks.

'Yes,' I reply.

'And are you angry with her because you're angry with him?'

'Perhaps.'

'Because the lumps will only go away when you let go of your anger. They will only soften with love.'

'I'll try,' I say, suddenly in tears myself.

'Yes, do,' he replies gently. 'For all your sakes. And in the meantime don't look at the lumps, just think of those lids as perfect.'

The play is booked to do a national tour. Dash is very excited at the prospect of seeing Durban, Cape Town, Port Elizabeth and East London. So am I. A season of sea and sun is not to be sniffed at. Linda, my battered friend from years back who now lives in Australia, arrives out of the blue to pay me a surprise visit. Despite the fact that she and Dash dislike one another on sight, the three of us end up renting a holiday apartment on the Durban beachfront.

One night our *ménage à trois* plus two other friends go out to dinner. Someone doesn't pay their share; I accuse Dash and things turn nasty. Eventually the bill gets paid and the others go off for a walk. Almost as soon as we get into the flat he lays into me, holding me up against the wall with one hand while punching me with the other. I am too shocked to feel either pain or fear. I just ride the blows. When it is over I walk out of the apartment and along the esplanade.

Funny, this is the same beach front where Annie and I used to pick up our rugby players. He's a rugby player too. My mind is in turmoil. What on earth am I to do? We are in a play together, the entire tour of which has been sold out in advance. I am committed to completing the run because I have signed a contract. Oh well, I have made my bed, I'd better lie on it.

That night I spend on the spare bed in the hotel room of another actress, who is also on tour in Durban. She has never been involved in any violence but says things don't look too good, especially my face.

I have to go back to our flat the next morning and Dash is beside himself with remorse. He says he has no idea what came over him and begs me, on bended knees, to forgive him.

Linda, too, begs me, to end the relationship. She says, 'Surely you know from what happened to me, that once a man has been violent it will happen again and again. Of course, he will promise that it won't, but it will. Please, believe me, I really do know what I'm talking about.'

I try for a few days to take her advice and maintain a separation but eventually all the beautiful flowers and his tears break my resistance. It's the way he cries that gets to me, scrunching up his fists and rubbing them into his eyes like a three-year-old. It just breaks my heart and I end up taking him in my arms and cuddling him. He loves me doing this and together we enter a fantasy world where we pretend to be bunny rabbits in our warren or bears in our den. It is only ever our adult selves that fight. Our child selves play together nicely.

At the end of the Durban season my friend returns to Australia and we travel on. In East London trouble breaks out again and this time we both suffer physical damage. I badly scratch his face and he gives me a black eye.

The company manager, who already suffers from angina and is now in serious danger of sustaining a fatal heart attack, practically forces the doctor, called in to treat us, into taking an oath of silence. He is terrified that the press will find out.

We both look so silly sitting in our dressing-rooms with an assortment of raw steak poultices and ice bags on our wounds that we cannot help laughing. Aided by a great deal of powder and paint the show goes on and so does our relationship.

Thank God Louisa is safe and secure in the dutch-gabled house, or so I think. No sooner have I left to go on tour than Annie comes out of the mental hospital. While Miss McKirdy is teaching and Auntie Edie is playing the piano for Jilly, Louisa is left in her care.

Every afternoon they walk to the bottle store to buy Annie's booze and, on their return, go into the doll's house in the back garden and play at tea parties. Louisa fills the plastic teapot with water and does the pouring for the dolls and herself. Annie pours her own, straight from the bottle. Usually, she manages to make it back to her bedroom before passing out but one afternoon when Louisa looks in to see if she is all right, Annie is sprawled out on the floor surrounded by empty pill bottles.

Louisa makes a dash for the telephone and rings her cousin, Grant, who comes up on his bicycle to lend support. He is an old hand at dealing with his aunt's suicide attempts and together the children shake her and jump on her and try to make her sick. When this method of revival fails they call an ambulance and she is rushed to hospital for yet another painful pump-out. Eleven-year-old Grant and seven-year-old Louisa are praised by the doctors for having saved Annie's life.

230

By now the play has reached the Cape and we are staying at Kalk Bay with friends whom I met when Robert and I lived there.

Each morning we wake up around ten with the sun streaming into our bedroom and the sound of the breakers crashing on the rocks outside our window. We make love and then stroll down to the beach for a swim. Around three we come back for lunch which is usually something light like lobster salad or grilled sardines, washed down with a bottle of cold Cape wine. This is followed by an afternoon nap and usually a little more love-making, then we shower and dress and drive to the theatre. After the show we dine at either a Chinese or Indian or Italian or French or Greek or Portuguese restaurant. Strangely, I've never been more unhappy in my life.

On our return to Johannesburg Dash suggests that I ask Mummy if he can move into my bedroom in the dutch-gabled house for his last couple of weeks in South Africa. I am terrified of doing this but Dash keeps on saying, 'For God's sake, you're thirty-five years old, married with a kid and you're still shit-scared of your mother?'

That night I walk resolutely into Mummy's bedroom to ask her permission. She is sitting up in bed, surrounded by pillows. On her bedside table rest a box of chocolates, her spiritual reading matter and her teeth in a glass. I sit down nervously on the edge of her bed and ask her if, having got to know Dash a bit better, her opinion of him has improved.

'He's all right, I suppose,' she answers, flattening the cover of *The Path of Truth* with the palm of her hand. 'I can't say I care for his style of dress.'

'Looking scruffy is fashionable,' I say, taking her hand and stroking it. I have always loved my mother's hands. They make me want to cry because they're so small and full of freckles.

'I am thinking of getting married.'

'You already are married,' she reminds me dispassionately.

'I know that,' I say. 'But once we're divorced.'

'I see.' Coldly.

'So I was wondering if you'd mind him staying in my room for a couple of weeks? Louisa could sleep in here.'

'God's laws are God's laws,' she says. 'They will not be flouted under my roof. He is welcome to sleep on the couch in the lounge. But anything else is out of the question.' And with that the subject and her eyes are closed.

For the last two weeks of the run we are booked to play in Pretoria where we will perform in front of the first multi-racial audience ever to gather in this Afrikaans stronghold. Halfway through the show on the first night, a teargas cannister is thrown by a dissenting member of the audience and pandemonium breaks out. As the curtain falls, Dash and I duck under it and I announce to the audience that once the teargas has cleared we will finish the play. To our astonishment a great cheer goes up and the majority of the audience shout back that they are determined to watch it. The evening turns from one of disaster to triumph with the star of the show being one Solomon Legoai, the first black man ever to sit in a 'Whites Only' theatre in Pretoria. He gets his photograph into all the newspapers by demonstrating to the audience how to survive a teargas attack. Two days later he telephones us to say that he has been fired from his job.

I can't stay in this bloody country. I've got to get out. But I'm so confused. I'm scared of facing Robert and I'm scared of just Louisa and I trying to make a go of it in England because I know how tough it will be. Dash has asked me to live with him in London. I suppose it's my best bet. Louisa can stay on here in the dutch-gabled house and I'll send for her as soon as I can.

232

Fifteen months after my return to South Africa I prepare to leave again.

Dash flies to London and I spend the last few days in the home of a friend. She is appalled that I am leaving Louisa in South Africa, albeit for such a short time. 'I could never be separated from my children,' she says, 'not even for a few days. I'd be worried sick.'

On my last night she throws a farewell party for me. Drinks around the swimming pool and then a delicious dinner served by her faithful manservant dressed in starched white uniform, complete with red sash. The following morning, nursing a mammoth hangover, I am chatting to her maid in an attempt to stop her vacuuming so close to my head when we get on to the subject of her two children. She tells me how they live with her old mother on a farm in the Northern Transvaal and how my friends give her one weekend a month to go and visit them and two weeks annual leave. In the last ten years she has seen her children less than six weeks in each year. But then, as my friend would say, 'Black people don't feel things the same way as we do.'

Dash meets me at Heathrow in his green MG sports car. The whole country is in the grip of the Winter of Discontent. Strikes and snow abound, mountains of uncollected rubbish slummify every street corner. He drives me to his bedsit in Hampstead which consists of one room, kitchen and a small garden. The bathroom and loo are shared.

Dash has made me promise to take the EST training, a self-development programme devised in the States, which takes place over two weekends in the ballroom of a London hotel. He says it will not only transform me but will focus me on what I wish to achieve in my life, all of which sounds great. He also makes me promise not to contact Robert until it is over.

At first I find this American-style enlightenment a totally terrifying experience, but Dash, who has already undergone the training, is wonderfully supportive and in the end I am as elated as everyone else as I celebrate the discovery of my own 'magnificence'.

I can't wait to telephone Robert and 'share' with him all the wonderful insights of the last few days and so I ring him as soon as Dash and I get back to the bedsit.

'Hi, it's me.'

'Who is this?'

'Me. I'm back.'

'I heard you were.'

'Oh Robert, I've just been through the most amazing experience. Can we come round and see you now. Dash is dying to meet you and I'm sure we're all going to get along wonderfully together.'

'Hang on,' says Robert. 'You do know it's three in the morning?'

'Time is nothing but an illusion,' I reply airily.

'Well,' says Robert. 'It may be to you but I've been waiting for this call for a very long time and I was hoping to feel a bit more ready. Never mind, we might as well get it over with. I'll meet you downstairs in half an hour.'

When we arrive I introduce the two men to each other and Robert makes us all coffee. I start to tell him about the training but all he wants to hear about is Louisa. Then I ask if I can have my clothes which he has in storage. Robert shows us into the bedroom where he leaves Dash and me to go through the suitcases containing my clothes. Dash is hugely fashion conscious and likes me wearing sexy clothes. Robert never seemed to notice what I had on. We make our selection and then, shouting goodbye, Dash carries several suitcases out to our waiting car. When Robert comes into the bedroom, I tell him that anything I haven't taken can be sent to War on Want. As I turn to go I hear a thump and looking round see him fall to his knees. I rush to help but he waves his hand and mumbles, 'I'm fine, really. Just for God's sake go.' I hesitate. 'Get out!' he rasps. Caught between my past and my future I decide to go with the latter.

Some weeks later, whilst Dash is in Spain filming a commercial, Robert and I meet again to talk through the arrangements of our separation. The conversation begins in a very controlled way. We come to an easy decision that Robert will keep the bits and pieces that we've accumulated in England and I'll have everything left behind in South Africa, most of which I've already given to Mummy, anyway. Robert goes on to explain that the impotency he'd been suffering from is now a thing of the past. My quizzical expression produces the information that yes, he has had a couple of girlfriends. This opens the way up for me to confess my past infidelities.

'Oh no, not Hans,' he says when I tell him.

'I'm sorry if that hurts you, but you have no idea how much it hurt me when you said to me, "I don't mind what you do so long as you always come home," ' I reply.

'But you know my philosophy always was, open the cage door and the bird won't fly.'

'Not this bird. This bird wanted to be shown it was loved.'

'But you were! You still are. I will always love you.'

I feel as though my heart will break but I say, 'Oh Robert, it's too late. Just too much water has flown under the bridge.'

In silence he walks me to Gower Street station to get the underground. 'It was nice to see you,' he says.

'Yes,' I reply, 'I enjoyed it too.'

We jig up and down to keep warm in the freezing air. Robert folds his arms, tucking his hands under his armpits to keep them warm. Why doesn't he put those arms around me? Why doesn't he say, 'You're my miracle woman! I love you! Please don't go. We've been through so much together, we fought the world together. You and I and Louisa are the three bears. I won't let you go.'

'Right then,' he says.

'OK then,' I say, 'which one of us is going to move first?'

'We'll move together,' he says.

'I'm going that-a-way.'

'I'm going this-a-way.'

We laugh and shake hands and then turn and walk in opposite directions. I can hear the sound of his footsteps moving further and further away.

Louisa arrives from South Africa and moves into the one-roomed apartment with Dash and me, sleeping in a makeshift bed in a corner. When we want to go out, Robert babysits. He arrives looking like Santa Claus, masses of beard and presents. Louisa climbs onto his lap and before Dash and I have even said goodbye, she is snuggled up in his arms listening to *The Lion, the Witch and the Wardrobe*.

Trying to find unfurnished accommodation in London is like trying to find a blackhead on a baby's bum but finally a small miracle occurs and we sign the lease on a lovely flat not far from Primrose Hill. It is badly in need of redecoration and once again I fly to my colour charts. To my chagrin I discover that Dash, unlike Robert, has strong opinions on decor and a violent argument erupts. The blow comes out of the blue but with the reflex action worthy of a seasoned boxer I return it and we compromise on a combination of Dried Earth and Magnolia.

Thank you for the earrings and the card. I am back in hospital. Mummy and Auntie drive me crazy so I am glad to get away from them. I have got a dreamboat of a boyfriend called Derek. All the patients think he is very good looking. He used to be an accountant before he had a nervous break- down. We can never be anything more than friends because he already has a wife and they are both Catholics. She lives in Cape Town. I am hoping to get a room in a hotel in Hillbrow and get away

from Mummy and Auntie. Honestly, they still treat
me as though I was a little girl. How is my darling
Louisa? Someone stole her dormouse card from my
bedside table. They steal everything in this place.
Please ask her to make me another.
   Love Annie

Smashing Dash straight back proves only a temporary
solution. One Sunday night, a few months later, we are
sitting up in bed having a discussion about books. He
is defending the fact that he never reads by saying that
he has no need of other people's ideas as he has plenty
of his own. I disagree. The next thing I know, Dash has
pinned me down on the bed and has punched me in
the face. The speed of the attack shocks me more than
anything else and the sensation reminds me of the time
Daddy taught me to swim by throwing me into the river
at Henley. On this occasion, as on that one, there is an
explosion of sound in my head followed by an eerie
silence.

Suddenly, I'm aware of blood all over the sheets
and of Dash helping me to the bathroom and of being
shocked at the sight of my own face in the mirror. My
main concern is that I have to appear on stage tomorrow
night with a split lip and a swollen mouth. I promise
Dash that I intend to tell my fellow cast members that
he is responsible and I keep my word.

Life with Dash is certainly never dull. At times good
fun, at others, like a bare-fisted knock down barroom
brawl. We go on hurting each other until one of us is
face down in blood and the other sprawled on the ropes.
We are both getting badly battered, not just physically,
but emotionally too.

But on one occasion Dash and I man the barricades
together. We are at a black-tie do thrown in honour
of my friend Charles's fiftieth birthday. Despite being
sought after as a handsome escort by well-to-do widows
and divorcees, everyone knows that Charles's sexual

proclivities tend towards men. Although I haven't seen him much in recent months, as he and Dash are not exactly fond of each other, I have noticed a steady deterioration in his persona. At times now, he seems quite remote from the fun-loving, witty character of the Blankshire days.

When we arrive, the uniformly good-looking guests are being served champagne and canapés by waitresses in black dresses and frilly white aprons. On introduction to the sunburned six-foot-two Kevin, I recognize him immediately as the ex-Bondi Beach lifesaver whom Charles always refers to in conversation as his 'flatmate'.

The caterers have done the hostess proud. We plough our way through silver platters overflowing with Scottish smoked salmon and Buluga caviar, succulent Irish oysters, crowns of spring lamb cutlets, kilos of Aberdeen beef and mountains of paper-thin Westphalian ham.

Charles is very drunk and after dinner I find him sitting in a corner of the chandeliered room, weeping into his whisky and muttering that his life is a total fuck up. Taking his hand, I start to comfort him when suddenly both of us become aware that Kevin is looming over us. Charles looks up, only to be met full in the face by Kevin's herculean fist. In the split second that it takes for this to happen, I recognize the look of familiarity in Charles's eyes and know this has happened before. 'Get these fucking straights out of here.'

'Don't you dare hit my friend like that,' I yell, pushing him away. He yanks me by the collar of my *Sunday Times* special offer silk blouse and pushes his face right into mine.

'You're the fucking straight I'm talking about, lady,' he spits. Then I find myself whizzing through the air before crash-landing into the opposite wall. As I ricochet off the Colefax and Fowler wallpaper I catch the sight of Dash long-jumping the drawing-room and bringing Kevin down in a rugby tackle on the dining-room table. Without giving it a second thought, I tear off my velvet jacket and join Dash in the fray amongst the Stilton and *crème brûlée*.

Together we make a formidable team and we're just getting into our stride when, to our amazement, we find ourselves taken on by the entire room, men and women alike. It's a case of homophobia in reverse and the next thing we know, we're being marched down the stairs and unceremoniously deposited in a heap on the pavement outside. My jacket and handbag bring up the rear as the front door is locked and bolted.

As one door closes another opens. After the run of a South African play at the Edinburgh Festival, I am offered a two-year contract with the Royal Shakespeare Company and Dash lands twelve episodes in a television drama. As work on his series doesn't start until I have opened in Stratford it is agreed that he will look after Louisa for the first few weeks that I am up there.

On the opening night of the first play of the season I telephone home, as usual, at six o'clock. Louisa answers the phone and informs me that Dash hasn't as yet come home. As she's now ten, she's quite capable of getting herself something to eat and having a bath, but the situation is still far from ideal. I promise to phone again as soon as I get the chance and at my first costume change I fly down the stairs to the public call-box at the stage door and ring again. Dash has still not returned.

Frantic with worry, I telephone the next-door neighbours but they too are out. Throughout the rest of the performance I ring whenever I get a few free moments until finally Louisa says, 'Please, Mummy, leave it alone now. I'll never be able to get up for school in the morning if you keep waking me up.'

Shortly after one o'clock I try again and this time Dash picks up the phone.

239

'Where the hell have you been?' I scream.

'I just didn't notice the time,' he slurs. 'Louisa's fine, she's fast asleep.'

'No thanks to you,' I shout, slamming down the phone.

The next day I ask permission to be excused from the director's note session and take the coach to London. At Louisa's school I explain to the headmistress that I have to take her back to Stratford with me immediately. Then we go to the flat to collect her clothes. As usual, Dash is full of remorse and promises through his tears, that no such thing will ever happen again.

'Sorry,' I say, 'I really don't think that I can trust you anymore.'

It seems that I am not the only one having emotional problems. Jilly's daughter, Morag, is having her fair share.

Thank you for the card and the lovely present. I know Mummy rang and told you about the wedding being called off but I wanted to write and explain what actually happened. Everything was organized and then the night before I suddenly realized that Peter and I hadn't really sorted out why we wanted to get married in the first place and I just felt I couldn't go through with it. When Mummy finished teaching I told her and she was wonderful. She listened to what I had to say and then told me that she had felt the same way the night before she married Daddy, but that she had gone ahead because she felt it was her duty. She said I was not to worry about the cost because my happiness was much more important than money and that whatever decision I made she would support me in it. I do feel terrible about the wasted expense because she works so hard. Things are very bad between her and Daddy and I know that their marriage has had an effect on us all. She works herself to death paying for

*everything and holding the whole family together.
Daddy is very sweet when he's sober but that's hardly
ever these days. What a family!*

*Granny was furious. She told Mummy that she
would never be able to hold her head up again and
Mummy said, 'What the hell has Morag's life got to
do with you holding your head up.'*

*Thank goodness you're so happy. Stratford must
be wonderful. Carol wants to follow in your footsteps
and be an actress. She is taking speech and drama
lessons with someone else and Granny isn't too
happy about that either.*

*Have you heard about Auntie Annie's boyfriend?
Derek! He's such a drip but she thinks he's wonderful. I suppose she can't be exactly 'choosey'.*

*The caterers brought all the food around here and
we took nearly all of it up to the dutch-gabled house.
Guess who scoffed most of it? Love to Louisa.*

Morag

Dash is away on location most of the time and I have
my work cut out rehearsing all day, running home to
attend to Louisa and getting back to the theatre in time
for the evening performance.

Just to complicate matters, Louisa has taken to
developing tonsillitis every time I have an opening
night. On one such occasion I return to our rented
cottage to find her with a roaring temperature and
tonsils covered in white gunge. As I rush around trying
to make her comfortable the telephone rings and the
babysitter informs me that she won't be coming in as
she has a bad case of the flu. In desperation I pick
the sick child up, cover her with a blanket and walk
out of the front door and up the pathway of the first
house in the street with a light on. 'I'm terribly sorry
to trouble you,' I say to the surprised looking man who
answers my frantic knocking, 'but I am an actress at
the Memorial Theatre and in an hour's time I'm due

to open in a play. My little girl is very ill and there's no-one to look after her. Could you take her in, do you think? I'd be most grateful.'

His wife has appeared in the hallway behind him. 'You just bring the little one in here, love,' she says. 'We'll take good care of her till you get back.'

The world can be an extraordinarily safe place.

For several months now, Dash and I have been getting on quite well and as he has often said that our un-committed status makes him feel insecure, I decide, 'What the hell, let's get married.'

We set the date for February and book flights to South Africa where we'll honeymoon. Thinking the wedding might upset Louisa we arrange for her to fly out there a week before it takes place in the Marylebone Registry Office.

On the morning of the wedding I wake to the sound of my inner voice telling me to call the whole thing off. Determinedly ignoring it, I dress in my wedding outfit, a tight-fitting plum and cream number topped off with a large plum-coloured hat. By now the voice is literally screaming at me, 'There is still time to call the whole thing off. Do not proceed any further with this madness.'

On the way to the Registry Office I stop the taxi, but instead of instructing him to turn around and take me back to the flat I ask him to wait whilst I dash into an off-licence and buy a flask of scotch. Weaving ever so slightly and completely at war with my intuitive self, I walk into the soulless courtroom and, in the presence of a small group of close friends, I marry Dash.

Louisa is waiting with a friend of mine at the barrier when we arrive at Jan Smuts airport. She looks like an escapee from a prison camp. Her beautiful blond hair, so expertly cut in the page-boy style the day before she left, has been chopped off. Her face is dirty and the dress she is wearing is filthy and stained.

'My God!' I exclaim putting my arms around her.
'What has happened to you?'
'Granny made Grant tie a piece of string around my
head and then she told him to cut off my hair with the
garden scissors. I cried but she told me to shush.'
'And what about all your lovely clothes?' I ask.
'Auntie Edie says they must be kept for "good".'
'Just like the "good" tea-sets and the "good" china and
the "good" glasses that they keep locked away. When do
they ever think this mythical "good" time is ever going
to come?' I say, feeling a tidal wave of despair wash
over me. What a way to begin a honeymoon.

When we arrive at the dutch-gabled house Auntie
Edie is sitting on the verandah crocheting and listening
to the church service on her portable radio. Flakes of
paint are peeling off the gables and the flower beds
could do with a good weeding.

'Hello, hello, hello,' says Auntie as we carry our cases
down the pathway. 'Your mother's at the hairdressers.
It's her regular day. She won't be long though.' Auntie
Edie has hardly changed at all. Straight away she tells
us that 'Annie is in hospital but due out any day now.'
Big Jeanie pushes open the fly-screen door and with
a grunt puts tea and biscuits on the verandah table.
I go into the bathroom and there I see all the old,
almost empty bottles I left behind years ago. No-one
has bothered to throw them out. Oh God, I think I'm
caught in a time warp. It's as though I've never left this
house, never married, never had a child, never been to
England, never divorced and never remarried. As I sit
on the loo, gazing out at the palm tree and the mint
patch in the back garden, I feel as though I'm just a little
girl of seven again waiting for Mummy to come home.

When she finally does, her first remark, just as in the
old days, is not one of greeting but of complaint, 'Oh,
Auntie, have I had a terrible time of it. The buses get
worse by the day and so do the queues at the bank.'
Dash and I might as well be people from across the

243

road for all the attention she pays us. You'd certainly never guess that we had just flown halfway across the world to see her and that we are newly wed to boot.

After a quick lunch of cold Cornish pasties washed down with luke-warm tea served in chipped cups, Miss McKirdy pushes back her chair and says, 'Now I really must get on with my accounts.' I glance at Dash and my look assures him that we won't be staying here.

Our next port of call is Jilly's where we all enjoy a good laugh at Mummy and Auntie's expense thereby turning the bitter fruit of our homecoming into a feast of mimicry and laughter. As there is no room for us at Jilly's house, we make some hasty arrangements to move into the guest bedroom at my friend's home.

On the day of the blessing ceremony it rains. Not a humid, torrential downpour with thunder and lightning and all the passion of a Transvaal storm but rather a steady, grey, English drizzle. Instead of the service taking place beside the swimming pool, family and friends have to crowd into the sitting-room and listen to the lecturer from the School of Truth reading a sonnet by Shakespeare and Kahil Gibran's advice on marriage from *The Prophet*, exactly the same service as he performed for Robert and me ten years earlier.

Auntie Edie pushes two scruffy-looking notes into my hand while Jilly presents me with a double bedsheet and two pillow cases hurriedly wrapped in Christmas paper. Miss McKirdy doesn't see fit to proffer any gift at all.

Finally it is all over and, as we collapse amongst the debris of wine dregs and limp lettuce shreds, Dash jokes that he feels as though he has sustained a lobotomy and I swear never to return to this God-forsaken country.

The horror of the honeymoon is only slightly relieved by a few days spent in the Drakensburg mountains where Dash and I, in a desperate attempt to provide ourselves with the memory of one magic moment, copulate wildly in a cave, cunningly concealed behind a liquid curtain of clear mountain water.

Then it's back to Johannesburg and the traditional farewell picnic at Henley-on-Klip. Terry, who is at present as dry as the Kalahari desert having just spent a week in an alcoholic's home, joins the rest of us on the tree-lined riverbank as we chomp our way through platefuls of grilled sausage, salad and watermelon. The only missing person is Annie.

Shaded from the heat by the breeze-filled branches of the weeping willows, I look across the lazy brown water to the opposite bank where another group of picnickers are keeping cool by jumping into the river from the roof of their boathouse. I find it hard to imagine that twenty-four hours from now I shall be rehearsing *Romeo and Juliet* in freezing Newcastle-upon-Tyne. This time Louisa and I will fly home together, leaving Dash to stay on for an extra week. While I am away on tour in the north, Louisa will live with Robert and his new wife, whom she adores.

Dash is a perfect party person. Surrounded by mates, he is the life and soul of the pub. The trouble is once he starts drinking there's no stopping him and what begins with a lunchtime pint ends when he is thrown out of the public house at closing time. His penchant for pub life becomes a bitter bone of contention between us when I return home for the company's London season.

I am getting fed up with a life which seems to consist of nothing more than working and waiting for Dash so, one Friday evening when Louisa has gone to spend the weekend with Robert, I decide to give him a taste of his own medicine.

After the evening performance my friend Natalie and I go out for a cosy meal washed down by several bottles of wine. As we are parking outside her flat in Maida

Vale, Dash's car screeches to a halt in the middle of the road beside us. He leaps out, yanks open the car door and pulls me out by the wrists. He must have followed us. 'Where the hell have you been? I've been waiting for you for hours.'

'Don't you bloody well talk to me about waiting. Let go of me and bugger off.'

'You're coming home with me,' he hisses between clenched teeth, and starts forcibly dragging me to his car.

'Take your bloody hands off me,' I spit, resisting him with all my strength.

'You belong at home with me,' he rasps as we tug-of-war on the pavement.

I am losing the battle. Another tactic is called for. 'Let me go or I'll scream the street down.'

'Be my guest,' he suggests.

I have a voice with as much natural power as that of your average sergeant-major, and after two years of daily voice training and nightly projection in a thousand-seater theatre it is in prime condition.

'HELP! POLICE! MURDER!'

The vibration swings the needle right off the Richter scale. Down the street windows fly open and, within what seems like seconds, squad cars converge from all directions. Suddenly we are surrounded by policemen, all trying to prise us apart. Dash is frog-marched away and pinioned against the trunk of a nearby oak. Shaking from head to foot, Natalie escorts me to the front door of her Edwardian-style residence. As she puts the key in the latch we are joined by a senior police officer who enquires as to my well-being. When I reply that, all told, I am none the worse for wear, he ventures to enquire if perhaps I've had 'just a little too much to drink'. Natalie draws herself up to her full statuesque height and in her grandest thespian tones says, 'I'll have you know, officer, that this lady is a member of the Royal Shakespeare Company and has, this evening,

246

been performing the role of Helen of Troy at a West End theatre.'

'Oh,' says the bemused guardian of the law, 'I do apologize.'

As soon as Dash has quietened down, the officers suggest that he climb into his car and drive himself home. He refuses, realizing that the moment he does, they'll have him on a charge of drunken driving. Thwarted, they settle for disturbing the peace.

On the journey to the police station his captors gloat at having a television personality in their custody, especially one known for his macho image, and taunt, 'Somebody we know is going to regret taking on the cops.'

As he is hauled out of the back of the van the driver leans out of his window and laughs, 'Don't worry about your car, mate. We'll take good care of it.' He spends a disturbed night in the cells.

It is several days before the two of us meet again. And then I issue my ultimatum. Either we seek professional counselling or it's all over. Reluctantly Dash agrees.

Thanks for your newsy letter. Thank heavens, things have quietened down a bit. Morag said she'd written to you. She and Peter are seeing each other quite regularly again. They are such a lovely couple I really hope that they can resolve their difficulties. I admire her so much for the decision she made, it took a lot of guts.

I am sorry that things are not too good with you and Dash. I, too, was in a constant dilemma as to what to do about my marriage. I spoke to my Christian Science practitioner and she told me that I was trying to force the issue, as usual, and that I should release the whole thing and let it take its own course.

Please try to read the article on Love that I am sending you. It talks of Love with a capital L, meaning

God. As children of God we must work to express His qualities and trust Him with our future and the unfoldment of it. Let His will be done.

What do you think of Annie having a boyfriend? She is looking extremely nice and seems almost like she used to be all those years ago.

We may yet make it to Britain this year. The girls are practising madly and I am affirming God's supply.

Tons of Love,
Jilly

However, Auntie Edie's version of events is somewhat different.

Your mother and I were pleased to read in the Johannesburg Star about your new play. Fancy it being a world première. You must be very pleased.

I am sorry to say that Annie has not been at all well. She got very excited and they had to give her shock treatments to calm her down. Your mother went to see her on Sunday and the sister told her that Annie had been very bad during the week.

Your mother and I are just getting over the shock of Morag cancelling her wedding. We were very upset. Jilly had so much expense and all for nothing.

The girls are practising very hard for the Highland Games in Scotland. I will try to give a hand with their fares over.

Tell Louisa that Freddie the Cat was run over. We are all very sad. Still, none of us can go on forever. Your mother sends her best.

TODAY IS THE DAY OF MY AMAZING GOOD FORTUNE. MIRACLES START TO HAPPEN AND WONDERS NEVER CEASE.

Every good wish,
Auntie Edie

Our joint therapy sessions prove quite enjoyable. In fact, Dash considers the whole thing an absolute hoot. He is adamant that his adoption has played no part whatsoever in his development as a person.

He says, 'I put all that behind me years ago and now I just want to enjoy life, which to me is very uncomplicated. I'm a very happy person.' After six sessions he decides to call it a day with the therapy business. I decide to continue, on my own.

Jilly's faith in 'God's supply' pays off and at the beginning of August she arrives in London en route to Scotland where her youngest daughter, Sheila, and seven of her pupils will compete at the Highland Games and the Edinburgh Festival. Like Mummy, Jilly will also take her Fellowship in Highland dancing.

I book seats for them to see a musical at the Theatre Royal, Drury Lane, which she describes as 'very polished', and afterwards, at dinner, we discuss her marital problems. Although she and Terry scarcely communicate with each other any more, she is still reluctant to use the law to remove him from their home. He has twice appeared on serious charges of drunken driving and in the last instance it was only the intervention of his son, Gordon, which stopped him being sent to prison. The boy made a personal plea to the judge, asking that his parent be released into his care. His request was granted on condition that Terry committed himself to a six-month drying out period in an alcoholic home.

Despite all this, Jilly still feels that she cannot break the vows she took on her wedding day. 'I promised to love him for better or for worse,' she says, 'and I feel I must.'

I point out that, in the meantime, her life is being ruined, she is not getting any younger and she's not helping Terry by refusing to desert a sinking ship. Perhaps, we counsel, if he were to hit rock-bottom his life could be saved.

Jilly says she agrees with that, it's just that he's the father of her children and, when all is said and done, she probably does still love him even though it doesn't feel like it at the moment. She is convinced that alcoholism is unreal and refuses to give it the acknowledgement of a name. Quoting Mary Baker Eddy, she says, 'Man is spiritual. Mortal existence is but a dream.'

Louisa is now eleven and due to start her secondary school education when the play I am appearing in is booked to go to Broadway. The Royal Shakespeare Company offers to arrange for her to attend a school in New York but I feel the time has definitely now come for her to put down secure foundations with friends and teachers at what will hopefully be her school for the next seven years. For the first time in her life I allow Louisa's needs to take precedence over my own and I hand in my notice.

> *Hi, how are you all in little old England! I'm great – just had a cup of tea and a ciggie.*
> *Home in hospital, for a rest with all my friends – oh what a relief!*
> *Natal is under floods – Amamzimtoti has sunk! However, we know that God is all in all.*
> *Thank you for your dog's footprint, Louisa. I wish I could draw like that! Will you teach me someday? Your cousin, Carol, could draw very well. I still have a picture of her mice somewhere. I hope your mother took her paintings with her when she went. My hair is on my shoulders, at last. Cheers.*
> *Annie*

Volcanic soil is rich. Crops planted in it grow quickly and produce good harvests – so long as nothing occurs to make the volcano erupt.

I get a television role which requires me to go on location to the winter quarters of a circus. Right from the start I realize that working with animals is both frightening and exciting and requires the utmost concentration.

The first rumble of trouble starts with Dash's constant phone calls. He keeps telling me how much he misses me and asking when he can join me. When I explain that because of the nature of the work, the director would prefer his actors to have no external distractions, Dash immediately becomes suspicious and infers that there must be something going on between us. Despite the fact that I am scheduled to do my most difficult scenes the following day, I tell him to 'come on up and see for himself'. It is agreed that he will arrive on the set around lunchtime, ready for the afternoon's filming.

I've already worked myself into a state by the time the meal break comes because for the first time in the week I'm having difficulty establishing control over the animals. The director takes me aside and says that the camera is picking up fear in my eyes. 'Is anything worrying you?' he asks. I assure him that everything is fine except, perhaps, for the animal trainer who is making me nervous.

By mid-afternoon there is still no sign of Dash and my concentration is completely broken. The director becomes increasingly impatient as in take after take I am unable to produce the confidence required to play the scene convincingly.

Around five o'clock the director, who is as shattered as I am, announces that we will try it 'one more time'. Just as we are about to begin Dash roars up in his car accompanied by a young actress of his acquaintance. They literally fall out of the car, hysterical with laughter. When 'quiet everyone' is called I can see them out of the corner of my eye placing their fingers on each other's lips. Somehow I get through the scene and the director, who by now knows that it will definitely not get any better, calls a wrap.

I am white with anger and humiliation as I storm

past Dash and his friend who now proceed to put on a display of intimacy intended expressly for my benefit. Then he follows me into the makeup caravan. 'So what kind of a day have you had?' he says, almost unable to form the words.

'What kind of a day do you think I've had?' I ask icily. Realizing that she is about to be caught up in a very nasty domestic scene, the make-up lady hastily proffers a jar of cleansing cream and a box of tissues and then, muttering something about checking the next day's shooting schedule, disappears hurriedly through the caravan door. Although we are out of sight we are not out of earshot and you can bet your bottom dollar that the rest of the cast and crew are huddled together somewhere nearby with hands clapped over their mouths, listening.

I am in such a state that I scarcely realize that I'm lighting several cigarettes at once, pouring the bottle of eye make-up remover all over the place and tugging at my wig as though it were a creature from the deep trying to strangle me.

He, meanwhile, is standing in the doorway, swaying gently with a drunken smirk all over his face. 'Christ Almighty, you are a bastard!' I say between clenched teeth as he smiles and nods his head. 'You are totally incapable of showing any kind of care or consideration for anyone except yourself! It clearly never occurs to you to think how anyone else may be feeling. You don't give a damn that today was supposed to be a really big day for me, you don't give a damn about how much I was looking forward to your coming up, how I wanted to show you the circus and the animals and for you to meet all the people who have become my friends. You don't give a damn about ANYTHING IN THIS WHOLE WIDE WORLD EXCEPT YOURSELF. Well, let me tell you, I have had enough of it, I can't take any more of it, this relationship has got me beat and you can just bugger off. But before you do that, let me ask you just one thing. How would you feel if this whole situation was reversed? How would you feel if it was you working and I was coming to see you and you're waiting for me to arrive? And you wait and you wait and you're worried sick that something has happened to me and you can't concentrate because you're thinking where the bloody hell am I and then finally I arrive and I am pissed out of my head and as though that weren't enough, I have also brought along some dishy young guy that I happen to have picked up along the way. How would you feel? Hey? How the bloody hell would you feel? Well, that's how I feel. So now that I've said what I wanted to say you can just bugger off out of here and take your little girlfriend with you because we are FINISHED.'

I have run out of steam and collapse sobbing at the dressing-table, my face a mess of cleansing cream and tears.

'What a performance! What a drama queen!' he says, applauding me. And then he's gone.

As per usual, when I get home he is sober and full of remorse. Somehow things get patched up yet again, but in my heart of hearts I know it is over, only I don't know how to end it.

Apologies for not having written sooner, but things have been pretty hectic here. Morag and Peter were married last Saturday. It was a very quiet ceremony held in our garden and attended by twenty-two people. The service was at three and then after the wedding photographs had been taken, tea was served at four.

Morag looked very pretty in her simple white wedding dress and so did Carol and Sheila who were the bridesmaids. The sun shone throughout.

The dreaded trio from the dutch-gabled house arrived, late as usual, and Auntie Edie managed to consume most of the food, as usual.

Mummy was rather quiet. I don't think she's been

all that well lately. She is suddenly looking old. Annie doesn't look too hot either. She has been having a lot of shock treatment and she looks really out of it. Terry is on the wagon, so there wasn't any chance of her laying her hands on any alcohol. Also her boyfriend, Derek, has given her an ultimatum that if she drinks, he will end the affair.

Terry has lost a lot of weight and is looking quite nice. He is living with his brother in Orange Grove and seems to be enjoying his new job.

Glad to hear that you are all well and happy. Working with that circus must have been fantastic. Sadly, we won't be able to see it because of the BBC's television boycott. I am enclosing an article from the Christian Science Monitor *on Forgiveness. It has helped me a lot.*

Tons of love,

Jilly

Dash is signed to do a six-month tour of a new play. While he's away Louisa and I settle into a tension-free life.

Each Saturday night after the show, Dash telephones to let me know his estimated time of arrival home for the weekend. At the sound of his voice a feeling of warmth rushes through me but as soon as his key turns in the lock my body goes numb and my heart starts to freeze over.

I never know what is going to come through the door, a man or a child. For some time now Dash has taken to speaking in his 'little boy voice' almost all the time he is at home. He refuses to discuss anything 'grown-up' and talking about money 'hurts his head'. Whenever I demand him to show some sense of responsibility, he whines and says, 'Don't ask me. I'm only small.'

Sundays are spent fighting. Louisa stays in her room with her dog, Dougal, an adorable mutt from Battersea

Dog's Home, her twelfth birthday present. When the row is over she emerges to play the role of counsellor, reconciling the warring factions. It breaks her heart when Dash scrunches up his fist to wipe the tears from his eyes and she cannot resist taking him in her arms and comforting him.

When he's not crying, he resents the relationship between mother and child, accusing us of ganging up on him. 'You don't even have to look at each other. I can feel your minds meeting,' he complains.

Louisa's wisdom is a source of constant amazement to me. One Monday morning after Dash has slammed out of the flat, she comes into the living room where I am sitting smoking and drinking coffee and enquires what the latest row has been about. When I say, 'Louisa, what am I going to do?' she replies, 'You know, Mummy, sometimes life works and sometimes it doesn't.'

Your mother and I are well and happy. Hope you are too. We are looking forward to Christmas. Your mother has been fetching Annie home at the weekends. Her friend Derek is a big help. He takes your mother shopping and is doing a bit in the garden, weeding and cutting the lower branches off the palm trees.

Morag is expecting her baby in March. She is still helping Jilly at the dancing and she also has some pupils of her own.

Carol is doing very well. She has got a job with the Sunday Times. She had a nice piece in the paper last week. We are hoping that Gordon will be home for Christmas. We think he is up on the Angolan border just now. It is very hot there; 100 degrees in the shade.

Sheila and Grant are studying for their exams. Tell Louisa that I am sending her some money to buy herself something nice. We are all going down

255

to Henley for Christmas. *Your mother sends her best
wishes.*

*I AM THE DAUGHTER OF THE KING. IT
IS MY FATHER'S GOOD PLEASURE TO GIVE
ME HIS GIFTS OF HEALTH, HAPPINESS AND
ABUNDANCE.*
    Every good wish,
    Auntie Edie

Throughout the Christmas celebrations of 1983 a
black cloud hangs over me. I sense that the approaching
storm is going to be a hurricane.

As Dash and I are dressing for the Hogmanay party
we are attending on New Year's Eve, an argument starts
as to what time we should set out for the evening.
'Seven-fifteen, I reckon,' says Dash.

'Oh, do you really think we need to go that early?' I
ask.

'Well what time do you suggest?'

'I would have thought seven-thirty would have left
us plenty of time to get there,' I reply.

'Seven-thirty!' says Dash. 'Well if we're going to
leave at seven-thirty I don't see why we can't leave
at seven-fifteen.'

'Because,' I counter, 'leaving at seven-fifteen means
we'll get there too early.'

'It doesn't need to mean that,' retorts Dash. 'I can
time it so that we arrive exactly at eight.'

'But we don't have that far to go. What's the point of
hurrying to leave early and then sitting outside waiting
to go in. I just don't see the point.' I am starting to sound
shrill.

'Just because you don't see the point doesn't mean
that there isn't one,' says Dash.

'What the hell do you mean by that?' I ask.

'Just what I've said,' he retorts. 'Your seeing or not
seeing the point doesn't mean there is or there isn't
one.'

'What are you talking about?' I shout.

'What are you talking about?' he shouts back at me.

'I thought we were discussing what time we should leave for the party.' I shake my head in disbelief.

'I thought we were doing that too,' he says.

'Well, what are we arguing like this for?' I say, beginning to shake from head to foot.

'I didn't start the argument. You did,' says Dash.

'OK,' I say, 'I agree with you. Let's settle the matter here. We'll go at seven-fifteen.'

'No!' he says, 'We'll go at seven-thirty because you always have to win every argument.'

I hear a terrible scream. It sounds like an animal caught in a trap. It is some time before I realize that the scream has come from me. Louisa rushes out from her room. 'Are you all right, Mom?' she asks.

'Yes, darling,' I say, breathing heavily, 'I'm OK.' Dash and I are staring at each other. We know we are close to the end. We are both too instinctive not to. In silence we finish dressing and at approximately seven-twenty we set out for the party. On the way there, Dash goes into his little boy mode. I clench my fists and try to ignore it.

When we arrive he does a complete volte-face and becomes macho-man supreme, flirting outrageously with every woman in the room. He keeps looking across at me as if to say, 'Well what do you think of this then?'

As the chimes of Big Ben herald in the first minutes of 1984 I am gripped by agonizing stomach cramps. It is years since I suffered from these colic attacks but now the old enemy has returned with a vengeance.

It is well after two in the morning when Louisa and I finally persuade Dash to leave but he insists on driving despite being very drunk. Throughout the journey I keep up an unremitting prayer as I sit strapped into the passenger seat. Louisa is just as nervous. I can sense her covering her face so as not to see how narrowly we are missing the curbside.

257

Somehow we make it home. Louisa and I let ourselves into the flat. He follows. Once inside she and I change into our nightclothes and the two of us climb into her bed. We can hear him struggling to open yet another bottle of wine in the kitchen. Holding onto each other we eventually fall into an uneasy sleep.

Suddenly I sit bolt upright as I hear a crashing sound, followed by bumping and thumping. 'He's probably thrown the bottle into the kitchen sink,' I think. Then all goes silent.

At six I get up to go to the lavatory and as I open the bedroom door I am greeted by the most horrendous sight – smashed plants, broken glass, upturned furniture, soil everywhere and Dash's prostrate form draped across the settee. With a scream I attack him, scratching, kicking and punching. I want to kill him.

'What have you done, you bloody idiot? What did the plants ever do to you that you should have destroyed them like this?'

'That's all you ever think of, those bloody plants. You love them more than me,' he says, grabbing hold of my flailing arms. I punch him in the groin and he doubles over.

My screams have woken our next-door neighbours who are now banging on our front door. Louisa opens it for them and they come running in. The wife takes hold of me and, sobbing hysterically, I am led out of our flat and into theirs. The husband gets out the hoover and sets about cleaning up the mess.

'That's it,' I say after several cups of coffee and endless cigarettes. 'This time he's done it.' When I telephone my lawyer he tells me that Christmas and New Year are the worst times to get an injunction order. Not because they are public holidays but because at this period more marriages come apart than at any other time of the year.

A couple of hours later I creep into our flat. Dash is still draped across the settee, dead to the world.

I pack two overnight bags, the dog's bowl and his biscuits and the three of us leave.

New Year's Day is not the easiest time to find emergency shelter, but fortunately we are taken in by an old friend from my radio days in Johannesburg. His home, overlooking the canal in Maida Vale, is expensively furnished and immaculately maintained.

As soon as we arrive, Dougal, normally a well-behaved animal, goes berserk. He charges around the apartment leaping onto and over the pristine white sofas, sending expensive Chinese figurines and onyx ashtrays flying in all directions and ends up tearing apart one of the embroidered satin cushions on top of the king-size bed. We can only apologize for the confused behaviour of our suddenly delinquent dog.

For the next two months our travelling circus moves from temporary home to temporary home until finally at the beginning of March the case comes up in court.

I am sitting with my actress chum in the corridor outside the courtroom when Dash arrives. We nod to one another. He looks ashen. According to my neighbours, not a drop of alcohol has passed his lips in weeks although he has kept them awake at night with his horrific howling.

The judge deals severely with the case, ordering Dash to leave the flat immediately and threatening him with arrest and jail if any further violence occurs. Despite all that has happened, I can't help feeling sorry for him as he stands in the dock, trembling from head to foot and battling to control his tears. He seems such a frightened little boy.

When it is all over the three of us go for a cup of tea in the Royal Courts of Justice cafeteria. As we make our way through the busy corridors, crowded with lawyers, clerks, senior counsel, policemen and social workers, it occurs to me how many people make a living out of other people's pain.

Bunch after bunch of red roses is laid upon the

259

corpse of our marriage whilst a veritable forest of love letters arrives through the letter-box. Promises of joining Alcoholics Anonymous are made, along with offers of sharing the ironing or paying for someone else to do it. But it's all too late. Even our shared Scorpio passion has burned itself out and I am left with nothing but a feeling of distaste at Dash's attempts to rekindle it. Every attempt at reconciliation ends in disaster until finally, and not before time, the coffin is lowered into the ground and a good deal of dirt heaped upon it.

Thank you for your telegram saying you had received the money. Glad you are feeling a bit stronger now. Your mother and I are very pleased that you are coming home. It will be nice for you to do a play again in Johannesburg.

Your mother hasn't been too well. Annie has to help her with her insulin injections. You will see a difference in her. The nights are still cold but the winter is nearly over. Looking forward to seeing you both.

Every good wish
Auntie Edie

Like two wounded birds, Louisa and I head for home. This time nobody is available to meet us at Jan Smuts airport but my friend sends her driver to pick us up. As the car draws up in front of the dutch-gabled house we can see Auntie Edie sitting in her usual place on the verandah, listening to her transistor radio and reading her *Path of Truth.*

Paint is peeling off the roof and the once immaculate garden has gone to wrack and ruin. The swing seat on the verandah is broken, wooden slats are missing from the chairs and the floral plastic cushions are filthy and torn.

260

Surprisingly, Mummy comes out through the fly-screen door to greet us. At the age of seventy-nine, Miss McKirdy has finally retired from teaching speech and drama at the convents. Tales of her falling asleep in front of her pupils finally filtered back to the nuns who thought it best for all concerned to pension her off. As it has always been her dream to die 'in harness', the enforced idleness of her retirement has had a devastating effect on her.

Her hair is now white and straggly; clearly there are no more visits to the hairdresser on a Tuesday morning. And when I take her hands in mine, I notice that they are covered with liver spots and crusty sores.

Over her egg-stained dress she wears a faded floral apron that once belonged to Granny Mac. Wrinkled flesh hangs from the underside of her thin arms and, as she shuffles along, her uncut toenails sprout through the holes in her pom-pommed carpet slippers.

She has become careless of removing her own facial hair and her sunken cheeks are devoid of powder or paint. Repeated falls over the curled-up edges of the worn-out carpets have caused nasty bruising of her arms and legs. She is almost as battered as the old Renault she no longer drives but keeps locked up in the garage. Only the clear blue eyes remain unchanged. They are still strong and challenging.

The smell of decay in the dutch-gabled house is over-powering, a combination of urine, onions and unaired rooms. Auntie laughingly tells us that Mummy has taken to putting the cooking pots out in the drive-way to dry in the sun. I watch in horror as she wipes the plates we are about to eat off with a filthy piece of cloth that once was a dish-towel. Big Jeanie has gone, and with her the smell of lavender furniture polish, Dettol and Vim. Declaring her bones to be too old for housework, she too has retired, to a farm in the Northern Transvaal, but without any pension in respect of her twenty-year service.

261

We are presented with another surprise when Annie emerges from the back bedroom to greet us. The whole image is clown-like, overpainted, blood-red lips open in a broad grin to reveal a set of toothless pink gums. Somehow, I never learn how or why she lost her teeth. She is dressed in an old, red-spangled evening top over a bedraggled Indian skirt from the sixties. On her feet she wears broken-down silver sandals. She holds out her arms for Louisa and then, clutching the child in a tight embrace, spins wildly about the room until, with a shriek, they both land on the floor.

Auntie Edie comes into the room to join in the fun. 'Isn't Annie looking beautiful? And keeping so well. I don't know what your mother and I would do without her. She's our little maid.' Oh Jesus! What a nightmare it's all turned into.

We are offered tea and rock buns which we decline, pleading a late breakfast on the plane.

I cannot possibly stay in this house. As soon as I get the chance, I telephone Jilly and tell her that, whether she wants us or not, we are coming to stay.

'I thought you might,' she says. 'Things've got pretty bad, haven't they? The kids tell me that the place is alive with fleas. So long as you're happy to muck in, you're more than welcome.'

Using the excuse of late working hours, Louisa and I remove ourselves as quickly as possible to Jilly's house down the road.

At the age of forty-seven, Jilly still has the body of a young girl which is not surprising as Highland dancing requires enormous energy and stamina. As she teaches, she leaps around, shouting and waving her arms, urging her pupils on to achieve the perfection she demands of herself. If she is not physically and mentally exhausted at the end of a day's teaching, Jilly doesn't feel she has done her job properly. For her there is definitely no gain without pain. She continues to weigh the rights and wrongs of having finally decided to divorce

Terry who is now seriously on skid row.

Morag is now the proud mother of a shy little girl who is the image of her father, Peter, while Jilly's other children all seem much more confident and relaxed now that their parents are separated.

Jilly doesn't keep a servant so everyone is given a weekly schedule of daily tasks. Her own schedule continues to be punitive. She rises at four a.m. and puts a chicken in to roast for two hours while she studies her Christian Science Bible lesson. The smell and sound of sizzling fat mingling with the repetitive monotone of Jilly affirming that God is Love, Truth, Health and Beauty have us all awake before five each morning.

In the evening we take it in turns to prepare the evening meal which usually ends in a full-scale political row between my nieces, my nephews and myself. 'You're all bloody brainwashed,' I shout at them. 'South Africa is Alice in Gondwana Land. You're all at the Mad Hatter's Tea Party.'

'You just believe everything you read in the British press,' they shout back. 'Just wait, just wait till you've lived here for a while and then see if you don't change your tune.'

Jilly sits at the top of the table blinking and nodding and trying to see everyone's point of view.

Sometimes she and I don't get a chance to talk to one another until well after eleven at night, when the children have all gone to bed and we can at last sit down at the kitchen table. Our seven-year age difference no longer matters as we talk well into the wee small hours on subjects ranging from our childhood to our wrecked marriages and the reasons for our existence at all. She sips pot after pot of herbal tea whilst I work my way with equal commitment through gallons of cheap Cape wine and packets of cigarettes. We scream with laughter at the goings-on in the dutch-gabled house. She describes how Miss McKirdy came face to face

263

with a burglar in her bedroom and declared, 'No-one comes into my home uninvited. Get out this minute!' And off went the intruder muttering, 'Sorry, madam,' as he carefully closed the door behind him. Apparently, in her statement to the young white constable who was summoned to the house after the incident she said, 'That native boy was the nicest looking man I've seen in years. Beautiful features. So strong and clean-cut. Poor devil was probably just desperate.'

Shortly after my arrival I start rehearsing. The play, a black comedy, is set in Johannesburg's gold-mining days and the multi-racial cast is the largest ever assembled at this theatre. I am excited at the prospect of working with black and Afrikaans actors for the first time in my seventeen-year career. Unfortunately, my co-star will not be there for the first week of rehearsals as he is busy making a film.

In Johannesburg the public transport and taxi service are skeletal and as the theatre is situated in the dangerous downtown section of the city, the first thing I have to sort out is some means of transport. Miss McKirdy refuses to lend me the Renault and Auntie has finally sold the old Hillman, so reluctantly the management agree to my having the use of the theatre Combi.

At first all the members of the cast appear to get on wonderfully well together, laughing, chatting and hugging in true thespian fashion. I am falling over myself in order to be accepted as one of the team.

However, from day one, it is evident that there is some conflict of acting styles and interpretation. My inner voice starts raising doubts, but these are, as usual, ignored or silenced.

The director's method of working, which is a very democratic one with lots of improvisation and character discussion, is proving to be somewhat of a problem with such a large and diverse cast. As the play is largely about exploitation, white on black and English on Afrikaner, there is an enormous amount of sub-text swirling around which we are all too afraid to deal with other than on a superficial, performance level.

Then my co-star arrives. Anton is rather unusual looking, tall and slim, with a large comical mouth. But when he bends down to shake my hand I am transfixed by the emotional depth and clarity of his eyes. They are like pools of green light. We spark from the word go and I find myself impatiently awaiting each day's rehearsal like a schoolgirl desperate for the tuck shop to open.

As we are playing characters who fall madly in love with one another, the director suggests that we do some improvisation sessions alone with her. She sits us down, facing each other, and asks us to gently stroke each other's hands and faces, to look deeply into each other's eyes, to kiss each other's fingertips and to whisper compliments and endearments into each other's ears.

When she asks what effect this is having on us, he replies, 'It's lovely, it feels gentle and safe.'

'Wonderful. Just wonderful,' I say. 'I feel like I'm floating in a pool of warm water.'

Later, in the bar when I ask her if Anton is married, she laughs and says, 'Good God, no!'

Rehearsals go forward apace. Anton is a very creative actor and we become deeply absorbed in each other and the development of our roles. When I am able to drag my eyes away from him, I find myself unable to watch the chaotic state of the rest of the production. The director seems to have lost control and everybody is throwing in their penny's worth.

Anton and I spend every available break together. He's an attentive listener and I find myself pouring my heart out to him, telling him the intimate details of my marriage to Dash. He shares stories of his childhood and early youth but won't be drawn into any discussion about his present life.

Whenever we rehearse our love scenes, I feel his

genuine physical response to what is supposed to be simulated passion. This makes me feel excited but confused at the same time. I go weak at the knees at his slightest touch and am battling within myself at the improbability of the whole affair. What little sleep I do get is deeply disturbed as I sweat and squirm in a fever of sexual fantasy. Nor am I eating properly, preferring to get by on a diet of cigarettes, wine and black coffee. I try talking to Jilly about the turmoil raging within me but sex is not a subject she is comfortable discussing. Besides, I don't want to lose her respect. Thirteen-year-old Louisa is my main confidante, listening patiently as I read the characteristics of the Piscean male in Linda Goodman's *Sun Signs*. As usual she has endeared herself to most of the company, including Anton, who hugs her warmly whenever they meet. As I have a great many costume changes in the play, Louisa is taken on as my dresser and remains remarkably calm and efficient however much I shout at her.

The opening night audience receives the play's explicit language, risqué sex scenes and the overt political comment in stunned silence. Later, at the first night party, the guests dexterously side-step any discussion of the production but, frankly, I couldn't care less as my attention is focused entirely on Anton.

Professing to hate parties, he stops only briefly to arrange to pick me up for a television interview the next day and then disappears.

As soon as I see him the following day, I know that he has undergone a complete change of heart. Instead of his usual sporty clothes, he is decked out from head to foot in skin-tight black leather. His eyes are hidden behind a pair of mirror sunglasses and when I look at him all I can see is a distorted image of myself.

The weekly arts chat-show goes out live and when asked if anything disastrous has ever happened to me on stage, I cause a national stir by using the words 'monumental cock-up' to describe one such incident. I had wanted to be the first person to say 'fuck' on South African television but, at the last minute, my courage deserted me.

It continues to drain away, as we drive to the theatre in silence and I come to the realization that I have indeed made the most monumental cock-up of my life.

I completely lose it. Every night after the show I go out to night spots where I drink and jive and smooch with anyone who makes himself available, including, in one instance, my nephew Gordon's best friend, an ex-Borstal boy, newly arrived from England. Louisa watches it all without comment but is there to pick me up, dust me off and put me to bed.

A week after we open, the two week's Notice to Close goes up on the board at the stage door, no doubt as a result of the roasting the show has received from the critics. My contract had been for six weeks but now I'll only do three. I was counting on the money but that's show business for you. One night I am drinking with some of the black cast members in the theatre bar when a discussion starts about the meaning of the word 'choice'. Several of them have been imprisoned for their beliefs. When I sound off about each person being responsible for what happens to them in life, one of them, an actor who was inside at the same time as Steve Biko, says, 'Black people in this country don't have any say in what happens to them. You try making a choice with a gun stuck in your back. If you don't believe me, how about taking us back to Soweto in your smart theatre Combi, and perhaps you can see for yourself.'

I had been vaguely aware that the black actors resented my being privileged in this way when their only means of transport to and from the theatre was in an unreliable and dangerous taxi or equally unreliable and dangerous bus.

'Fine,' I say, flushed with alcohol. 'Let's go.'

On the outskirts of the township we are stopped at a roadblock. Young white soldiers stand with guns at the ready while the sergeant orders everyone out of the van except Louisa and me.

'No, it's OK. You two can stay there while we search this thing.'

We decline his offer and join our friends in the freezing Transvaal night.

In a tone reminiscent of the one used in the police station all those years ago, I demand to see the commanding officer who arrives some fifteen minutes later.

'OK, lady, what I want to know is what are you doing with these people?'

'I'm driving them home.'

'I can see that. What I want to know is, why?'

'They're my friends.'

'What were you doing with them until two in the morning?'

'Working.'

'Is that a fact? I think we'd better get you breathalized, lady.' He radios for someone to get the gear.

My heart is pounding but I have my audience to think about. 'Great!' I say. 'You haven't found any guns or dynamite under the floorboards of the Combi, you can't get these guys because their passes are in order, so now, thank you very much, you want to arrest me for having a few drinks. Well, let me tell you something, I am dying to be arrested. I can't wait. I can't wait for the press to get hold of it. Headlines everywhere. Actress and daughter thrown into jail. C'mon, c'mon let's get the handcuffs on.'

Everybody's sniggering now and he's had about enough.

'Look, just get into that Combi and thank your lucky stars that I'm prepared to send a convoy with you. Because I can tell you, lady, you wouldn't last five minutes in that township. These people here, the ones you think are so wonderful, would very happily tear you and your kid apart to get this Combi. Drop these boys where my sergeant tells you, OK, then get the hell out of here. I don't want to see you again.'

Back in the Combi my friends applaud and cheer. 'You socked it to them, baby. Now we can see where we've been going wrong.'

We all roar with laughter and I am filled with admiration for the generosity and uncrushable spirit of these people.

In all the years I have lived in South Africa I have only ever seen townships from a distance. Now, in the cold light of dawn, I see for the first time the hovels in which black people are forced to live.

With only a week of the run to go, I plan my final assault on Anton. As we come off stage I say to him, 'If you can't play the part like a man, at least try not to play it like a bloody queen.'

'Christ, that's it!' he says, throwing down the towel he is using to wipe his face. 'I've had it up to here with your unprofessionalism. I'm having the director brought in.'

The next day I am summoned to the theatre. Louisa comes to give me moral support but waits outside in the Combi. When I walk into the rehearsal room Anton is already there, pacing up and down with a face like concrete. As soon as he sees me he says to the director, 'Right! I want to complain about the behaviour of this actress. I'm not being allowed to get on with my job because of her pathetic badgering, night after night after night. Then last night she made a vicious attack on me and my work and quite frankly I'm not prepared to put up with it. Either you tell her to stop this insane behaviour, or you can have my resignation here and now. I can't work with a lunatic.'

'Anton, please. Listen to me,' I say, tears starting to pour from my eyes, 'I love you.'

'Could we just try to keep this discussion on a professional level,' the director says.

'I can't,' I say. 'I know I've made life hard for him on stage but it's been difficult for me too. I can't stand by and watch this man refuse to accept reality.'

'Well, it may be your reality,' she says just a little tersely, 'but it isn't necessarily his.'

'I just don't believe that,' I reply tenaciously, which causes Anton to explode.

'Just shut your bloody mouth, woman, and listen for once in your life to what somebody else has got to say. You come out here from bloody England, you chuck your weight around, you trot out the biggest load of rubbish about acting and life and God knows what else and then you presume to tell me what I need and what I want. You need a bloody shrink, lady. Don't you know you're the laughing stock of this town? God, even the blacks are laughing at you behind their hands. All this liberal crap you're full of, sucking up to them with bloody lifts back to Soweto. Sis! You've got no dignity, lady. No wonder your husband smacked you around. I mean who could blame the poor guy? You're enough to drive anybody berserk. You're lucky you haven't been murdered. And as for that poor kid of yours that you drag around with you, fetching and carrying and watching you make a complete idiot of yourself – Jesus! Haven't you got any self-respect?'

'I think this has gone far enough,' says the director. 'Please, let's just try and get through this last week.'

She looks at Anton, 'All right?'

'Ask her,' he mutters, taking out his car keys.

I'm in a state of shock. 'Sure,' I hear myself whisper, 'that's fine by me.'

Back in the car I give Louisa a resumé of his speech. When I get to the bit about her, tears well up in her eyes. 'It's true, Mummy,' she says, starting to shake.

'How can you say that?' I gasp. 'We have a wonderful relationship. I don't know what I'd do without you.'

'But it's so hard for me, Mummy. I love you but I just hate the way it's always "darling this and darling

270

that" and you're all over me when it suits you. But you can't wait to get rid of me when something better comes along. I'm sick to death of always being thought of as your shadow. I'm a person too, you know, Mummy, I'm not just your daughter. And I'm fed up with having to pick you up out of the gutter. It's no good you telling me to leave you there. I can't. I've been looking after you for so many years now I don't know what else to do. It's just that I've never had a chance to be a child myself because you've always been the child and I've had to look after you.' Her voice trails off into uncontrollable sobs.

When the pupil is ready the master appears.

At the beginning of our last week Louisa and I pay a visit to the dutch-gabled house. As we get out of the Combi, the fly-screen door bursts open and out flies Annie clutching a pink winter dressing-gown around her. Like a whoosh of wind she turns the corner of the house, zooms past the rose garden and disappears into the orchard. Louisa and I gape after her in amazement.

Almost at the same moment Jilly drives up in her battered Volkswagen. She and her youngest daughter, Sheila, climb out and join us on the pavement.

Mummy appears at the fly-screen door, puffing nervously on her cigarette and waves us in.

'Thank God you girls have come,' she says. 'Auntie Edie and I can't do a thing with her. She's had us up all night. She refuses to take her pills and she won't lie down.'

Auntie Edie joins Mummy at the fly-screen. 'Oh dear God,' she says, 'have we had a time of it. Your mother and I are just worn out with the whole business.'

At that moment Annie gusts up to us like a tornado. As she draws level with Auntie she spits 'lesbian' into her face.

'Dear God!' says Auntie. 'That girl's got the devil in her today.' She clutches her throat and staggers towards a corner chair, resuscitating herself by picking up her

271

crocheting. She is halfway through making yet another pair of orange and pink bed-socks.

Mummy's hand moves involuntarily to her box of Rothman's. She speaks as she lights a fresh cigarette, putting the match into the saucer of a cup of cold tea. The makeshift ashtray is already overflowing with cigarette ends and dead matches. 'I have given my life to that girl. I have given and given and given and all I have got in return is— ' she breaks off as she searches for the word to describe the awfulness of what has been dished out to her. 'She is my cross and my Gethsemane.'

Auntie Edie nods sagely. The winter sun streams in through the Venetian blinds making bars on the walls. The six of us are standing or sitting in a variety of positions around the room. Three generations – Mummy and Auntie Edie, Jilly and me, Sheila and Louisa. We are all wondering where Annie has got to. I go through to the room that used to be mine and is now used by Annie. It is still furnished the way I left it, but the velvet settee has so many cigarette burns that it looks like a bullet-riddled corpse and the walls are smeared with coffee, lipstick, ballpoint pen and grime. The lamps are overturned, the curtains hang off their hooks, clothes spill from drawers and the floor is strewn with old photographs and yellowed newspaper cuttings. Whenever Annie goes doolally she searches frantically through her past, as though trying to find the answer to why it all went wrong.

The back door slams and Annie stomps up the passage and into the room.

'What the hell have you done to my things?' I shout at her. I am very angry. 'All this stuff belongs to me and look at it now.'

'Don't talk to me,' she says, pacing up and down the room. 'I've got a bloody cancer in my stomach the size of a snake. Do you know that?' She takes a deep drag on her cigarette and then uses her dirty, half-painted red fingernail to flick the ash onto the carpet.

272

'Don't do that,' I say. 'Don't you have any respect for anything at all?' But she's off again, down the passage, out of the back door and into the garden.

Jilly and the girls have joined me in the bedroom. For a few moments we stand looking at the anarchic scene and then not knowing what else to do or say we trail back into the small sitting-room. I am complaining bitterly about Annie and the chaos she has created when suddenly she is in amongst us, like a fox amongst chickens. Everyone seems to be talking at once. Words are flying about in the air like feathers.

Suddenly Annie thumps Mummy in the chest and pushes her up against the wall between the settee and the radiogram. On it stands a picture of her at the age of five. Anyone looking at the beautiful child in the portrait and the grown woman standing above it would have difficulty believing that they were one and the same person. Only the eyes give it away – the adult's are still huge and brown but, unlike the child's which glow with angelic softness, hers now spark like an exploding plug in a faulty socket.

'So, I am your cross and your Gethsemane, am I?' she shouts, her face pushed right into Mummy's. Miss McKirdy glowers back at her but she's scared, you can see it in her eyes. We are all scared. Annie holds Mummy pinned as she swings around on the rest of us. There are now seven women in the room. Auntie Edie pushes the front door shut to prevent neighbours and passing natives from hearing the row.

Annie's face is horrible. She hasn't shaved for days so it is covered in a black stubble. A gash of blood-red lipstick smeared across it almost merges with the mess of black mascara under her eyes. Her unwashed, lifeless hair is teased and lacquered into a tangled bird's nest on the top of her head. 'I am the one with the cross,' she says. 'And do you know why? Because I have a cancer right here in my stomach.' With her other hand she makes a fist and punches her slack belly. 'It's the size of a snake and it's here, right in here,' hitting the belly again. 'And it's eating me up.'

Mummy twists her head and speaks to us as though Annie weren't there. 'Do you see what I have to put up with?' she says.

Annie grabs Mummy's face and twists it to face her own. 'Look at me when I'm talking to you,' she says angrily. 'Look at me when I'm telling you about my cancer.'

Gently, Jilly puts her hand on Annie's arm and says, 'Listen Annie, listen to me. I want to tell you something about cancer.'

'Yes, China. Yes?' she responds, wiping her sweaty forehead with the back of her hand.

'Cancer,' Jilly goes on, 'is not a reality. People think it is but it's only an illusion brought about by man's erroneous thinking. The penalty people pay for believing in this illusion, which they call cancer, is the pain and disease itself. Do you understand me? You can actually give yourself cancer if you don't try to correct your thinking.'

'Och,' says Auntie Edie from her chair in the corner, 'she looks lovely and there's nothing at all the matter with her.'

'Why don't you, just once in your life, try telling the truth,' I throw at her over my shoulder.

Jilly and I have spent hours discussing this truth business, how in our home there has always been a denial of what is actually going on, a total refusal to accept things the way they really are. Jilly and I have resolved to confront this deception at whatever cost, and now we each take one of Annie's arms and draw her between us to form a battle line. Miss McKirdy stands opposite us, facing her three daughters.

Then Jilly says, 'You see, Annie, this thing in here,' she pats Annie's stomach, 'this thing that you say is a cancer is really just a whole lot of . . . negative thoughts and feelings.' Both Mummy and Annie nod their heads. 'And if you could just try to get rid of them by speaking about them, you would be able to allow God's love to fill you instead of . . .'

'The snake,' I finish her sentence for her and take up the speech. 'If only you would really say what you feel about things, if you really told the truth for once, really got it out, then it wouldn't be down there any more.' I pat her stomach.

Jilly does the same and we both start rubbing it rhythmically. Annie has relaxed a little throughout all this but is still glowering at Mummy. 'You want to tell her, don't you?' I say. 'You'd like to tell her the truth about how you really feel about her.'

If this is to be The Big Confrontation, then let's get on with it. I can feel the disapproval of the two younger girls. They don't want to witness the spilling of blood and guts.

'Come on,' I persuade further as Jilly and I continue to massage her stomach. 'Let's get down to the nitty-gritty here, let's hear what you really think of Mummy.'

'Because you know, Annie,' says Jilly, 'that is where your cancer lies.'

'I know, China,' says Annie, sounding completely normal but with tears welling up into her eyes.

'Well then, let's hear you say it,' I urge. 'TELL HER!'

Annie's face crumples. Her lips start to quiver. She looks like a frightened little child as she says in a small voice, 'I can't.'

'Nonsense,' Jilly and I say, almost in unison. 'You can if you try,' says Jilly.

'Just put one word after the other,' I add.

Annie has gone quite limp between us. 'I do love her,' she says. 'You see, I do, I do.'

'No you don't,' I say determinedly. I'm having difficulty keeping up the gentle massage whilst dealing with my own erupting emotions. 'I'm sure you hate her.' I am baiting Annie now. I want blood, I want revenge for all the hidings and harsh words I have suffered from my

275

mother. I also want to show everyone that I no longer fear her. 'Well if you won't tell her, then I damned well will,' I say, turning to face Mummy square on. I am breathing heavily and my heart is pounding. 'Why do you think this girl is like she is? Hey? Why?'

Mummy looks at me. She is frowning slightly.

'Why do you think I went to live SIX THOUSAND MILES AWAY FROM HERE? WHY? Why do you think Jilly married the man she did and fucked up her life? Because you bloody forced us to.' I have never sworn like that in front of my mother. I see the shock come into her eyes. 'It's all because of YOU.'

The boulder is rolling down the mountainside, gathering momentum as it goes. Nothing can stop it now. 'Jilly and I managed to get away from you because we were strong enough, but she wasn't. She was too sweet and loving,' I say, shaking Annie like a rag doll. 'You got your hooks into her good and proper and she couldn't escape from you because you held her in a stranglehold.'

As I am saying this, I am deeply aware of how much I love my mother and how I wish she had loved me enough to want to hang onto me. Her head is pulled right back as though she is trying to avoid being spat on. She is stunned, but still in control. Beside me, Annie suddenly finds her voice. She leans forward, still supported by Jilly and me.

'I do love you,' she says, 'but I also hate you for what you did that night . . .' She is gasping for breath. 'That night on the ship after I did the Sailor's Hornpipe.'

Mummy glares at her and makes a little 'what' question mark movement with her head.

'Don't pretend you don't know what I'm talking about because you do. Yes! You know what I mean.'

The intensity of Annie's speech affects everyone in the room. We are all deeply aware that she is not only speaking the truth, but is trying to share some enormous secret. She is no longer hysterical. What she

276

is saying is coming from somewhere deep inside her yet so close to the surface that one feels it is about to explode. Quite out of the blue, she has referred to their trip overseas, God knows how many years ago. I was seven years old when they went and now I am nearly forty.

Just saying that has taken a lot out of Annie and now she slumps forward and almost faints. Jilly and I catch her as her knees buckle. 'Come on, finish what you've got to say,' says Jilly, frantically keeping up the massage. 'Come on, you're not finished.'

'Come on!' I say. 'Tell us what happened that night on the ship after the Sailor's Hornpipe. Come on, you've got this far, don't give up now!'

Apart from the sound of the clock ticking away in the next room, everything is suddenly terribly silent. Jilly and I are praying for Annie to find the strength to say what she has to say. It's as though we have stepped into Aladdin's cave and the genie and his lamp are about to appear and reveal the mystery of Annie's mental illness. Please God! Let her get it out and maybe she'll be cured. We see the words forming somewhere down inside her. She makes a retching movement as if she is about to vomit them up. She swallows hard, trying to hold them down. We see them force their way up into her throat again. They have reached her mouth. She and Mummy are staring at one another, unblinkingly, their eyes locked. Annie's lips tremble as she tries to form the words into an organized shape. She is about to speak them when she suddenly snaps her mouth shut and swallows hard.

'No!' I scream. 'They mustn't go down there. They must come up, out into the open. She's got to hear you say them.'

But it is hopeless, the moment has passed. At first her head moves slowly from side to side indicating a refusal to say anything further. Then the movement quickens until her whole body is shaking convulsively. Finally, she collapses totally and hangs, sobbing, between Jilly and me.

Mummy recovers her composure quickly. Her head is shaking but it is a very controlled movement. She almost shrugs her shoulders. She has a strange look on her face, as if she is suddenly bored with the whole scene. Quite casually she says, 'Well, what was all that about?' and moves away to get a cigarette.

The next day Jilly and I arrange to take Annie out. Something has changed between the three of us. We are united again as we once were, years ago.

Mummy is resting in her room when we arrive to fetch Annie who is waiting for us looking happy and relaxed. She is cleanly dressed and nicely made up.

'What sort of a night did you have?' we ask her.

'Oh . . . OK,' she says. 'We all just went to bed after you left.'

We drive across Johannesburg to a friend's home in the northern suburbs. Like all the other homes in this affluent area, it is large and set in an acre of ground surrounded by a high security wall topped off with broken glass to deter potential burglars. Into this fortification is set a decorative wrought iron gate, now locked and bolted. We ring the bell and the maid comes out from the kitchen. She carries with her a bunch of keys that the keeper of the Bastille would have been proud to possess. Smiling sweetly, she undoes all the various locks and bolts.

'Your madam likes you to be safe, hey?' I say and the maid laughs, showing us a set of perfect, white, pearly teeth.

'Haw! Too much, too much,' she says.

My friend is at work so only the second car is parked in the garage. We all wipe our feet on the doormat before walking into the house which is tastefully decorated in autumnal shades with the occasional splash of orange to brighten things up. A selection of embroidered cushions is arranged with mathematical precision on the huge cream settee. My friend works long hours in the city and so is seldom at home. She is a single parent and complains constantly that the upkeep of the house, swimming pool and tennis court is a constant drain on her resources.

As a reward for making it to the patio without creating so much as a ruck in the afghan rug or leaving a smidgeon of oak leaf on the beige carpet the maid asks us if we would like some tea.

'That would be lovely,' we say in unison, sounding like one of Miss McKirdy's choral verse choirs.

Annie and I are heavy smokers so Louisa, who is with us, is sent indoors to fetch an ashtray. Sitting in the shade of a huge, old avocado pear tree, I am reminded of the one Robert and I had in our back garden. It's funny, whenever I mentioned having an avocado pear tree to people in England, I always felt that they thought I was making it up, as though they didn't believe avocados grew on trees. Mind you, I didn't know brussel sprouts grew on stalks until I lived there.

The tea arrives and is poured and passed around. We sip genteelly and nibble on dainty biscuits as we comment on the beautiful blue of the pool water and how expensive it must be to employ a full-time gardener. At that precise moment, he returns from his lunch-break and begins clipping the grass around the edge of the patio. Thank God it is still too early in the spring for the grass to be mown.

In South Africa, one so often gets the feeling that servants make their presence felt by doing something noisy or irritating just to say, 'I'm a real live human being and I'm just letting you know it.'

With a toothless grin he returns our greeting and I get the feeling that Annie would be a lot happier chatting to him than to the two of us.

'So,' I say, 'how do you feel about yesterday?'

Annie smiles and shakes her head. 'I don't know,' she says.

'Do you think you got something off your chest?' I ask. She shrugs.

'Do you feel any better?' asks Jilly.

Annie nods. 'A bit,' she says. We are all silent for a moment.

It's my turn again. 'Don't you think you'd feel a lot better if you told us everything that happened that night in the cabin, on the ship with Mummy?'

Annie bites her lip and looks at me. Then she looks at Jilly. She reaches out and touches Jilly's hand affectionately. 'Our china doll,' she says, 'don't you think she's beautiful?' she asks, turning to me.

'I do,' I reply. 'Very beautiful. But that's not what I asked you. I asked you if you wouldn't feel a lot better if you got out whatever it is you are keeping inside you, because obviously something happened that night on the ship and it's still very close to the surface with you. How many years ago did all that happen? And yet yesterday you came out with it as though it had just happened. How long ago was it when you went overseas with Mummy?'

'Oh God,' says Annie. 'I haven't a clue.'

'Well,' Jilly says, 'how old were you?'

'Twelve,' says Annie, quick as a flash.

'And how old are you now?'

'Forty-four,' says Annie, again, as quick as a flash.

I am thinking there doesn't seem to be anything wrong with this girl's memory. 'How many shock treatments do you say you've had?'

She laughs. 'About a hundred and ninety three.'

'So what happened,' I ask, 'on the ship?'

She studies my face for a long time. Louisa strokes her hand. 'Little Louisa,' says Annie, looking at her, 'always so quiet.'

'I have to be,' says Louisa. 'With my mom, someone has to be quiet.'

'You cheeky so-and-so,' I say and we all laugh. Louisa and I have done a great deal of talking in the last few days.

'Come on, Annie,' says Jilly, 'we want to help you.'

'We're your sisters,' I say, 'we love you and we want you to be well again. You know yourself from going to AA meetings, when you stand up and say, "I am an alcoholic", you're well on your way to getting hold of the problem.'

Annie nods.

'So tell us what happened. For God's sake, we're not going to tell Mummy what you say. We think she's done enough harm as it is.'

'No, that's not quite fair,' says Jilly, always a stickler for the truth. 'She's also been very good to Annie. She's stuck by her through thick and thin.'

'She has, China,' says Annie. 'She really has.'

'But she's only human,' I say. 'She can get things wrong too, you know, she's not a saint.'

Annie laughs. 'The nuns at the convent used to think she was.'

'I know they did,' I say. 'And it was bloody tough on all of us. When Reverend Mother used to say, "Oh, your dear mother, what a wonderful woman she is" – we could hardly say, "Oh no she isn't. She's fucking awful."'

We all laugh. I am pushing my luck a bit. Jilly doesn't at all approve of bad language. I'm sure she only lets me get away with it because I'm in the theatre.

'Do you believe in God, China?' asks Annie.

'You know I do,' says Jilly. 'I also believe that if you harbour anger and resentment you can develop a serious illness. I don't think for one moment that you have cancer but I do think that it's dangerous to allow negative thoughts to foster inside you.'

I chip in, 'Get rid of them. Set them free. You'll feel a lot better. Look how much better you are already.'

Louisa goes indoors to get more hot water. Annie

reaches for Jilly's hand which she clasps in her own and says, 'You know Mummy was very friendly with the captain on the ship.'

'Ye-es,' we both say.

'Well,' she goes on, 'Mummy was very cross with me, you see, because I wouldn't practise. I was sick of practising. I just wanted to have some fun.'

'Sure,' I say. Jilly nods in agreement.

'The captain asked me to dance at the fancy dress ball and Mummy said I should do the Sailor's Hornpipe, you know, with it being a ship and everything, but I was so fat I could hardly get into my costume because I'd been eating all those cakes and things in Scotland. All those high teas, you know.'

'Disgusting food,' I say, and Jilly agrees.

'Oh I loved it,' says Annie, 'I could have eaten it till the cows came home.'

Louisa has arrived with the hot water and we break off to pour, stir and light new cigarettes.

'Go on,' encourages Jilly.

'Has anything happened yet?' asks Louisa.

'No,' I say. 'But we're getting there.' We all settle down again.

'You were telling us about doing the Hornpipe,' I say. Annie looks at me and her brow furrows. A shadow seems to cross her face. She looks at Jilly and then back at me. I am starting to get a little bit impatient with her. 'Come on Annie,' I say. 'You're safe with us. We are your sisters, for God's sake!'

She looks down at her hands which are shaking terribly as Jilly puts an arm around her trembling shoulders, catching hold of the ancient cardigan which has slipped down her back. I recognize it as having once belonged to me. Jilly readjusts it tenderly around her hunched shoulders.

'It's all right,' she tells Annie quietly. 'It's all right. Mummy was cross with you, and then what happened?'

Annie is crying now, causing her mascara to run

in black rivulets down her shaved cheeks. She uses her right fist to rub away the tears which only makes an even worse mess of her face. We wait while she takes short, neurotic draws on her cigarette. Finally, after a long pause, she begins.

'She . . . she threw me out of the cabin.' The tears have turned to sobs now.

'She threw you out,' prompts Jilly. 'And then?'

'And then,' says Annie, 'she told me . . .' She is really sobbing now. 'She told me she was sick to death of me.' She wipes her runny nose with the back of her hand. 'I went to the party and danced. It wasn't very good, but I got through it, you know. And then I . . . then I . . .'

'Yes, you . . .?' we all three chorus.

There is another long silence. 'Then I went down to the cabin . . .' We all nod our heads. She swallows hard, and hiccups from the sobs. 'But she wasn't there.'

'Mummy?' I say. 'Where was she?'

'Hang on a sec,' says Jilly, 'give her a chance.'

Suddenly the words come rushing out in a torrent. 'She was with the captain, in his quarters. I just went running in there because I knew where to go, you see, cause I'd been there before with her and I just saw them . . . you know . . .'

'Mummy and the captain?'

She nods.

'Have a little tea,' says Jilly.

'You're doing so well, Auntie Annie,' says Louisa, squeezing her hand. Annie gives her a little smile.

How about that, I think. The old girl and the captain! 'What did she say to you?' I ask. Annie twists her soggy tissues between nicotine-stained fingers. Her nails are in a terrible mess, all different lengths and shapes, some bitten, some broken off, some half-covered in chipped nail varnish, some with dirt under them.

'Was she cross with you?' I'm pushing now, getting more and more impatient. 'What did she say to you, Annie?'

283

'Come on,' says Jilly. I can sense she, too, is beginning to lose patience. She's just better at concealing it than I am.

'Come on, Auntie Annie,' says Louisa.

Annie stares at us. Her eyes have a stubborn look in them. She sighs and shuts her mouth, expanding her diaphragm. There lies our answer. Down there in the depths of her.

I once saw a photograph of a python that had swallowed a buck. The snake's stomach had expanded to accommodate the bigger animal. You could see the shape of the buck quite clearly inside it. Annie, like the python, has swallowed the secret of that night. She knows what Mummy said to her. She hasn't forgotten a single detail of that experience, but for some reason she's determined to keep the information stuffed inside her.

What on earth could my mother have said to her?

She breathes deeply once more, her mouth closes, her eyes flicker from side to side and then shut tight. She concentrates hard, her brow furrowed. She makes little noises in her throat and we can see the words coming up. Her body rocks back and forth as she pushes downwards as though constipated, a look of agonizing pain engulfing her face. Then she takes a sharp inward breath and tries to speak. The words are on the tip of her tongue.

'She said . . .' We lean forward. We are on the edge of our chairs. 'She said . . . she . . . she . . .'

'Yes?' says Jilly. 'Yes?'

Annie swallows. Hard. She clenches her fists and shuts her eyes tight like someone desperately trying not to see what is right there in front of her.

'Oh, for God's sake!' I scream, leaping to my feet. 'Tell us what she said!' Before I know what has happened, my arm has swung out and I have cracked Annie across her face.

'Don't!' says Louisa, jumping up and grabbing my arm.

'What on earth did you do that for?' asks Jilly, alarmed.

'Well it's so damned frustrating,' I shout. 'Why the hell can't she spew it out, for fuck's sake.'

Annie has turned to stone. Her body is stiff. She sits immobile, her fists clenched in her lap, her eyes tight shut. God, I've blown it. I've ruined it. My damned impatience. Goddamn it! Will I never learn.

'I think we had better go home,' says Jilly, standing up and collecting her things. 'It's been an upsetting afternoon.'

We collect up the tea things, tidy the chairs and make our way back through the house. As we get to the front door, Annie says, 'Do you think I could go to the lav, please?'

'Sure,' I say. 'There's a guest one through here.' I lead her down the passage and push the door open for her. She goes in. We hear the key turn in the lock and then the sound of vomiting.

The door to the kitchen opens and the maid sticks her head out. She has a worried look on her face. I smile and indicate that there is nothing to be concerned about. Her head disappears back into the kitchen and she shuts the door. When Annie comes out I say, 'I think I'll just pop in quickly.' I'm worried in case she's left a mess in there. But all is fine. I catch up with them just as they get to the gates. 'I'm sorry, Annie,' I say. 'I really am sorry to have hit you like that.'

She shuffles on without looking at me.

Before flying back to England, I make the now ceremonial visit to Henley. Along the way I pass a pseudo-Spanish mansion in all its stucco and wrought-iron glory. Scarlet and purple bougainvillea cascade over the phoney *el tora* balconies, three brand-new cars, one German, one British and one Japanese stand in the driveway while an azure-blue pool shimmers in the noonday sun. All this in full view of the passing motorist. Also in full view of the passing motorist, but completely concealed from the occupants of the mansion by a huge white-washed wall, stands the servants' quarters. Sheets of corrugated iron, bits of old cars, tin baths, barbed wire, rusted wire bedsteads and cardboard boxes provide shelter for those who serve the madam and master. While their offspring play in the red dust amongst the scrawny chickens and emaciated dogs the children of their employers dive bomb each other in the swimming pool.

Louisa and I return to London in the early autumn of 1984. Although it is lovely to be back in our little home, I am suddenly aware of the fact that from now on it will be entirely up to me to bring home the bacon. I will have to find work that provides us with some security. I can't just sit and wait for the phone to ring.

In a couple of months I will be celebrating my fortieth birthday, which means that acting-wise I will be moving into the most oversubscribed section of the *Spotlight Casting Directory* – the age-group in which ninety-three per cent of Leading Ladies listed remain safely unemployed for most of the year. By the same token, the idea of retraining as a computer operator or an estate agent doesn't exactly excite me. So what to do?

One evening, I force myself to sit down and go through the Situations Vacant column in the *Evening Standard* newspaper. It isn't long before I am yawning widely and, in a state of deep depression, I close my eyes. "Oh God, what shall I do?" I ask out loud and to my surprise a little voice within answers, 'Use what you know'. 'The only thing I really know about is the theatre,' I say. 'Well use that', comes the answer.

'How?' I ask.

'Take people backstage and show them how the theatre works'.

286

'What a brilliant idea,' I say, sitting up and opening ny eyes, 'that's exactly what I'll do.'

Thank you for your letter, it was super hearing from you. I'm pleased you had an enjoyable 40th birthday, even though it was so quiet. Talking of birthdays, did I tell you that I am giving Auntie a party for her 90th on Sunday? We have invited forty people and Uncle Rob will give us a song. He is 92 and fit as a fiddle, still plays bowls every day and is Grand Master of the Transvaal masons.

Mummy will play the piano and although Annie is still in hospital we are hoping she will be let out for the day.

Talking of loneliness, I can understand how you feel. When one's marriage is not good you long for the separation which you feel is the answer to all your problems. When you are apart in the beginning, you are so relaxed and relieved because you have been removed from an unhappy situation. You enjoy the freedom. However, once the pressure is off, and if you have things to put right in yourself, you start to feel differently. In my case, I began to realize how important it is to care about the other person. To understand what they feel and think. I still find myself very selfish and thoughtless. Issues which I used to feel were so important now seem rather trivial and things which seemed trivial before are now important.

I think that one does so much soul-searching and I certainly have found many things about myself which I do not like. I also feel shattered when I look at Terry and see a stranger. In my case, I don't believe I even tried to get to know him, I was so busy always being right. I am trying to stop seeing myself as better than him – I realize that no-one is better than me and I am no better than anyone else, and that is taking education and success into

account as well. We are all spiritual ideas reflecting
God's qualities. We are all capable of expressing
all God's qualities. It is what we are inside that
counts.

Tons of love
Jilly

It is a well-known fact in the theatre business that the
minute you focus your attention on something other
than acting, offers of work immediately come rolling in.
It is typical, therefore, that I have just got my new backstage tour business up and running when I am asked to
do two plays, one following the other, and amounting
to nearly a year's work. As I am as yet unable to choose
which hat to wear, that of businesswoman or actress. I
decide to don both, plus of course, the one I am already
wearing, that of a single parent. Louisa and I don't see
a great deal of each other in the months that follow but
we are both happy and relaxed and surviving.

It's strange the way shattering news often arrives when
you least expect it. One Sunday morning early in the
following summer I am lying in bed watching the lace
curtain blowing gently in a soft breeze and feeling
quietly happy when the telephone rings. It is Morag on
the line from South Africa. 'We have some bad news.'
My heart begins to thump and the saliva instantly
leaves my mouth. 'What is it?'
'Mummy has cancer and it's gone so far there's
nothing they can do.'
Despite being forty I still think of my mother as
Mummy and my thoughts immediately go to her.
'Oh my darling,' I say, 'that's terrible.' Then in an
effort to comfort her and myself, 'But she is an old lady,
so it's not totally unexpected.'
There is a pause, then Jilly's eldest daughter says,
'Not your mum, our mum.'
'Your mum?' I scream, leaping out of the bed. 'Your

mum can't have cancer! She's a Christian Scientist!'

Jilly and Mummy are both in the Johannesburg General hospital. Jilly is in the cancer ward and has received one chemotherapy treatment. The doctor attending her is horrified at how far the killer disease has spread. It is everywhere, both inside and outside her body. He simply cannot understand how she has managed to conceal her condition for so long. The children tell him that apart from a peculiar smell and the fact that her blouse often seemed wet, they had noticed absolutely nothing until she finally collapsed. After just one treatment Jilly checks herself out of the hospital and puts herself back in the hands of her Christian Science practitioner. She refuses all sedatives and pain-killers, affirming that she will be cured by God and God alone. There is nothing her family can do but support her decision. She's that sort of person.

By now you will have heard the sad news about Jilly and your mother. I am enclosing an affirmation which you and Louisa must learn by heart and keep repeating every time you think of them. I am forming a wall of prayer to surround them. Every person who rings up I tell to pray.

THE HEALING POWER OF GOD'S LOVE REACHES OVER OCEANS AND CONTINENTS TO THE GLOBE'S FURTHEST ENDS.

Every good wish
Auntie Edie

Mummy is in the geriatric ward and is being treated for diabetes and suppurating sores on her legs. She is discharged at almost the same time as Jilly.

Auntie Edie and Annie are promoted to commander-in-chief and adjutant. Auntie Edie takes over the banking and the shopping while Annie makes an efficient and caring nurse. Tea bags are saved to be used time and time again and mince and mash become the staple diet. Annie complains that she is suffering from hunger but Auntie Edie is in seventh heaven as she cuts the supermarket costs and watches her building society balance grow. She saves old newspapers in cardboard boxes under the bed, wears her lisle stockings until there is hardly any stocking around the darn and refuses to waste good soap on anything as foolish as washing.

After a month Miss McKirdy is readmitted to hospital but the badly trained staff in this state-run institution treat her more like a parcel of decaying meat than a patient. Private medical care in South Africa costs more than a retired elocution teacher can afford. Piles of unswallowed pain-killers lie on her bedside table because no-one can be bothered to fetch her a drink of water. Her sores fester in dirty dressings but her courage remains undaunted.

Discharged for the third time she is made as comfortable as possible at home. Annie helps her to sip a little barley water while Auntie Edie holds the bowl of gruel. Throughout her final suffering she constantly apologizes for being a nuisance and never once complains. In the early hours of a cold day in August she dies in the front bedroom of the dutch-gabled house and is laid out in the same bed in which she gave birth to her three daughters.

Jilly is well enough to attend the funeral, along with Annie, Auntie Edie and the rest of the family. Louisa and I are unable to attend due to my contractual commitments in the theatre.

Miss McKirdy's coffin is carried into Dove's Funeral Chapel to the sound of a piper playing the beautiful lament, 'Flowers of the Forest', but as it leaves the tempo changes and she is sent on her final journey to the upbeat strains of the Highland Fling. Her two daughters accompany the body of their mother to the crematorium where they watch as her mortal remains glide silently into the furnace.

The Sisters at the convent have asked me to pay tribute to dear Miss McKirdy who is now with God. She was highly revered and loved by them.

Miss McKirdy was renowned for the excellence of her choral verse choirs at the Eistedfodds and for the entertainments she provided at the St Patrick's concerts in the Johannesburg city hall. She also produced plays and operettas and taught Highland dancing.

Miss McKirdy's enthusiasm and interest in all she did, coupled with hard work, ensured success in whatever role she chose, whether it be as wife, mother or teacher. She weathered the storms of life with a cheerful manner and her personality was such that she made a strong impression on all who dealt with her. We shall long remember her deep voice and regal manner, not forgetting her ever-present though rather battered suitcase and faithful Renault car. We thank God for her eighty years of vigorous life and the happy memories she has left us, not only of herself but, speaking as a parent, of our children excelling themselves through her demand for excellence.

May God bless you, Miss McKirdy, and may your soul rest in peace.

At roughly the same time as the funeral is taking place, Louisa takes my hand in hers and gently strokes it. We are sitting on the Brighton beachfront, looking out over the cloudy grey waters of the English Channel. We cannot hear the gentle soothing sound of waves on pebbles because of the deafening noise of traffic moving bumper to bumper along the Grand Parade but our hearts reach out over oceans and continents to the globe's furthest ends.

Auntie Edie's Wall of Prayer seems to be working as Jilly shows positive signs of making a recovery. Terry has returned home to nurse her and take over the running of the family. Then suddenly, after three months of 'reprieve', comes another devastating collapse. Auntie Edie writes to say that she will pay for Louisa and I to fly out to South Africa for Christmas.

We are all looking forward to seeing you both. Annie is preparing your old room for you. Don't get a shock when you see Jilly. Her hair has all fallen out so she wears a scarf. It will grow again. Morag's new baby is beautiful. Full of smiles. They call him Michael.
  Every good wish until we see you,
  Auntie Edie

On arrival at Jan Smuts we are met my Morag and her little family and the sight of my adorable great niece and nephew lightens my spirits. As we drive up outside Jilly's house I see her sitting on the verandah, a scarf tied tightly around her head. The gauntness of her face and lack of hair only emphasize her beautiful features. As I walk up the path to meet her, she smiles warmly and I see that she is missing one of her front teeth. She can hardly see out of her right eye now as the cancer has reached her brain. Under the garden chair on which she sits lies a plastic bowl covered with a small towel. This is for emergencies. Sometimes she cannot make it to the bathroom to be sick. Beside her, in a neat pile, are her Christian Science Books, Mary Baker Eddy's *Science and Health with Key to the Scriptures* and *Prose Works*.

Terry comes out to say, 'Howzit, duck-tail?' He looks slim and strong and they hold hands as she talks to me, smiling and nodding and asking all about my life in England. She is delighted by the news that my business venture is doing so well and that I am beginning to enjoy my life of freedom and independence.

She describes Mummy's funeral in minute detail and shows me a photograph of the simple floral tribute that she herself arranged and placed on Miss McKirdy's coffin with a card that said, 'With love from your three daughters'.

The subject of cancer is never mentioned as we giggle about the two remaining occupants of the dutch-gabled house and Annie's boyfriend whom Jilly describes as 'a bit creepy'. Apparently he has a penchant for covering every female in sight with wet but impassioned kisses. Jilly says it's a family joke that whenever he appears all the girls leap into the pool, whatever the weather, and refuse to come out until he's gone.

Jilly is also rather concerned that he might be after Annie's inheritance. We decide to set the wheels in motion to get a trust fund set up for her in order to ensure it's safety.

'You know what she's like,' says Jilly. 'She could just take everyone in the hospital to Durban for the weekend.'

'Or blow the lot on booze,' I add.

Auntie Edie is waiting at the fly-screen door when we draw up outside the dutch-gabled house. She rather resembles a scruffy old garden sparrow, tiny and frail with the odd wisp of white hair around her wizened face and a few brown stumps for teeth. However, her spirit is as strong as ever. 'Hallo, hallo, hallo,' she shouts through the door as we come down the path. 'Welcome to sunny South Africa. Just look at that Louisa, hasn't she grown! She's taller than you now, do you know that?'

It is a hot December day and as we step inside the house the smell of decay is overpowering. Even at a quick glance one can see that everything has been allowed to fall into a state of total disrepair. Annie and Auntie have been living here on their own since Mummy died.

'Auntie,' I say firmly, 'something has to be done about the condition of this house. We must get somebody to clean it up.'

'Och, don't be daft. There's nothing whatever the

293

matter with this place. It's lovely. You're too fussy, altogether,' she replies. 'And don't talk to me about having a servant, they're all a bunch of thieves and liars.'

'But what about Big Jeanie? She wasn't like that,' I say.

'Don't talk to me about HER,' says Auntie. 'That one stole all your mother's good silver and most of her jewellery.'

'That is a lot of rubbish, Auntie Edie,' I say. 'You know perfectly well what happened to Mummy's silver and jewellery.'

She gives me a fierce look and says, 'We're managing very nicely on our own and we don't need any help from anyone.'

'But Auntie,' I continue determinedly, 'there are masses of nice black women out there – kind, motherly women – who'd be only too happy to take care of you and this house and it wouldn't cost much.'

'They'll clean you out as quick as look at you. And that's the end of it. I don't want to talk about it any more.' And off she goes to fetch her radio and her *Path of Truth*.

'She's a bloody stubborn old woman,' I say to Louisa. 'She's like an old warthog that's got itself stuck in a hole. God knows, she's got more than enough money to pay for help. She must have thousands in that building society account of hers. What's she bloody saving it for?'

Louisa has a knack of looking at things with dis-passionate clarity at times. 'She's made her choice, so let us make ours,' she answers.

My friend has built a guest cottage in the garden of her home and she invites us to stay there. We make the excuse to Auntie that, as it's midsummer and very hot, Louisa will have a pool to swim in. I'm awash with guilt as I tell her because she looks so disappointed and sad. 'Och, just suit yourselves', she counters defensively, 'I'm not at all bothered.'

Selling the dutch-gabled house does seem to be the only solution. Jilly is dying and Annie has already telephoned to say that she hates Auntie Edie and refuses to live with her. She wants to move into a flat with Derek so will I please organize the wherewithal for her to do so.

Well, I cannot leave this incontinent old woman of ninety-two living by herself in a big house on the outskirts of Johannesburg and besides, I'm here now, so I might as well make the best of the time and get everything sorted out nice and tidy.

It should be easy but it isn't. Auntie Edie proves unbelievably obstinate about going into an old-age home. First days, then weeks pass as we plead and cajole, beg and threaten. We bring in neighbours and friends and lawyers and even the grand master of the masonic lodge but to no avail, she refuses to accept the notion of change. Oh, she listens and nods but when I try to get any sort of commitment out of her, she simply looks away and clears her throat.

With Louisa's help and that of my nieces and nephews, I set about disposing of the contents of the dutch-gabled house. Family photographs are carefully divided into three separate piles, one for each of Miss McKirdy's daughters. Pictures of Mummy and Daddy and family groups are divided evenly between us. Morag takes Jilly's pile down the road while Annie's and mine are left on Mummy's bed in the front room. Over the weekend Annie comes home from the hospital and when I go to collect my pictures on Monday morning, they have disappeared.

In a frantic state I drive out to the mental hospital to question Annie but she refuses to speak to me. Instead, she pulls the blankets over her head and will not answer any of my questions. I get the nurse to check her locker but they are not there. I search through the rubbish in the lane at the back of the house but they are not there either. Where the hell can they be? What has she done with them? As I cannot take any of the heavy old furniture back to England, these faded sepia photographs represent my inheritance and I am deeply disturbed by their loss.

Apart from the contents of 'Auntie's antique cupboard', most of which she gives to Sheila, there is almost nothing of value left in the house. Our trophies are donated to the Highland Dancing Association of the Transvaal, a charity collects tho old clothes and the hundreds of books, the furniture goes to auction and the badly out-of-tune piano is advertised in the evening paper.

Auntie Edie is now threatening to go and live alone in the stone cottage at Henley. But this, too, has been allowed to deteriorate into an overgrown 'ghost house' as her penny-pinching ways have now reached almost pathological proportions. It's as though she doesn't want anything that will improve the quality of her life, as though her comfort and her convenience are of no importance at all.

But of course she can't live there alone. She might be murdered in her bed or, worse still, have an accident and lie injured and alone on the floor for days.

We manage to persuade her to have a medical check-up and she only agrees because the doctor is a young woman from Glasgow. The report states that apart from incontinence she is as strong as an ox and could last for years.

Christmas day dawns hot and sunny. We are spending it at Jilly's. The yuletide party is to consist of Annie and Derek, Auntie Edie, Louisa and me and, of course, all the members of Jilly's family apart from Carol, who has emigrated to Australia with her journalist husband.

As Annie and Terry are both on the wagon, I shall be the only one drinking, and so on my arrival I hide my litre of Zonnebloem Riesling in the pantry behind the breadbin.

Around noon Gordon goes to collect Annie and Derek from the mental hospital but returns with only Annie. Apparently, Derek really meant it when he warned, 'Drink and it's over between us.' As a result of her surreptitiously slugging a can of Lion Lager at the hospital's carol-singing ceremony, he has categorically ended their affair.

Devastated, Annie is now hell-bent on seeking 'oblivium' and follows me wherever I go in the hope of laying her not-so-clean little hands on whatever alcohol I might have hidden away.

Jilly is sitting up in bed looking desperately ill but still managing to smile despite the horrific pain she is suffering. Her courage is almost unbelievable. Although practically consumed by cancer she is still determined to endure the pain without medication of any kind.

We all gather in her room and inevitably the chat gets round to that of relationships. When I ask Annie if she would like to get married, she replies after a moment's thought, 'Yes, I suppose so, but I'd rather have a brandy and coke.'

After our Christmas lunch of cold turkey and salads, Terry carries Jilly out into the garden to watch us all having fun in the swimming pool. He has presented her with a canary in a cage which he now fetches and puts on the table beside her chair. She tries to join in the laughter but when the pain becomes unbearable Terry picks her up and carries her back inside.

He is the only one in the family able to dress her cancerous wound without being sick. His big motor-mechanic's hands caress her emaciated body with almost unbearable tenderness. He loves her to distraction and she, too, has finally found it within herself to love him completely in return. Together they appear to have discovered a love neither of them dreamed possible.

It is early evening when I go in to kiss her goodbye. She is lying on the rumpled sheets with her eyes closed.

In a quiet voice she repeats over and over again, 'God is truth, God is beauty, God is love.'

On New Year's Eve the family gathers at Morag's home. Jilly arrives exhausted, having vomited throughout most of the car journey, and is carried into the spare bedroom where she is left alone to rest.

A few moments before midnight, I am suddenly overwhelmed by emotion and, rushing into the room, I almost scream at her, 'Oh God, China, please don't die. I can't bear it if you leave me.' Then I throw myself into her arms.

'I don't want to die,' she says with tears streaming down her face, 'I'm very scared.'

'I love you so much,' I sob, 'I've always loved you so much.'

'I have always loved you too,' she says, cradling me in her arms.

'I know we'll be together, for all eternity,' I say, 'but I don't want to live in a world without you.' She smiles and strokes my hair.

We can hear 'Auld Lang Syne' playing on the radio and, as the clock strikes twelve, we both know that this will be her last New Year.

> Should Auld acquaintance be forgot
> and never brought to mind;
> Should auld acquaintance be forgot,
> And Auld lang syne,
> And here's a hand my trusted friend
> And gie's a hand o' thine,
> We'll take a cup o' kindness yet
> For the sake of Auld Lang Syne.

Eventually the dutch-gabled house is sold over Auntie Edie's head and the electricity supply cut off. After a long, hard fight she finally accepts defeat and on a sunny afternoon in late January she emerges onto the verandah carrying her little transistor radio and a framed portrait of Uncle Billy in his Transvaal Scottish uniform. In her handbag is her building society book, her *Path of Truth* and a piece of white heather. Her war of independence is over. She has finally agreed to move into a residential hotel, albeit only on a temporary basis.

I unscrew the brass plate, bearing our family name, from off the front gate and then taking one last, final look at the dutch-gabled house with the four palm trees in the front garden, I climb into the back seat of Morag's waiting car.

Auntie Edie is wiping her eyes with an Eau de Cologne-soaked hanky. The sleeve of her dress has slipped and I can just see the strap of the old black petticoat resting on her soft, white skin. Clutching the pathetic remains of her worldly possessions she says in a small voice, 'I just wish I was dead.'

Our final day in South Africa is spent at Henley, a place of my childhood and of my dreams. This is my spiritual home to which my ashes will one day return in order that my dust may once again mingle with the dust of Africa.

Along the river, three properties from ours, many moons ago, a local archaeologist unearthed the remains of a prehistoric village and as children we used to run in and out of the labyrinth of passages once walked by peoples of an ancient civilization. Perhaps I was one of them. Perhaps in a previous lifetime I swam in the brown waters of the river, smelt the perfume of woodsmoke, heard the cooing of the doves and fell in love with the red earth. Perhaps that would explain my soul's attachment to this place.

On arrival at Jan Smuts airport, I concentrate solely on the details of departure. I haven't been to say 'good-bye' to Jilly — neither of us are up to that. We make do with a quick 'au revoir' on the telephone. The plane takes off into a terrifying electric storm and it feels as though my heart, like the aircraft, might just split in two.

299

It was really super hearing from you. Glad to hear that you are settling down after your hectic trip. I can well believe that you are looking forward to going to Kenya and the sun again. I too dislike black rainy days.

Mom spent last week here. It was hard work but I loved spending the time with her. She was wonderful with the kids, so patient. For some reason they call her Bobby instead of Granny.

It is amazing how quiet she is and yet she creates such a presence. I found the few days after she returned home so strange. It was as though I had lost a child. I miss her terribly and would love to nurse her all the time but it just isn't practical with the children being so little.

I have been in a very depressed state but am feeling better now. As you said in your letter – 'One day, when we can see the whole picture, perhaps it will make sense.' All I know is that this particular frame of the film is a very painful one.

Mom now needs constant physical help as she can no longer move on her own. On Wednesday she said she was very afraid of dying but had reached the stage when she no longer cared any more. The pain must be unbearable.

Auntie Edie is not too good. She is very bitter and keeps telling everyone how awful we've been to her. People have noticed a big deterioration in her. She is no longer the happy, optimistic woman we all knew. Maybe time will heal the hurt she feels. We certainly didn't mean to upset her, we only wanted to make sure she was properly looked after.

Anyway, she moved out of the hotel and in with her friend, Phylis, who lives a couple of doors down from Granny Mac's old house in Booysens. God knows how they have managed to fit her in as the house is pretty full already.

Daddy dropped into the hospital with some

300

cigarettes for Auntie Annie at the weekend. He says she is in a terrible state about the break-up with Derek and the house being sold. I don't know why, but she's blaming you for all that has happened and they've had to give her shock treatment again. Never a dull moment.

Derek phoned me and asked me to come and collect her things from his room in the boarding-house as he is in the middle of yet another nervous breakdown. Can you believe all this madness?

Grant is having a hard time with Mom's illness. He told me that he pulls socks over his ears to stop himself hearing her scream. Poor kid.

Write soon and tell us all about your filming in Kenya.

Tons of love,
Morag

Whilst on location in Kenya I meet up with an old friend from my acting days in Johannesburg. We haven't seen each other for more than ten years but sitting under the stars, sipping beer and swapping stories, our friendship is renewed. J. has done very well since leaving South Africa and moving to England where he is now highly thought of both as a writer and actor. He is tickled pink by my stories of life in Blankshire, and suggests that we team up and create a television series based on that period of my life.

'Good idea,' I say and change the subject.

'No seriously,' he says, 'I'll call you when we get back to England and we'll start.'

Miraculously, Jilly keeps going for another three months, and then in early April she is admitted to a hospice and given morphine. The family gathers around her bed and each in turn gives her their permission to die.

From the blinded eyes there is scarcely a flicker, but the cracked and bloodless lips still continue to affirm

God's Truth and Beauty and Love. A few moments more and then, with a tiny exhalation of breath, her soul vacates her withered body and zooms straight to heaven.

Jilly's funeral is held in the same church in which she and Terry were married. At about the same time as the hundreds of mourners packed into the little church are singing Jilly's favourite hymn, Louisa and I slide into a pew at St Martin's in the Field, Trafalgar Square. It isn't long before we are giggling helplessly. A demented looking man in a tartan scarf is tuning the great organ and two tramps are snoring loudly in the row behind us, creating a cacophony of sound perfectly in tune with Jilly's sense of music and humour.

Yes, we did lose a very precious person when we lost our China Doll. It is a tragedy, really. I miss her, naturally, but the one I cannot get over is Mummy. To me, she was the outstanding member of our family. I just cannot get over her death. She gave me so much love. No other member of the family loved me like her. I am so privileged to have been the one to be with her at the end.

She gave so much love to her three daughters but I think that I am the only one who appreciated what she did for us. I have no regrets that I stood by her to the very end.

I am not at all happy living with Auntie in this back room. Phylis is kind to me but I pray every day that I will be able to move into a boarding-house soon. As you know, Auntie doesn't wash or look after herself. She smells of urine all the time and she treats me like a three-year-old child. She is so possessive, it is unbearable.

Did you take Mummy's engagement ring with you when you left? She gave it to ME, you know, the year before she died and I would like it back, please.

I miss Derek terribly. There is no sign of a

reconciliation. I was such a fool to lose the man I love for a can of beer. Alcohol is a terrible thing. I am so lonely without him.

Please pray that I can get away from Auntie and be on my own.

P.S. I wear Mummy's wedding ring all the time. I would never sell it, no, not even for a beer.

Annie

Two weeks after Jilly's death, J. contacts me and we arrange to begin work on the comedy series. He is fascinated by the idea of a white South African working as a domestic servant and he starts asking questions about my childhood. Flipping back through the pages of my memory, two stories leap out and demand to be told. The first is the incident of the marriage licence in the Hillbrow police station and the second is the hiding I got from my mother for missing her. The next thing I know I am sobbing my heart out. The Great Grief has begun and we are both aware that this is no longer a comedy series but the beginnings of a book.

My horoscope for the week ending 18 April 1986 reads 'You are entering a period of great change, from which you will finally emerge stronger and wiser'.

I am awash in every sense of the word. Not only do I howl for hours on end during our writing sessions but I become obsessed with washing clothes. My behaviour is not unlike that of an alcoholic in that I keep excusing myself but instead of pouring a secret drink I fill the machine with yet another load of washing. As I watch the garments going round and round in the soapy water so my thoughts go round and round, analysing, going over, remembering, discovering, as gradually my grief rises and rises, in a never ending flow, from the very centre of my being.

J is wonderful to work with because not only has he taken on the role of writer, therapist and friend

303

but, displaying almost unbelievable patience, gradually draws my 'voice' out of me encouraging me to 'fuck the grammar for the time being and just tell the story'. We also manage to piss ourselves with laughter.

Good News! I moved into a small hotel in Hillbrow. I have a nice clean room and the food is very good. It wasn't working at Phylis's what with Auntie Edie and eighteen cats. Too much!

I am so happy and feel I am my own boss now. The lawyer in charge of my trust fund pays my board and I have my pension to live on. I have still never set eyes on Derek. He is not interested. I am still in love with him but there is no chance. I have made a few friends at the hotel. They are quite nice.

At last I have Blue Boy, my budgie, back with me. He is so clever. He says 'budgie boy' with a Yorkshire accent. The woman who looked after him is from there.

I bought some daffodils the other day for my room. It made me think of you two in London.

I never see the rest of the family. For some reason they are not interested in me.

When you sold the house, did you sell my medals and cups? No-one seems to know what happened to them – I am very disappointed because they are all I have got to show for my hard work. Write soon. Love to Louisa.

Annie

When her friend, Phylis, can no longer cope, Auntie Edie finally accepts her fate and goes into the Eventide Old Age Home where the nurses deposit her, screaming and kicking, into a bath of hot, soapy water. She dies clean, on Easter Monday.

Her funeral is well attended as Auntie Edie was much loved. The man from the School of Truth performs the ceremony and it is while the tributes are being read that Morag notices three 'penguins' sitting in the congregation and thinks how odd that is as Auntie Edie had nothing to do with the convents. Later, when they shake Morag's hand in the condolence queue, they ask where Miss McKirdy's daughters are and she has to tell them that Miss McKirdy was a spinster and had no children. 'But aren't you Jilly?' they ask. 'No,' she replies, unable to bring herself to tell them that not only are they at the wrong funeral but that Jilly, too, is dead.

Sadly, neither Annie nor Terry are in a fit state to take their places in the family pew as both are drinking heavily. It is two years since Jilly's death and her family are in disarray. Terry doesn't seem to care whether he lives or dies and spends weeks at a time passed out in the front seat of his truck parked in a street beside the Radium beer hall. Carol has returned to Australia, Gordon is 'walking the beaches' somewhere in the Cape and the two younger children, Sheila and Grant, are left to fend for themselves.

In April 1989, almost three years to the day after Jilly's death, Terry is found slumped at the wheel of his truck in the parking lot of the Halfway House Hotel between Pretoria and Johannesburg. At the age of fifty-one he has sustained a massive heart attack. His death comes just two months after that of his brother.

Homeless, motherless and loverless, Annie is now presenting a real problem. Jilly's children are trying to rebuild their shattered lives and have nowhere to put an alcoholic, manic-depressive, schizophrenic aunt.

Auntie Annie is out of hospital and staying in some dreadful boarding house in Hillbrow. It is difficult to believe that the two of you are sisters. You have such a love of beautiful things and she looks and lives like a bloody hobo. On Friday I picked her up to take her to the Post Office to get her pension and to say that she was in cloud cuckooland is the understatement

of the century. She was on an incredible high. She
never stopped chatting and combing her hair. She
said she had been up since 4.30 in the morning,
picking roses to prove that life is eternal.

She couldn't find the key to the cupboard in which
her pension book was locked and so she and all the
other residents decided to break down the door. By
the time we reached the Post Office she no longer
had the pension book which I think she threw out
of the car window. Every time we passed a booze
shop she wept.

Eventually she was in such a state, I decided to
take her to the hospital where they admitted her
immediately. I phoned yesterday and was told that
they had her on the maximum medication but it was
not having any effect and that they were starting
her on shock treatment again. If she refused they
would have her certified and committed. The whole
situation is so sad I just don't know what to do about
it. Maybe one day we will understand why we as a
family have experienced so much sorrow.

Tons of love,
Morag

The riddle of what Mummy said to Annie, in the cabin
when she was twelve years old, continues to haunt me.

Then one day in early 1990, driving to Bristol with
a friend, the conversation turns from what my mother
could have said to how children are never believed
by adults as evidenced by my mother's reluctance to
believe Annie when she was attacked by the man on
the golf course. 'I can just hear her saying, "Well,
you know what a vivid imagination that girl has" —'
Suddenly I stop in mid-sentence.

'THAT'S IT!' we both scream at the same time, and
the car nearly swerves off the motorway. I rush on
excitedly, 'Oh my God, I can just picture it. Annie
comes running into the cabin, discovers Mummy and

the captain in some compromising position, and then is told that what she is seeing is nothing more than a figment of her imagination.'

Her sense of reality must have done a complete flip. Could it be that from that moment on she was only able to make sense of things by taking refuge in unreality? Did Miss McKirdy sacrifice her daughter in order to save herself?

When I think of Annie, cowering in the corner of a lock-up cell, her huge brown eyes vacant with fear, her mind numbed with drugs, her heart frozen with hate, I wonder if this is where the years of her 'mental illness' began.

This is not something I can possibly write to her about. Or discuss over the telephone. It will have to wait until I see her again and we can talk face to face.

I never get the chance. On 19 July 1990, she disappears from the mental hospital. Morag telephones me with the news the following day. My immediate reaction is anger followed by frustration. What has she gone and done now, just when so many things are beginning to make sense? Typical bloody Annie!

When I finally speak to someone at the hospital on the telephone, I am told that she went for a walk after breakfast and has not been seen since. The matter has been reported to the Krugersdorp police and as far as the hospital authorities are concerned it is now out of their hands. Besides, she goes on to say, 'So many patients go missing every week that they don't even bother to count them anymore.'

'But that's outrageous!' I shout. (God, how I wish I could keep my 'cool' at times like this. My Scorpio passion always gets the better of me.)

'I agree,' comes the reply, 'and I've written to the authorities but they don't take any notice. The policy of this hospital is that if a patient decides to abscond there is nothing we can do about it.'

'But surely, you have some security in that place, surely there is someone on the gate who can say whether she went one way or another when she walked out?'

'No,' says the superintendent, 'there are no fences or guards. Patients can come and go as they please.'

'But she was committed into your care, by the courts,' I continue. 'Surely that means something?'

'We are responsible only so long as a patient is on the premises; once they leave it is no longer our concern.'

'Will you please tell me what kind of emotional state she was in prior to her "absconding"?' I ask.

'She had been in the lock-up section for several days before she disappeared but her psychiatrist felt that she was much improved and therefore had ordered that she be returned to the open ward.'

'Does her psychiatrist think that she may have committed suicide?'

'Well, she had spoken about "wishing it was all over" but then she's been talking like that for years so no-one took it very seriously.'

'I must say,' I continue, 'you don't sound very concerned.'

'That is not the case at all,' she retorts. 'Everyone is very sad that she has gone because she is a very loved person. Even the men from the workshops went searching for her, because they know and like her very much. And I, myself, am very sad about this business.'

'Not half as sad as I am,' I say.

Through the generosity of a friend, who forks out over a thousand pounds for my airfare to South Africa, a flight is booked and I prepare to leave.

A friend suggests that I consult a medium and so the day before my departure I book an appointment. As she cuts the cards, the psychic energy in the room is making every hair on my head and body stand on end. I am shaking as she says, 'I see a terrible tragedy, a catastrophe, the beginning of something and the end of it. I see plotting, intrigue and cover-ups. A man with ginger-coloured hair is involved. I see police, doctors and lawyers. I see a long rocky road and I see the need for balance between head and heart. I see protection and ultimate victory. I see that you are going on a sad and disturbing journey to a place in the sun. Does any of this make sense to you?'

This woman, who has never visited South Africa, then goes on to give me, as I will discover later, an almost photographically accurate description of the landscape around the hospital. She tells me to look for a military establishment, a church or chapel, a hole with water in it, mountains in a northwesterly position, a rocky path with thorn trees on one side and barbed-wire on the other, an overflow, a watershed, something that glitters but is not gold, for the number six and for many other things. She also tells me that there is intrigue, conspiracy and dark forces at work within the hospital itself. She says that I will meet with opposition but that I should maintain my balance at all times and simply allow myself to go with the flow. But she cannot say, for certain, what has become of Annie other than her being in a state of confusion and panic. 'She can't breathe, can't breathe, can't breathe.'

Striding across the tarmac at Jan Smuts Airport, I am suddenly struck by the realization that the dutch-gabled house and its occupants are no longer there. The thought almost makes me faint, but with an enormous effort I push it from my mind and hurry to meet Morag and the kids in the arrival hall. The warmth of their greeting acts like a balm to my wound and in no time we are cracking jokes and laughing hysterically.

After a quick cup of tea and catch-up on family news, I play her the tape and she says, 'I think I know the place this woman's talking about. Let's try and find it and then we can visit the hospital afterwards.' With that she and I pile into her Suzuki jeep.

On the main highway, near the mental institution, we

see a sign which reads 'Army Commando' and turning off onto a dirt road we hump and bump our way across some appalling potholes until we come to a barbed-wire fence and a guard post where two young soldiers are standing talking to one another.

'Excuse me,' I say, rolling down the car window and waving to get their attention, 'I would like to speak to your commanding officer.'

'That's me,' says the better-looking of the two, as he comes over to my side of the jeep.

'Well, you see,' I plunge straight in, 'my sister has disappeared from the mental hospital over there,' pointing across the veld, 'and a psychic in London has given me a description of some kind of water-hole near a church. Would you have any idea where that could be?'

Without batting an eyelid at the somewhat eccentric content of my speech, he calmly answers, 'Ja, I know exactly the place she's talking about. It's an old, disused mine shaft, over there by the township.' He points to a place somewhere in the distance. 'It's filled with water now. It's called Blougat.' The other soldier has joined us and he nods in agreement.

'Ja, I'm sure that's the place because there's a Catholic church right nearby.'

'Thanks,' I say, returning my head to the jeep like a tortoise to its shell. 'We'll go and have a look.'

'Tell you what,' says the officer, 'I'll take you there myself just as soon as I've finished this,' and he indicates some paperwork he is holding in his hand.

A few minutes later we are bumping back along the potholed road, trying not to choke from the dust whipped up by his speeding car.

Recrossing the main highway, we take a minor road on the other side of it which leads down to a bridge over a stream bordered on either side by tall bluegum trees. We park the vehicles and climb out.

'Blougat's through here,' he says, indicating a path

which leads between the trees. The path is rocky and difficult to walk on as it winds its way through the undergrowth and then, almost without warning, breaks out into open country. We follow it through tall, lion-coloured grass until it becomes a rocky ledge bordered by thorn trees on one side and barbed-wire on the other.

Suddenly the soldier stops and points to something down below and for the first time we realize that we are standing on the edge of a precipice with the rock-face sheering away to reveal a large pool of water glinting in the noonday sun.

'That's Blougat down there,' says the young officer.

'That huge hole was once a mine shaft?' I ask.

'What were they mining for?' asks Morag.

'Gold, of course,' says our guide. 'But they didn't find any. Only fool's gold.'

I look at Morag. 'It glitters but it's not gold,' I say.

As we stand looking down at Blougat, the peaks of the Magaliesberg lie precisely to the northwest and we can clearly see the spire of the Catholic church a short distance away in the township.

Having established the spot we drive to the hospital. Here we are met with anything but friendly assistance. We are informed that Annie's psychiatrist is at present unavailable and that the superintendent is away attending a conference.

We sit and wait. Finally, we are ushered into an office where we are met by an extremely nervous looking man who says, 'Look, I am only your sister's psychiatrist and cannot be held responsible for what has happened to her.' The man is clearly in such a state that one almost feels sorry for him. However, when he warns us not to question any patients or staff as this would constitute a breach of the Mental Health Act, our pity soon turns to outrage.

We ask for her Book of Life, an identification document every white South African is obliged to carry by

311

law, in order that we may use the photograph in it for publicity in the newspapers.

We are refused. 'Sorry,' he says, 'but this document has been placed in our safekeeping and we cannot just hand it over to any Tom, Dick or Harry.' When I point out that, far from being any Tom, Dick or Harry, I am her closest relative and have flown six thousand miles to find her, he shakes his head and repeats that it is his responsibility to see that her book is kept under lock and key.

'Perhaps,' I say, 'if you'd taken as much care of her as you have of that damned book, she might be here now.' After a protracted argument we finally succeed in getting a photocopy of her identification papers and this time we head for the police station.

South Africa is close to a state of civil war as factional fighting rages between the ANC and Inkatha and the township near the hospital has been the scene of some horribly savage fighting. The police and the army are on full alert. The disappearance of one mental patient is scarcely going to cause them concern. There are so many people missing in this brutalized country that one more won't make much difference.

We park the Suzuki jeep under the shade of a syringa tree and make our way to the charge office where we are ushered in by a smiling black policeman. A pimply white youth behind the counter asks what he can do for us and I tell him that we wish to speak to his commanding officer. He picks up the telephone and within minutes we are ushered into an office on the other side of the building.

After a great deal of polite handshaking we explain about Annie's disappearance and ask to see the hospital's report. This, it transpires, has been incorrectly filed and has therefore lain unlooked at for over a week. We all wait in silence as the commanding officer reads the details and then asks, 'What exactly do you want us to do for you?'

'We want a team of divers,' Morag says with the kind of straightforwardness that her mother was renowned for, 'to make a thorough search of Blougat.'

The police officer explains about the acute shortage of manpower 'what with the troubles and everything', but promises to take the matter to the colonel to see what can be organized. Satisfied that we have done everything in our power to get a search going, Morag, Sheila and I return home to prepare the family reunion dinner.

The following morning, the three of us make another sortie into the area accompanied by our soldier. Driving in his Chevrolet with a machine-gun lying across his lap, we enter the no-go area of the township. Hundreds of black, hate-filled eyes watch us suspiciously as we get out of the car and begin to show Annie's photograph to a group of children outside the mission church.

Their sullen silence tells us that we stand little chance of receiving co-operation in what amounts to a war zone and, as a belligerent looking mob begins to converge on our vehicle, we beat a tyre-spinning retreat.

Once more, we head for Blougat where we follow the rocky path through the dense undergrowth until it reaches the river.

While picking our way across it by means of stepping stones, Morag suddenly lets out a cry and points to a tin of deodorant spray bobbing near the water's edge.

'Sixth Sense,' she shouts, 'it's her Sixth Sense!'

'What?' Sheila and I ask bemused. 'What Sixth Sense?'

'The name of the deodorant,' she cries. 'It was Auntie Annie's favourite. I took her a can and she liked it so much she asked me to get her some more. But I couldn't, because they no longer make it. And now look, there's the identical can lying in the water.'

'But our sixth sense is intuition,' I say. 'It's our psychic sense.'

We have reached the opposite bank and we follow the flow of the river as it makes its way over rocks and stones to form a largish pool which could be described as a watershed. The sun is really hot now, despite it being winter in the Transvaal, and we are all sweating profusely as we clamber over the rain-starved vegetation and start our descent to the ground below. The overflow from the pool cascades over a wall of stone, creating a waterfall which tumbles down over more big rocks until it reaches its final resting place, Blougat, the Blue Hole.

Having reached the grassy bank on the water's edge, we see to our utter amazement that painted on the largest rock, in big, white letters are the words LOVE IS . . .? and beneath that is written, quite clearly, the number six.

The next thing I notice is that the trees growing in profusion around the disused mineshaft are mimosa trees, Annie's favourite, while on the opposite side to where we are standing, Sheila points out the word VICTOR written on the rock face. It seems strange that none of these things had been visible from the path above. Are they messages or merely twisted interpretations of our overstretched imaginations? Whatever they are, all four of us confess to feeling a sense of something unlike anything we have ever experienced before.

Two days later, a full-scale police operation is mounted. Hundreds of black and white police, male and female, comb the khaki-coloured hills, while a team of divers prepare to search the dark, mysterious waters of the disused mineshaft. As the frogmen disappear beneath its surface, firmly attached to safety ropes, Morag, Sheila and I take up positions of vigil along the path on the precipice overlooking it. There are rocks and stones and boulders everywhere and the winter sun is beating down on the tinder-box dry earth.

The sound of a deep voice startles me out of my reverie. Standing beside me is the colonel, a good-looking man in his mid-forties, tanned and well built. After wiping his hand on a white cotton hanky, he extends it to clasp mine in a firm grasp. 'Hello there. How's it going with you?'

'Not too bad,' I say, warming to his easy manner.

'Ag, it's a bad business this,' he says.

'Yes it is,' I agree. We watch the proceedings from our vantage point above Blougat. Beneath us the divers are laughing and calling to each other as they move around the sides of the old mineshaft. The noonday sun travelling overhead suddenly catches the surface of the water and the colonel and I are momentarily blinded by an explosion of golden light.

'Do you miss the sun, in England?' he says.

'I do,' I say. 'Very much.'

'Why did you go to live there?' he asks, shielding his eyes.

This is a tricky one. Right now I need this man and his police force, so I can hardly say, 'Because of something that once happened in a police station over twenty years ago.' Instead, I smile and say, 'Because I didn't like apartheid.'

He laughs and says, 'Ag, but apartheid's nearly finished, so now you can come back home and live here again.'

I shake my head and look across to the blue peaks of the Magaliesberg. 'It's not as easy as that,' I say. 'I've made a new life for myself in England. I think it's too late to put the clock back now.'

A shout comes from the men below. 'We'd better go down,' he says, holding out his hand to offer me support. We clamber down the hillside, slipping and sliding on the stony, dry veld. We are both covered in red dust by the time we reach the bottom.

The divers have discovered a large quantity of dynamite sticks which they mistook for salami and which they were throwing at one another underwater. For them, the whole episode amounts to nothing more than a day spent enjoying themselves in the sun.

Finally, the fruitless search is called off when the sun starts to sink behind the ochre-coloured hills. We make our way home, tired and depressed.

That night there is very little laughter around the dinner table. The unfillable hole left by Annie's disappearance is beginning to be felt. In silence, we sit listening once more to the tape lest some clue remain overlooked.

Because we are not entirely satisfied with the way in which the divers conducted themselves, we request that another team be sent down into the dark waters of Blougat. But again, the search renders nothing and we sense that the colonel and his men's patience is wearing a bit thin.

'Annie!' I scream that night lying on my bed, 'Where the hell are you?'

We now decide to consult another psychic. Jean comes to us highly recommended and a week later I am sitting in her pleasantly furnished sitting-room while she holds in her hands the hairbrush surreptitiously removed from Annie's locker by one of the more accommodating staff at the hospital.

'This person is not in spirit,' she says. 'Otherwise, this brush would feel cold, and it is distinctly warm to the touch.'

'Can you give me any clue as to the whereabouts of the owner of the brush?' I ask.

'She is near water and with a community of nuns or monks or some such similar group of people,' she replies.

'Oh my God,' I say, starting to feel as though I am going mad myself.

'You have no need to worry,' she says. 'She is very happy and enjoying a long rest. She is very tired.'

'I can't make head nor tail of all this,' I say. 'We've

had throbbing heads, mountain ranges, all that glitters is not gold and now monks. I just don't know what to think any more.'

'Well,' she says, 'perhaps you would like to consult someone else. I can recommend a man who is excellent at this sort of work and I shall be only too happy to give you his telephone number.'

This time I am accompanied by Morag and Gordon as we arrive at the home of a tall, Mediterranean-looking man by the name of Joseph. His rather funereal appearance belies a warm and compassionate personality and, feeling sufficiently all right about the proposed seance, we take our places around the black mahogany dining table. 'Well,' he says gazing at the cards laid out before him on the shiny surface, 'she is very happy and in love and has no desire to be found by you or anyone else at all. In fact, she almost regards you as the enemy.'

'Oh,' I say, feeling suitably stung by his remark, 'that's nice!'

He then goes on to recite the details of an extraordinarily convoluted plot involving members of the hospital staff. Dark men and ginger men and dark women and blond women and people blackmailing chemists and medication being smuggled out and inheritances being promised and safe houses and love affairs and bad men and good men and their female counterparts and possibly black magic.

Promising to read the cards on a daily basis and to keep us informed by telephone, he ushers us out into the chill night air. In a state of stupor we drive home in almost total silence.

Days slide into weeks as we battle to get media coverage. No-one seems remotely interested in running the story. In a country like South Africa life is cheap.

Eventually, Annie's picture and a small piece on her disappearance appear on the front page of the *Johannesburg Star*. Suddenly newspapers throughout the country are printing articles on the number of people who have gone missing from mental institutions. I am astounded that hundreds of patients have disappeared from Annie's hospital in the last five years, and questions are being asked in parliament. This leads to a television station featuring Annie's story in prime viewing time, but despite this extensive coverage not a single clue emerges to assist us in the search. The trail appears to have gone completely cold.

No doubt because of all this, every attempt to elicit more information from the hospital authorities is met with the same reply. 'In accordance with the Mental Health Act we are not allowed to supply any information regarding a patient at this hospital, irrespective of whether the patient has absconded or not. No, we're sorry but all medical reports are confidential and cannot be released, in fact will never be released. By the same token, we cannot give any details of the names of the drugs a patient is prescribed or in what quantity they were administered. No, it is not permitted to talk to or question a member of staff or a patient and should any unauthorized person be caught doing this, they will be immediately removed from the premises of this hospital. No, the police do not have a right to conduct an investigation without the full consent and permission of the superintendent. Under the provisions of the Mental Health Act a mental hospital cannot be investigated.'

We are beaten before we begin. The subject, it would seem, is closed. Annie has simply disappeared into thin air.

After two more weeks in which Joseph's psychic scenario becomes ever darker and weirder, I decide to return to England.

This time there is no farewell visit to my beloved Henley. For as long as I can remember, Auntie Edie had promised that I would inherit that acre of sacred (to me anyway) ground but just before her death, no doubt believing that I had totally betrayed her, she changed her will and left the property to Sheila, Jilly's youngest daughter, who sold it to buy a home for herself and Grant nearer to Johannesburg.

On my arrival home my spirit moves into a very dark place. I am angry and frightened at having been deserted, at having been left alone in an empty house while the rest of the family have moved somewhere else. At times, I feel as though I no longer have the energy to hold onto life, and yet at the same time I am obsessed with the fear of my own death.

One morning, I wake having had this dream. Jilly, Annie and I are doing the conga along a road. Jilly leads, then Annie, then me. Suddenly I am standing on the edge of a precipice looking down on a six-lane highway along which are thundering trucks and juggernauts. I am afraid to step off into nothing but Jilly who is already halfway across looks back over her shoulder and says, 'If you believe there's a road, there's a road.' Summoning up all my courage, I step off the edge and discover that I can walk on air but as I reach the middle I lose faith and start to sink. When I am close enough to the highway to hear the rumble of the traffic, I say to myself, 'Come on, look what's happening to you. Get your faith back before it's too late.' I breathe deeply and, like a helium balloon, rise again to the higher level. Jilly has gone and so has Annie and I don't remember getting to the other side.

Having attended none of the funerals of those I have lost, having seen no corpses, no coffins, no hearses; in other words, never having looked death in the face, I now realize the necessity of doing just that, if I am to survive at all.

Epilogue

Conversation With A Dead Mother

I wasn't at your funeral, Mum, so I never really said goodbye. It has always worried me that I didn't cry when you died. Grief should be expressed. I said at the time that I had done my crying when you were alive but now all these years later, sitting here at my own private funeral clutching a bunch of your favourite flowers, iceland poppies, I realize that that is not true.

You know, Mum, I remember the world lit up when you came home. When you weren't there it was as if we were all waiting for something to happen. I hated Auntie Edie and Lena Mashlangu only because they weren't you.

But I don't remember you ever coming through the door and taking me in your arms and loving me. You never came down to my size and looked at me and talked TO me. You were always on the move, going somewhere, giving orders, organizing things. Wherever you were running to or whatever you were running from, this little child was left feeling very unimportant and neglected.

'Nonsense,' I can hear you say, 'you were like Topsy. You just grew'd. You never gave any trouble, you just got on with life.'

I had to get on with it, Mum. I didn't have any choice. If I had complained you'd have given me a lecture instead of lifting me onto your lap and kissing me and telling me that you loved me. I can see myself now, at a very young age, maybe two or three years old, hanging onto the gates at the top of the driveway, waiting for you. It's funny but I still experience terrible feelings of anxiety and fear whenever I wait for someone I love.

I shall remember to my last breath sitting squashed up beside you in the front seat of our car and feeling the warmth of your fur-coat and smelling your perfume, Evening in Paris. I would say my prayers quickly and then snuggle up, wishing with all my heart that the journey would never end.

I loved consoling you and being your tower of strength. Like the time we stood at the fly-screen door and watched Daddy weave his way drunkenly up the garden path. 'Oh God, how will he ever manage?' you said, your voice sounding small and scared.

'God will look after him, Mummy,' I told you.

'You are a wonderful child,' you said. 'I really don't know what I would do without you.'

You said the same thing to me when you made me go in the ambulance and sign Annie's committal papers. You told the psychiatrist that all of your three girls were brought up exactly the same. That's not how Jilly and I saw it. We never stood a chance when Annie was around. Jilly used to say she didn't care but I'm sure she did.

I see now that getting involved with a married Catholic whose children you taught at the convent and then leaving South Africa were ways of getting back at you, of levelling the score. I can also understand why you treated me the way you did whenever I returned to the country and the mother you felt I had deserted. My own years of motherhood have taught me much about the pain of loving.

Although you were such a defender of truth and justice, you never saw the iniquity of the apartheid system. You just accepted it as the law of the land. The closest you came to any kind of criticism was to say 'poor devils' as we drove in our car past the endless queues of black people waiting for their buses to take them home to the townships. Daddy called those buses 'green mambas' and showed little compassion for the gaunt-faced men, women and children shivering in the freezing Transvaal cold. Like so many whites, you salved your conscience by giving a *bonsela* to the boys and girls who brought your tea at the various convents. I think our servants were treated as fairly as the unfair system allowed but like all the other white madams you harped on endlessly about their ingratitude. The women who worked for you may not have liked you, but I'm sure they respected you. You were a person who commanded respect.

On three occasions you touched me to the very depths of my being. One was six months after Daddy died. We were on our way to Durban and we stopped for petrol at a small town. You were being particularly irritating and I stomped off to the lavatory. I turned around to see what the hell had happened to you and there you were, standing in the middle of the dusty forecourt, clutching your handbag with an expression of total terror on your face. You didn't seem to know who you were, where you were or what you were doing. At that precise moment, I knew that Daddy's death had suddenly hit you and how much you loved and missed him. I also knew, for the first time in my life, how vulnerable you were.

Then there was the time I took you to the General Hospital for a check-up because you were falling down and injuring yourself. The doctor suggested that you might have had a mild stroke. 'Such rubbish!' you said, your blue eyes blazing. 'There's nothing the matter with me.' Very gently he asked you to walk in a straight line across his office. Summoning all your will, you rose majestically to your feet and, with your head held high and your chin thrust proudly forward, you placed one shaky foot in front of the other. Suddenly your arms began to swing rhythmically at your sides as though, somewhere, in the distance, you could hear the sound of bagpipes playing 'Scotland the Brave'. Then, like some Celtic matriarch, you swept across the floor in a style so magnificent that he and I felt inspired to rise to our own feet and applaud.

Later, sitting in the back of the car, you were so quiet that I turned around to see if you were all right. Your sad, blue eyes gazed vacantly out of the window but you couldn't have seen any of the trees and houses that we passed because of the tears spilling from them and rolling down your sunken cheeks. How I loved you at that moment.

You've been gone for years now and I'm still as confused about you as I ever was. During the writing of this book, I have gone from tearing your picture into shreds and stamping on the bits to a kind of empty sadness.

Now as I sit here trying to say goodbye, I can only ask you to help me write these last few lines.

Suddenly you are no longer dead, but alive in me because I am your daughter. I carry as much of you within me as my daughter will carry of me within her. Good and bad.

It seems the time has now come to let go of the past, and to forgive and set free. For it is only by doing that, that I, too, can forgive myself and in turn be forgiven. The process is cyclical.

I know that in my last hours I will call out to you, as you cried out to Granny Mac. And I know you'll be there.

I once told a friend that I regarded the world as a very safe place. She smiled and said, 'You got that from your mother.' What greater compliment can I pay you. Goodbye Mum.

Conversation With A Dead Father

I was at your funeral, Dad, and I did say a proper goodbye to you but I couldn't possibly leave you out of the epilogue. Incidentally, it was just as well that you were dead on that occasion because Uncle Rob sang the hymns with such gusto that, had you not been, I'm sure you would have climbed out of your coffin and clobbered him.

Holding you in my arms just after your death has to be one of the happiest memories of my life but it wasn't until almost a year later that my grief was finally expressed. I was on a double-decker bus and an elderly man slipped on the stairs and cut his head open. I went to his assistance and, as I smoothed his blood-soaked white hair, I was suddenly overwhelmed by a feeling of such loss that I thought my insides had fallen out. I literally howled in pain. Poor man! He must have been very confused.

Sometimes, sitting in the sun, I remember how we used to creep up behind your deck-chair on Sunday afternoons in the back garden and decorate your hair with garlands of nasturtiums and rose petals. We would pee ourselves laughing as you smote the air and shook your head and spat out all manner of imagined irritations. I wonder, were you really asleep? Or did the clown in you love to make us laugh?

Like all comics, you had your tragic side which was never more evident than when you were drunk, both nasty drunk and sad drunk. At times like that you seemed so let down and betrayed by yourself. I remember you saying, 'I am so mad at myself, I could kick myself around the house.' I know that feeling very well indeed.

Despite the tempestuous nature of your relationship with Mummy, I think you two did love each other a great deal. It's funny, you know, but looking back, you were far softer and much more 'the mother' than Mummy ever was. She was 'the man' in our household which probably accounts for the fact that we three girls had our viewpoint on men badly abused.

A couple of years after your death, I dreamt that you came to see me at Henley and you arrived through a bust of Beethoven. You looked wonderfully well and chatted happily, telling me what a pleasant place the hereafter was but how it was necessary to go through customs before entering it. Then you announced that it was time for you to return and asked if I would assist you by creating velocity.

Robert, who was sleeping beside me, woke with a shock to discover me sitting up in bed, furiously banging my knees together. When he asked me what I was doing, I replied disdainfully, 'Getting Daddy back to the other world, what does it look like, for heaven's sake!'

So now, Tubby Tilkins, with a quick knee bang and an au revoir I'll do just that. See you at the customs post.

Conversation With A Dead Granny

I've come to your funeral, Granny Mac, carrying a small posy of cuttings. There's a bit of geranium, a sprig or two of mint, some thyme and a few stems of ivy. I always assumed it was because you were far too Scottish to buy plants at a garden centre that you took cuttings from other people's gardens, but maybe it was because you didn't think plants should be bought and sold. I can see you now, at Henley, in your floral cotton pinafore, bending down to check the soil and debud a plant or two in the process. In all honesty, I think I have you to blame for my flower-thieving ways and my obsessive love of all plants and flowers.

Like you, I too love dogs and babies and auction sales. To this day I laugh at the story of you and your neighbour sitting in Barnetts saleroom when the auctioneer shouted 'Sold to Mrs Lipshitz in the front row' and she jumped up and shouted back 'De name is Lips vitout de Shitz, tank you!'

You could be so kind and generous and honest and strong.

And you could also be domineering and small-minded and cantankerous and cruel. But when it came to mending a bird's broken wing or cuddling a child on your ample lap you were everything a grandmother should be – strong and wise and warm.

Granny Mac, medicine woman of the clan, please continue to guide and protect me always.

327

Conversation With A Dead Aunt

Over the years you grew into a kind, broad, big personality, largely as a result of Granny's death and the teachings of the School of Truth. In fact, as an old woman, people really adored you, especially little children. They gathered around your piano in droves, knowing you always had two things for them — time and peppermints.

In many ways, you were more of a mother to me than my own mother ever was. For ten years your letters and affirmations of God's love kept me going in my darkest moments. Your loyalty to me during the years of the Great Isolation earned you my undying love and respect. I never meant to hurt you, Auntie, I only ever wanted to help. Please forgive me. You were always gracious to Robert and you adored Louisa. I can see you now jigging her up and down on your lap to the tune of the Highland Fling. She loved you too, very much.

> *Anty panty, I've lost my anty panty*
> *I lost her in the Troongate*
> *And I don't know where to go*

328

Conversation With A Dead Sister

I should not have missed your funeral. It might have helped me to accept the reality of your death although I don't think that I will ever get over losing you. When you died, so did part of me.

On the pew beside me I have a bunch of garden roses, pink and red and yellow, fragrant and freshly cut. You always loved your garden even though you spent so little time in it. Your whole life was a race against the clock. You must have known that you had so much to do and so little time to do it in.

From the time I was a little girl, I looked up to you in every possible way. You were my big sister, my heroine, my princess, my saint and my goddess. I thought you the most beautiful, the most clever, the most just, the most honest, the most strong, the most clean and the most absolutely perfect person I had ever met. I couldn't find anything wrong with you and I still can't.

But you must have had a dark side, otherwise you wouldn't have been human. Sometimes I think that the more you denied your body, the more it demanded to be acknowledged and the more you suppressed your emotions, the more they fought to be free.

What I do know is that your life and death were something very special. We are all touched by the Divine but you, somehow, were more than most. Throughout your life you searched for the truth that would set you free. I believe in death you found it.

329

Whenever I think of truth, I think of you. Whenever I think of beauty, I think of you. Whenever I think of love, I think of you.
Well, that's God, isn't it?

Conversation With A Missing Sister

When I spoke to the superintendent after your disappearance she told me that you were the most loved person at the hospital. It was the same story wherever you went. Everybody loved you. I did, too, you know, until you went mad. Your madness frightened me so much that I just wanted to be shot of it and you. I think we all did.

When you first went into hospital I was so relieved that other people were looking after you but I was distressed by their methods. Destroying your wonderful spirit with their relentless drug regime and shattering your neurones with blasts of electricity hardly seemed the way to draw out and heal your gentle mind. Instead of trying to blot out your memory, why didn't they try to find out what you were trying to forget? I don't believe, in all the years of your alleged treatment, anyone ever properly listened to you, and I think you had a lot to say.

I was forever at a loss to know what to talk about when I visited you in those sad, sterile places. There were times when I desperately wanted to help you untangle the mess inside your head but the psychiatrists so convinced me of their superior knowledge and ability that I didn't even try.

Over the years my pain and guilt turned to anger. Somehow you always managed to grab the limelight and steal the show. You never missed an opportunity to upstage me. Or so I thought.

Then came your disappearance and with it a lot of soul-searching. The more obsessive I became about finding you, the more I realized that I was searching for a part of me – my own madness perhaps.

Once, I dreamt that I was going to a funeral which was taking place in the area we used to call Fairyland at the convent. I turned to the person beside me and said, 'I think it's Annie's funeral but you never know with her, anything could happen.'

332

Final Conversation

I have now come to the end of a long journey, and my companions along the way have taught me a thing or two.

I have learnt that it's not what life dishes up to you, but rather how you deal with it.

I have learnt to stay with the pain and to face the fear.

I have learnt that it is about going within and about trusting a power greater than oneself.

I have learnt that learning never ends, and that the pain of loss never leaves you.

Yet I dream of us all being together at Henley, sitting on the benches under the Pride of India trees with a cloudless blue African sky above. We are laughing and chatting and feeling the warmth of the red earth beneath our feet. We are saying how beautiful the wisteria is and marvelling at how it survives the winter frosts each year.

We watch the sun as it slowly sets behind the willow trees, turning the river gold with its light. Fireflies land on the mosquito netting and we hear bullfrogs in the reeds and smell rain and woodsmoke drifting across the veld.

As night falls we watch in wonder as the stars come out to create the miracle of beauty known as the Southern Cross.

Then we go inside and light the paraffin lamps and sit at the trestle table on the *stoep* and eat our evening meal. When it is time to go to bed, we lie down on the old horsehair mattresses and safe within the thick, stone walls, for there is nothing to fear, we listen to the sound of rain falling on a land in which everyone is free.

Postscript

On 30 December 1990, I held a funeral ceremony for the members of my family on Primrose Hill in London. It was a windy but clear day as a small group gathered under the leafless branches of an old plane tree on this ancient burial site. The congregation consisted of Louisa and J. and four other dear friends. My present family.

I read the funeral sermon from the *Book of Common Prayer*, Shakespeare's sonnet, 'Let me not to the marriage of true minds admit impediment', and the Twenty-third Psalm. Then I cut a tartan ribbon in two, one half of which I buried in the ground and the other I kept. After pouring us all tumblers of whisky, we sang the Hallelujah Chorus from Handel's *Messiah* with gusto. Then raising our glasses we drank a toast to the dead and the living.

From London Zoo across the road came the sound of a lion's roar and we knew that Africa had answered.